The Mississippi Choctaws at Play

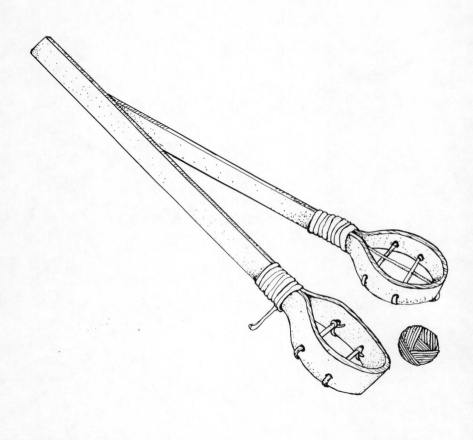

KENDALL BLANCHARD, 1942 -

The Mississippi Choctaws at Play:
The Serious Side of Leisure

UNIVERSITY OF ILLINOIS PRESS
Urbana   Chicago   London

Publication of this work was partially funded by a grant
from the Faculty Research Committee,
Middle Tennessee State University.

Library of Congress Cataloging in Publication Data

Blanchard, Kendall, 1942-
    The Mississippi Choctaws at play.

    Bibliography: p. 183
    1. Choctaw Indians—Games. 2. Indians of
North America—Mississippi—Games. I. Title.
E99.C8B45   796′.08997   80-26527
ISBN 0-252-00866-9   AACR1

In memory of my father,
Craig Allan Blanchard
(1918–63)

CONTENTS

Preface   xiii

1. Choctaw Team Sport: Work or Play?   1

2. Choctaw Sport in Historical Perspective   23

3. Sport and Choctaw Identity   64

4. The Economics of Choctaw Sport   102

5. Choctaw Social Organization and Team Sports   113

6. Sport, Myth, and Ritual in Choctaw Society   145

7. Change and the Significance of Sport   167

Appendix A: The Football Game Projective Test   179

Appendix B: Football Projective Plate Schedule   181

References Cited   183

Index   192

FIGURES

1. Location of Choctaw Communities in East Central Mississippi   5
2. Catlin's Ball Player, *Tullock-chish-ko*, "He who drinks the juice of the stone"   *31*
3. *Toli* Rackets (*kapoča*) and Ball (*towa*)   *33*
4. Catlin's Choctaw Ball Game; ball up   *38*
5. Football Projective Plate 1   *93*
6. Football Projective Plate 2   *94*
7. Football Projective Plate 3   *95*
8. Football Projective Plate 4   *96*
9. Choctaw Kinship Terminology (male ego)   *115*
10. Choctaw Kinship Terminology Pattern Compared to Typical "Crow" Type   *116*
11. Standing Pine Women's Softball Team, 1975: Kinship Definition   *119*
12. Importance of Team Competition and Individual Performance Factors in Mississippi Sport Behavior   *122*

TABLES

1. Mississippi Choctaw Population by Community, 1974 6
2. Occupational Classification of All Persons in the Mississippi Choctaw Labor Force, by Sex and Total, 1974 9
3. Football Projective Plate 1 (responses as to identification of players): Choctaw versus Anglo, 1974 91
4. Football Projective Plate 1 (responses as to perceived normality of event): Choctaw versus Anglo, 1974 91
5. Football Projective Plate 2 (responses as to identity of recipient of spectator attitudes): Choctaw versus Anglo, 1974 91
6. Football Projective Plate 3 (responses as to intention of participants): Choctaw versus Anglo, 1974 92
7. Football Projective Plate 4 (responses as to valuation of perceived coaching style): Choctaw versus Anglo, 1974 92
8. Football Projective Plate 4 (responses as to presumed affection for primary subject): Choctaw versus Anglo, 1974 92
9. Responses to Ideal Female Somatotypes: Rankings of Choctaw and Anglo Samples Compared, 1976 99
10. Somatotype Projective Test (responses relative to perceived curvilinearity): Choctaw versus Anglo, 1976 100
11. Somatotype Projective Test (responses relative to perceived linearity): Choctaw versus Anglo, 1976 100
12. Somatotype Projective Test (responses relative to perceived muscularity): Choctaw versus Anglo, 1976 100
13. Ranking of Mississippi Choctaw Communities Relative to Overall Social Prestige as Perceived by Four Informants, 1977 123
14. Multiple Affect Adjective Check List (MAACL): Scores of Athletes Compared to Those of Nonathletes among Choctaw and Non-Choctaw High School Students, 1974 142

ILLUSTRATIONS
(between pages 112 and 113)

1.   Mississippi Choctaw Stickball Player, 1908
2.   Mississippi Choctaw Stickball Player, 1908
3.   Man Beating Drum for Dance at Choctaw Stickball Game, 1908
4.   Choctaw Group, 1908
5.   Nanih Waiya Mound, Mississippi
6.   Choctaw Home, Pearl River
7.   Choctaw Home, Pearl River
8.   Choctaw Man and his Stickball Sticks
9.   Choctaw Chanters
10.   Between Classes at Choctaw Central High School
11.   Choctaw Boys Playing Makeshift Baseball
12.   Choctaw Social Dancers
13.   Stickball Game Action
14.   Stickball Game Action, 1977 Choctaw Fair: Bogue Chitto versus Pearl River
15.   The Old and the New: Stickball and the Church
16.   Stickball Game, Water Break, 1977 Choctaw Fair
17.   Stickball Team Marching to Game
18.   Choctaw Stickball Player
19.   Choctaw Drummer
20.   Choctaw Central High School Band in Choctaw Fair Parade, 1976
21.   Bogue Chitto Stickball Team in Choctaw Fair Parade, 1976
22.   Making Stickball Sticks at the Choctaw Fair
23.   Dinner on the Grounds at Standing Pine
24.   Track Season at Choctaw Central High School
25.   Choctaw Central High School Football Team in Action
26.   Choctaw Central High School Football Team, 1974
27.   Girls' Basketball Team, Choctaw Central High School, 1977
28.   Women's Basketball, Recreation League Action
29.   Men's Basketball, Recreation League Action
30.   Tucker Baseball Team, 1967
31.   Men's Recreation League Softball Action
32.   Women's Recreation League Softball Action

33. Choctaw Dixie Youth All-Star Baseball Team
34. Pumping Iron during the Recreation League Physical Fitness Program, 1976
35. Practicing the Art of Self-defense at Choctaw Central High School

PREFACE

The Mississippi Choctaws, avid sportsmen who enjoy life but also take their play seriously, are the subjects of this book. The work describes the formal recreational activities of the Choctaw people and the seriousness that characterizes these events. In this study, as well as elsewhere, sport anthropology provides a convenient perspective not only for analyzing sport behavior itself, but also for describing other dimensions of the cultural experience. In the latter sense, what is purported to be "the anthropology of sport" can be viewed as general ethnography.

This work concludes that the seriousness with which the Choctaws define many of their leisure-time activities can best be explained by the way in which these pursuits are interwoven with the basic elements of their total life-style. Team sports also serve to maintain tradition and preserve Choctaw cultural heritage and identity.

It is further suggested that this commitment to play—the serious side of leisure—can be instructive in the twentieth century. Approaching recreation with a work ethic brings a sense of meaning and satisfaction that may serve as an important substitute for actual employment. In a time when population growth and technological change threaten to restrict many to worklessness or less than full-time employment, such a recreation ethic may help to make the leisurely life meaningful.

In writing this volume I have tried to achieve a style that combines elements of descriptive narrative with solid, scientific prose and by so doing to humanize the analytic detail. For this reason, I have used Choctaw personal names wherever possible, except in the chapter on ritual, in which I thought the issues might be too sensitive to risk their inclusion. I have also extensively used direct quotes and comments by the subjects themselves; in many cases exactly as they gave them to me; in others, edited at the request of individual informants.

At the same time, because this description of Choctaw sport behavior is written by an anthropologist, it also employs categories, selected jargon, and a theoretical framework consistent with that professional viewpoint.

I have written the book with the hope that it will appeal to the anthropology student, the physical educator, and the layperson, as well as to the Choctaw people themselves. If the anthropologist is to justify his role as "myth teller" (Richardson, 1975:528–29), he must tell the story of his subjects not only for colleagues and students but also for the native raconteurs from whom he has learned it. I have listened to the Choctaw sport enthusiasts who remember how it used to be, talk of it as it is, and dream of how it will be. I hope that amateur athletes among the Mississippi Choctaws will enjoy hearing an anthropologist retell their story.

In all cases where I have employed Choctaw words, I have written these in the style of the new orthography recently developed by the Mississippi Choctaw Bilingual Program (Joe et al., 1976). In this system, the only significant differences of importance to this particular work relative to older Choctaw orthographies are the following:

1. The *sh* and *ch* sounds are transcribed as *š* and *č*, respectively;

2. the nasalization of vowel sounds is indicated by the placement of a cedilla under the appropriate letter (e.g., *a̧, i̧, ȩ*);

3. the older *u* (e.g., *anumpa*) has been replaced with a lengthened *o* (e.g., *anompa*).

I use the word "stickball" for the classic Choctaw two-racket game because that is how the Native Mississippians themselves refer to the game if they do not employ the traditional term *toli*. Stickball is the parent form of lacrosse and should not be confused with the game of stickball that is played in the streets and sandlots of the American urban North.

Several other terms that I use throughout the text also require some explanation. The word "Anglo" is a common expression used by Native Americans to describe white Americans in general, and is intended to mean all white, non-Indians. "Native Mississippian," on the other hand, is an expression of my own creation and is simply an alternate term for "Choctaw." In several cases, I refer to Mississippi Choctaw society as a "tribe," and in other contexts refer to Choctaws individually as "tribesmen." Though the term is fraught with both theoretical and political difficulties, it is still used by the Choctaws to refer to themselves in many instances and has important legal implications for their current status vis-à-vis the federal government. It is in this latter sense that I am employing the term and its variations.

I was initially attracted to the Choctaws because of their historical fascination with team sports, from the intercommunity stickball matches of the past to the high school and recreation league ball games of the present. Having met several members of the Choctaw community at a conference in Nashville the previous year, I decided to go to Mississippi during the spring of 1974 as part of a general research project dealing with sport behavior as a means of conflict resolution. Over the next three and a half years I spent ten months working in the area; as a consultant to the tribal recreation program, as an ethnologist working on a variety of field problems, and as a participant in community life. During these months I was funded by research grants from Middle Tennessee State University. Some of the research for this volume was also conducted in Washington, D.C., at the Library of Congress and the Smithsonian Institution, while I was a postdoctoral fellow at Johns Hopkins University. During that time, September 1976 to May 1977, I was supported by a grant from the National Endowment for the Humanities.

I am primarily indebted to the Mississippi Band of Choctaw Indians for their openness and willingness to tolerate me and my esoteric concerns. Tribal chiefs Phillip Martin and Calvin Isaac were supportive throughout the project. Other members of the community providing invaluable help include: Jackson Isaac, Baxter York, Albert Farve, Carl Tubby, Gloria York, Roger Bell, Delaura Henry, Hulan Willis, Mavis Steve, Delbert Thomas, Jim Gardner, Doyle Tubby, and Jimmy Gibson.

I am also grateful for the logistical assistance and insight afforded me by tribal employees Marty Gamblin, Dr. James Smith, and Lonus Hucks. Anthropologist John Peterson of Mississippi State University went far beyond the demands of professional courtesy to share with me his extensive Choctaw files and to comment critically on my research. In addition, Alyce Cheska, Raymond Fogelson, and Phillips Stevens, members of my profession who share an interest in the study of play, colleagues John Boles, Billy Fogelman, Steve Fox, Frank Glamser, Eugenia Shanklin, and Marilyn Wells, and editor Nancy Krueger, have made many important suggestions regarding both style and content, but I must assume complete responsibility for the book's theoretical assumptions and for any structural weaknesses.

My wife Katherine also deserves special thanks for her ability to listen to me repeat my Choctaw stories and act as though she never heard them before.

Credit for many of the photographs goes to Edward John and Carl Tubby of the Pearl River community in Mississippi as well as to the Museum of the American Indian.

KENDALL BLANCHARD

CHAPTER 1

Choctaw Team Sport: Work or Play?

It's a hot July afternoon in east central Mississippi. A light breeze disturbs the kudzu and almost lifeless needles of towering pine trees and blows across the baseball diamond behind the high school at Pearl River. The backstop of timber and chicken wire sags as though broken by the heat, the browning grass reflects the wear and lateness of the season, and scattered shoots of wild oats sway silently in the outfield, inviting one more bounding ball or crunching cleat.

An old, fading white Chevrolet sedan pulls slowly into the asphalt parking lot beside the ball field and comes to a bumping halt against the curb. The door opens and the driver emerges, removing his green-billed cap and mopping his perspiring brow with a single motion. Standing beside the car, he looks intently across the expanse of the baseball diamond.

Bending over and reaching back into the hot and dusty-smelling car, the driver ignores the three children playing in the back seat and reaches for an expensive Wilson baseball glove. The woman on the other side of the front seat leans over the crying baby in her arms and pushes the fancy piece of equipment into the outstretched hand.

Grasping his prize of soft leather and nylon, the Sunday afternoon athlete backs away from the car, places his cap carefully over his thick black hair and onto his head, and with some annoyance flicks at a small red-clay smear on his worn but impeccably clean, green-striped uniform. He leans back against the car, thrusts his baseball glove onto his left hand, pounds his right fist methodically into the pocket of the still new-smelling glove, and waits.

Albert Willis* is Choctaw, thirty-two years old, currently unemployed, Baptist, married, a father of four, a resident of the Connehatta community, a high school graduate, and trained as a welder. But more important, he is a baseball player, and today is the most critical day of the week. His team, the Deputies, faces a scrappy ball

---

*The name Albert Willis is a pseudonym, as are all the names in this brief anecdote. However, others used in the book are actual names.

club from Tucker, and he is scheduled to pitch. For several days he has been preoccupied with the thought of this particular recreation league contest: how should he pitch to Butch Jimmie, Tucker's stocky home-run hitter; how will he hold "Streak" Isaac on first if he should get on base; how can he keep the ball out of right field, the one weak spot in the Deputies' line-up; and is anyone going to be using magic or medicine in today's game?

Albert is not an anxious person, but today he is nervous. Baseball is an important part of his life, perhaps the *most* important. Unlike his many different jobs, there is great consistency to his ball playing. He has been on the same team for five years, and has always pitched or played left field. He has missed only one game during those five seasons, and that was because he was out of town.

Playing baseball is not just play for Albert, though he may refer to it as such. It is a serious enterprise, an essential dimension of his life-style.

It means continuity and predictability. He *might* have another job next week, but barring bad weather or a death in the community, he *shall* play ball.

It means responsibility and obligation. His teammates, many of whom are immediate relatives, depend on his being there, so he must show up every time a game is scheduled. On this occasion, he is at the ball field thirty minutes before game time. Just last week, however, he was fired from his job of three months because of his consistent tardiness.

It means personal pride and recognition. When he plays well, his wife, his children, his neighbors, and even his opponents and their fans treat him with admiration and respect, and he feels good about life.

It means time. This week he has driven almost forty miles; next week he will drive fifty to get to the ball game.

It means spending money: for uniforms, gloves, cleats, cleaning, and team expenses such as league and tournament entry fees. It must all come out of his own pocket.

It means community involvement. In many ways, the ball field is the center of Choctaw life. It is here that the relationships between the several local groups are acted out and defined, old friendships are renewed, and old antagonisms perpetuated. Both the pleasant and the traumatic events of community life can occur in this context. Just two months ago, during a softball game at Tucker, an irate player disputed an official's call and in the ensuing argument hit the third-base umpire over the head with a bat and killed him. Folks were still talking about that event. Albert knew them both well. The two men were relatives, and the fight should not have happened, but the impulsive protester had been drinking. Anything can happen at a ball game.

It is urgent, but it is also entertaining. Albert enjoys playing baseball, despite the occasional moments of despair brought on by losing to a rival like Tucker. He gets great pleasure in interacting with friends and relatives who come and help to make the games significant social events. Still, it is not the immediate pleasure that brings Albert out into the heat on these sweltering, summer Sunday afternoons, but rather the ultimate satisfaction that comes from the realization of personal goals. There is always a goal, though it may not be the same from one Sunday to the next: to win, to look good on the pitcher's mound, to hit a towering home run. However, what does not change is his underlying commitment to the game itself and to those with whom he plays.

While it is not a profession, a job, or financially profitable, baseball is in many ways like work for Albert. By his own admission, it is the point around which his whole life revolves during the spring and summer. It provides a meaning and sense of satisfaction he finds in no other activity. For him, working at play is an important and intrinsically rewarding experience.

Certainly, Albert is not unique in the seriousness with which he approaches sport. Neither can this attitude be seen as one characteristic of all Mississippi Choctaws. Some members of the Choctaw community do not participate in any organized sport activities, much less let them become all-consuming passions. On the other hand, many non-Choctaws exhibit this same total commitment toward their athletic activities. Witness, for example, the amateur tennis buff who misses work to finish a match, spending a sleepless night in anxious anticipation; or the sheet-metal worker who changes jobs to pitch for a softball team on the other side of town. In fact, it is an experience not unknown to most Westerners who have ever had any athletic ambition.

However, because of the high level of community participation in their recreation activities, both past and present, the Mississippi Choctaws are perceived at this point as unique. Their history provides an ideal situation within which to consider the meaning, benefits, and costs of the serious side of leisure.

The People

The Choctaws of Mississippi today live in seven communities located across the east central portion of the state: Pearl River, Bogue

Chitto, Standing Pine, Tucker, Bogue Homa, Connehatta, and Red Water (see Figure 1 and Table 1). The approximately 4,000-member group is the faction left behind after most of the other tribesmen moved to Oklahoma following the signing of the Dancing Rabbit Creek treaty in 1830. The size of the group that refused to move was further cut by the second removal of 1903.

Because of their geographical isolation, dispersion, and limited contact with government and missionary agencies until recently, the Mississippi Choctaws have retained their cultural distinctiveness to a greater extent than have their Oklahoma kinsmen. For example, as late as 1970, 74 percent of the households among the Mississippi group still spoke Choctaw as the first language in the home.

The area in and around Neshoba County, the focal point of Choctaw settlement in the state, is characterized by an altitude that ranges from 339 to 431 feet and an annual average precipitation of 55 inches. The soil, primarily large beds of marl and fertile red brakes, is sufficient to support a moderately productive agricultural economy. The countryside is largely covered with timber: pine, hickory, sweet gum, sassafras, dogwood, cypress, and oak.

The Choctaws speak a Muskogean language, and are related both historically and linguistically to the Chickasaws, Creeks, and Seminoles. They have been in this general area of the Southeast for hundreds of years, farming, hunting and gathering, and playing ball.

The basic unit of Choctaw social organization today is the highly endogamous local group or community. The older exogamous clan system has long been replaced and forgotten. Similarly, the traditional pattern of matrilineal descent, exposed to the pressures of English kinship terminology and Western law, has gradually given ground to a patrilineal emphasis.

Politically, the affairs of the Mississippi Band of Choctaw Indians are administered under a constitution and tribal form of government. The *miko,* a traditional leadership role, is now a tribal chief elected every four years by the Choctaw people.

While most of the Choctaws have affiliated with one of several churches active in the area (e.g., Baptist, Methodist, Catholic), many elements of traditional ideology persist, symbolic of the Native Mississippians' determination to retain their cultural heritage despite their active participation in the broader events of contemporary American history.

The continuing emphasis on sport and recreation in Choctaw tradition, from stickball to softball, makes the Choctaws ideal subjects for a study examining the world of work and play. The Choctaws'

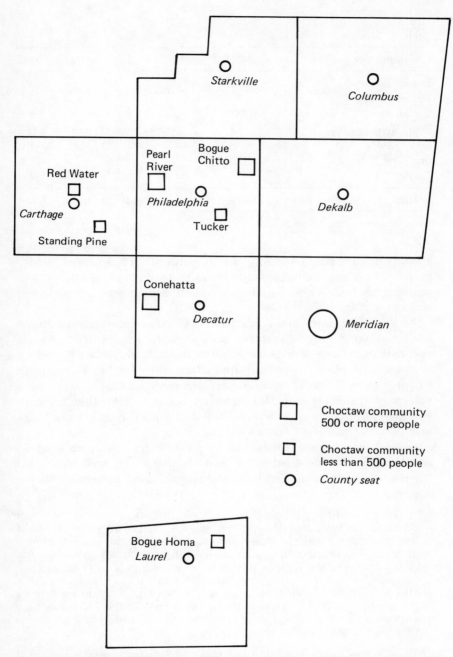

Figure 1. Location of Choctaw Communities in East Central Mississippi (adapted from Peterson, 1970a:7)

Table 1. Mississippi Choctaw Population by Community, 1974[a]

Community	Male	Female	Total
Bogue Chitto	422	408	830
Bogue Homa	56	74	130
Conehatta	287	304	591
Pearl River	583	600	1,183
Red Water	198	220	418
Standing Pine	139	139	278
Tucker	174	175	349
Total	1,859	1,920	3,779

[a]From Spencer et al., 1975:8–9.

attitude toward play has a long and colorful history, and that history may hold an important message for modern man as he attempts to manage his health and structure his daily activities to adjust to the realities of life in the 1980s.

At the same time, this emphasis on Choctaw play and leisure is not intended to suggest that they are a lazy and unproductive people nor that they have a negative attitude toward the value of work.

In the first place, the Mississippi Choctaws have been caught up in the twentieth century, and have internalized many basic work values of the West even though they seem to take their play so seriously. Yet the way in which they deal with the realities of work and play is uniquely Choctaw.

Second, the Choctaw tribe has long had a reputation as a labor-conscious and hard-working group. Romans (1775:83) described them as the most conscientious, industrious, and patient of Native Americans.

> Their way of life in general may be called industrious, they will do what no uncompelled savage will do, that is work in the field to raise grain; and one may among them hire not only a guide, or a man to build a house, or make a fence, but even to hoe his grounds; nay they will for payment be your menial servants to the meanest office; . . . they are ingenious in making tools, utensils and furniture; I have seen a narrow tooth comb made by one of these savages with a knife only out of a root of the *Diolpyrus* that was as well finished as I ever saw one with all the necessary tools; this shows their patience.

The Choctaws were among the most successful farmers, not only in the Southeast, but in Native America in general. As one nineteenth-century writer noted: "The Choctaws have long been known to excel all the North American Indians in agriculture, subsisting to a considerable extent on the product of their fields" (Cushman, 1899:250). In fact, on many occasions in the leaner times of the year, neighboring tribes, such as the Chickasaws, were dependent on them for corn and other staples.

To the Choctaw, work (*tǫksali*) is a noble activity basic to group survival and one's worth as a person, a pride-producing and prestigious pursuit. In one of the Choctaw origin myths, the *mịko*, the traditional Choctaw political leader, addresses his people:

> We are a brave and exceedingly prosperous people. We are an industrious people. We till the ground in large fields, thereby producing sustenance for this great nation. We are a faithful and dutiful people. We packed the bones of our ancestors on our backs, in the wilderness, forty-three winters, and at the end of our long journey piled up to their memory a monument, that overshadows the land like a great mountain [Nanih Waiya]. We are a strong, hardy and very [mobile] people. When we set out from the land of our fathers, the Chata [Choctaw] tribe numbered a little less than nineteen thousand. We have traveled over a pathless wilderness, beset with rocks, high mountains, sun-scorched plains, with dried-up rivers of bitter waters; timbered land, full of lakes and ferocious wild beasts. Bravely we have battled and triumphed over all. We have not failed . . . [Swanton, 1931:21–22].

At the same time, the enemies or the evil factions among the people are characterized in Choctaw myth as indolent and slovenly.

While such patriotic pronouncements reflect an element of ethnocentrism, they also suggest a clear work-ethic ideal fundamental to the Choctaws' conception of themselves.

During the nineteenth century, child-rearing practices among the Choctaws stressed industriousness, stamina, and persistence as virtues. Children were forced to swim in the coldest weather, lift heavy weights, run, and engage in activities, such as chunkey, that would improve their manual skills. Choctaw parents worried lest their children succumb to laziness (*ịtakobi*). In order to cure this disease, "they made them play ball and run races. Sometimes they scratched them with a nettle to improve their circulation and cure them of laziness by forcing them to scratch themselves" (Swanton, 1931:127).

Choctaw children are still encouraged to stay active. One young adult member of the Pearl River community told me about her own experience as a child: "Parents never wanted kids to have idle time. They would assign you to do things; chores around the house. Once you got through with that, if you came back in the house, Mom would always say, 'Go outside and play.' I think maybe play was to occupy our time, rather than see us sit around and watch TV or something."

One's ability and reputation as a worker were also important considerations in the traditional Choctaw marriage process. After a young man had decided on a mate, he had to approach her parents, state his intentions, and hope for a favorable response. In most cases, the primary consideration in the ensuing decision was the prospective groom's ability to support a wife. As one older Choctaw, Jim Gardener, recalls:

> In the old days, when a boy wanted to marry a girl he came to the girl's father and asked him first. If the father said "No," it was the law, and the girl must obey. . . .
> If you had a daughter, you wanted her to marry somebody that was a good worker and a good hunter. Sometimes, if a boy came to a father to ask him for his daughter, he would tell the boy he did not want his girl to go hungry, so he must see if the boy is a good hunter.
> "Go get me a turkey."
> He would have to go, right then, and get that turkey. If not, no wife.

While marriage patterns and courting techniques have changed, Choctaw parents still worry lest their son or daughter take a lazy mate. Industriousness remains one of the most attractive personal characteristics.

Despite their general emphasis on the importance of work, the unemployment picture among the Mississippi Choctaws is grim, but for reasons beyond their own control. In 1974, the Choctaw community had a total labor force of 1,481 persons—742 males and 739 females (see Table 2). Of that total, 27 percent were unemployed. Since that time, the increase in the size of the work force, the general economic recession, and the cutback in government funds have further complicated the unemployment picture.

The reasons for Choctaw unemployment are obvious. Only with the passage of the Civil Rights Act in 1964 did many industrial and clerical jobs in the surrounding, predominantly white communities become available to Native Americans. Also, as the 1974 Choctaw Demographic Survey reported, "the overall education and skill levels of the average Choctaw remain low" (Spencer et al., 1975:29). For example, 86 percent of the labor force that year had "few or no job skills" (Spencer et al., 1975:29). Also, many kinds of employment entered into by the Choctaw worker are temporary, either as a result

Table 2. Occupational Classification of All Persons in the Mississippi
Choctaw Labor Force,[a] by Sex and Total, 1974[b]

Occupational classification	Total		Male		Female	
	No.	Percent	No.	Percent	No.	Percent
Professional/technical	14	.9	6	.8	8	1.1
Administrative/managerial	31	2.1	23	3.1	8	1.1
New Careers program[c]	21	1.4	11	1.5	10	1.4
Clerical/misc. white collar	55	3.7	7	.9	48	6.5
Sales workers	3	.2	3	.4	0	.0
Craftsmen/foremen	46	3.1	43	5.8	3	.4
Service workers	286	19.3	107	14.4	179	24.2
Operatives	174	11.7	71	9.6	103	13.9
Transport operatives	54	3.6	52	7.0	2	.3
Laborers, nonfarm	222	15.0	194	26.1	28	3.8
Farm managers/laborers	53	3.6	49	6.6	4	.5
Private household workers	8	.5	0	.0	8	1.1
Trainees	116	7.8	70	9.4	46	6.2
Unemployed	398	26.9	106	14.3	292	39.5
Totals	1481	100.0	742	100.0	739	100.0

[a]The "labor force" includes both persons who are employed and persons who are
unemployed, but available for work. Not included are persons who are students,
disabled, retired, or otherwise not available for wage employment.
[b]From Spencer et al., 1975:23.
[c]New Careers trainees, generally, were employed on the white-collar skill level.

of design or circumstances: "The majority of Choctaw workers remain heavily dependent on jobs with little security, in that their jobs
are based on short-term programs (e.g., service workers employed
in short-term developmental programs) or on other contingencies,
such as weather conditions (e.g., pulpwood haulers, laborers) and
economic conditions (e.g., operatives, laborers)" (Spencer et al.,
1975:29).

As Table 2 suggests, Choctaws are employed in many different
types of jobs, but the majority of these are unskilled: farmhand,
assembly-line worker, construction crew, general maintenance, gar-
dening. Also, coupled with their uncertainty, most of these jobs offer
limited financial incentive. In 1974, the average hourly wage for an
unskilled Choctaw laborer was $2.08, and yet for all workers and
occupations among the group it was only $2.48 an hour (Spencer
et al., 1975:28).

Although faced with depressing unemployment and low-income problems, Mississippi Choctaws remain an industrious people who manifest a desire for material accomplishment and a work ethic comparable to that of the Anglo-American world but unlike this world in that it does not preclude an even greater passion for play.

This positive attitude toward leisure, or *nąištatta ikimikšo*, translates roughly as "nothing to do." A good-natured, fun-loving people, the Choctaws throughout their history have used much of this free time to enjoy games and sports, from chunkey and stickball to baseball and basketball (see Chapter 2).

Play (*wášoha*), a consistent element in Choctaw child-rearing and education as well as in the daily routine of the adult life, is viewed as both an enjoyable and purposeful pursuit. Play is not seen as simply an idle passing of time; it serves a meaningful purpose in the Choctaw·world.

For this reason, Choctaws often view the recreation program as the most important phase of contemporary tribal government. With many facilities that can be used for recreational purposes and an annual budget of about $50,000, this program is the focal point of formal Choctaw play. With basketball, baseball, softball, and swimming for all ages, this tribal activity affects, either directly or indirectly, the lives of all the Mississippi Choctaw people. In fact, a survey I conducted in 1975 revealed that 87.5 percent of persons between the ages of sixteen and forty in six of the seven Choctaw communities participated in at least one of the recreation activities sponsored by the tribe that year, as player, spectator, or both.

During most of the year, sports enthusiasm runs high among both players and fans alike. Ball games are often viewed as serious business and approached with a commitment which resembles the Western work ethic. These activities are understood as obligations, demand an adherence to rigorous time schedules, define explicit goals and tasks, require deliberate effort, have many deferred rewards, and exist for more than just the pure pleasure of playing.

This tendency for the Choctaws to work at play is probably an old one. While archeological and ethnohistorical data are insufficient to ascertain conclusively, it is safe to suggest that the ancient Choctaws made a distinction between work and play, recognizing the importance of labor on the one hand and leisurely celebration on the other. However, typical of tribal peoples around the world, the Native Mississippians approached the play phenomenon with a seriousness that often muddled the clarity of the distinction between the two states. As Turner (1973:28–29) notes, the "play" or "ludic" aspects of tribal and agrarian ritual and myth are, as Durkheim says, *"de la vie sérieuse,"* i.e., they are intrinsically connected with the "work" of the collectivity in performing symbolic actions and manipulating symbolic actions so as to promote and increase fertility of men, crops, and animals, domestic and wild, to cure illness, to avert plague, to obtain success in raiding, to turn boys into men and girls into women, to make chiefs out of commoners, to transform ordinary people into shamans and shamins, to "cool" those "hot" from the warpath, to ensure the proper succession of seasons and the hunting and agricultural responses of human beings to them, and so forth. Thus, the play is in earnest and has to be within bounds.

Choctaw play still has its "bounds," and it is these that circumscribe the serious side of leisure in their world.

Working at Play: The Rationale

The Choctaws are not alone among peoples of the world in their tendency to work at play. This approach to leisure has some positive, adaptive features and can be viewed as a productive attitude within certain types of socioeconomic environments among Choctaws and non-Choctaws alike.

The Western world is faced with the prospect of increasing amounts of leisure time, that is, time not devoted to necessary vocational, personal, or household activities (e.g., job, eating, sleeping, child care). The average American adult already has between twenty-five and fifty hours of such unobligated time each week, while the young and the elderly have even more, from fifty to seventy-five hours (Southern California Research Council, 1967:17). As the work week shrinks, this figure will continue getting larger.

With the growing mechanization of Western industry, it is reasonable to predict an increase in the number of unemployed persons who ultimately may have to accept leisure as a way of life, either by choice or as a result of unavoidable circumstances. In any case, the future is filled with large amounts of free time for the "working" public, and the question is, "How do we use it?" As some writers have suggested, the leisure-time boon may be more problem than blessing (see Charlesworth, 1964).

Part of that problem is in the fact that in the industrialized West, leisure is defined in relation to work or activity directed toward a particular goal. Ideally, leisure is "a state of being in which activity is performed for its own sake or as its own end" (de Grazia, 1962:15). For many, however, leisure is justifiable only as it occurs between clearly defined periods of work.

In such a work ethic–oriented social context, many persons will employ a laboring-man model for defining their own self-worth. One person feels guilty if too much time, vacation or otherwise, is spent away from the job. Another seriously questions his own value as a person because he is not "gainfully employed." For these, the reality of increased leisure time is at best unpleasant. How, then, do we lower free-time anxieties and make leisure more meaningful in a work-bound society?

One way of using leisure time is by playing. Play is defined by Johan Huizinga (1949:13) in his classic *Homo Ludens* as

> a free activity standing quite consciously outside "ordinary" life as being "not serious," but at the same time absorbing the player intensely and utterly. It is an activity connected with no material interest, and no profit can be gained by it. It proceeds within its own proper boundaries of time and space according to fixed rules and in orderly manner. It promotes the formation of social group-ings which tend to surround themselves with secrecy and to stress their difference from the common world by disguise or other means.

While the Huizinga definition is of limited cross-cultural utility, it is a frequently employed concept of play and it does point to some of the phenomenon's fundamental characteristics. In this context, "play" is viewed as self-contained and providing its own immediate meaning and justification. This justification or implicit goal is the activity itself rather than the results or by-products of the activity. Play is play for play's sake.

Because play is often viewed as nonproductive, it has negative overtones for the work-conscious segment of the American public. One may take time to play, but must be careful lest he play too much. Also, there is a popular myth that suggests that play is a childhood characteristic unbecoming to ideal adult behavior. Even among those who accept the notion that a certain amount of adult play can be constructive, play is often defined in opposition to work.

Play can also be viewed as an important part of the work process. M. Csikszentmihalyi has analyzed several professions and sport ac-tivities (e.g., surgeons, rock climbers), attempting to isolate and de-scribe the techniques these commitments employ in the achievement of "peak experiences." He suggests that most are motivated and rewarded intrinsically, without direct regard or demand for material or extrinsic reinforcement. These intrinsic rewards are defined ulti-mately in terms of what he calls the "flow experience": "In the flow state, action follows upon action according to an internal logic that seems to need no conscious intervention by the actor. He experiences it as a unified flowing from one moment to the next, in which he is in control of his actions, and in which there is little distinction between self and environment, between stimulus and response, or between past, present, and future" (1975:36).

For Csikszentmihalyi, "play is the flow experience par excellence," and thus essential in the process of enjoying the work event on the one hand and avoiding boredom and anxiety on the other. In coping with a world of shrinking material rewards and expectations and limited resources, it is important that the worker be motivated by the intrinsic enjoyment of the "flow" rather than the extrinsic goal of increasing consumption and accumulation.

Mergen (1978:197) has described the ways in which the American shipyard worker makes his job more pleasurable and ultimately acceptable by injecting heavy daily doses of play. "The competitive spirit, company sponsored athletics, day dreaming, joking, tricks, gossip, costuming—all have important functions in making shipyard work more like play." The suggestion is that the play attitude can be a productive posture toward work.

If the two activities, work and play, can be meaningfully integrated within the work context, why not also in the play environment? In other words, if one can play at work, why can he not also work at play? This serious approach to leisure might function to make compulsory free time more palatable in the work-bound Western world.

One of the central themes of this volume is that in approaching certain forms of play with a work-like attitude, one can often achieve intrinsic rewards commensurate with those of a "job well done" in a labor-conscious society. It is also suggested that such rewards make possible an effective adaptation to a forced leisure environment. In effect, serious play can take the place of work and reduce the anxiety that comes with worklessness or the uncertainties of temporary laboring or professional roles.

The sport and recreation scene of the Mississippi Choctaws is used as a setting for considering the ways in which a play-conscious people structure the symbols of work and leisure and achieve meaning and satisfaction in their play, specifically in their team sport forms of recreation.

The Anthropology of Sport as Perspective

The perspective for this analysis is afforded by the emerging anthropology of sport. Generally treated as a facet of the broader realm of "play," sport behavior was largely ignored or treated only tangentially by anthropologists until recently. As a result, the literature contains only limited material on athletic activities in non-Western or tribal society previous to the mid-'60s. Robin Fox's (1961) article on Pueblo baseball, Corrado Gini's (1939) analysis of Berber baseball, and James Mooney's (1890) study of Cherokee stickball are a few exceptions. Such phenomena are usually viewed as incidental to the broader cultural environment and too "frivolous" to merit scholarly attention.

In recent years a new interest in the sport phenomenon has developed among anthropologists. In May 1974, the Association for the Anthropological Study of Play (TAASP) was organized in London, Ontario, in conjunction with the annual meetings of the North American Society for Sport History and under the advisement of B. Allan Tindall, the member of the anthropology community most instrumental in the founding and early growth of the association.

Since its inception, the organization has increased the size of its membership to almost 250, including physical educators, recreationists, psychologists, sociologists, and historians, as well as anthropologists. Publishing a newsletter and holding annual meetings, usually in conjunction with regional and national anthropology societies, TAASP functions to channel the growing amount of research, presentations, and publications related to the anthropological study of sport and play. As a result of the new interest and organization, literature on the subject has expanded immensely in the past five years (see Lancy and Tindall, 1976, Schwartzman, 1976:289–328, Stevens, 1977, and Salter, 1978, for recent bibliographies).

The anthropology of sport is significantly different from other scholarly approaches to the analysis of this behavior primarily because of the special topics to which it addresses itself. This subdiscipline of cultural anthropology focuses on the following major problems: (1) the meaning and description of sport behavior, particularly in non-Western and preliterate societies; (2) the cross-cultural definition and analysis of sport; (3) sport as a factor in acculturation, enculturation, and cultural maintenance; (4) sport as a form of human conflict and a context within which to consider the issues of aggression and violence; and (5) sport as a perspective on other facets of cultural behavior.

Also, the anthropology of sport deals with many significant issues of applied value; for example, the development and implementation of athletic, recreation, and physical education programs in multicultural or multiracial environments, or the use of sport as a facilitator of international awareness and understanding. In this connection, the sport anthropologist is often employed as a consultant or instructor by physical education and leisure-program directors to deal with special problems.

Finally, the anthropology of sport is different from other social scientific approaches to the phenomenon because of the distinctive historical, theoretical, and methodological characteristics of its parent discipline, anthropology. In general, the anthropological perspective, though overlapping these in some areas, complements other approaches to the study of sport, such as those growing out of psychology and sociology.

This volume treats most of the major questions posed by the anthropology of sport. It is primarily a description of Choctaw recreational activity, but it is also an ethnographic treatment of the Choctaw world in general. Sport provides a unique angle from which to describe and analyze the various dimensions of culture. This is especially instructive in cultures like that of the Mississippi Choctaws, in which athletic events are interwoven with total life-style, from economic and social to political and ideological components. The study of sport behavior from an anthropological viewpoint is important for general data-collecting as well as descriptive, interpretative, and applied purposes. As anthropologist Raymond Firth (1931:95–96) has suggested, in connection with his classic analysis of the Tikopian dart game:

> Sport, as an integral feature in the life of many primitive peoples, offers a number of problems for investigation. Some of these are concerned with questions of organization, of the nature of the factors which differentiate a vague play activity from a regularly established game with clearly defined procedure, hemmed in on every side by rules of strong sanction. . . . The relation of primitive sport to other aspects of the social life, its unique cultural value on the one hand, and its inter-reaction with economic, aesthetic and religious affairs on the other, presents a field of research which merits even more attention than it has already received.

The anthropology of sport research, like any other subdivision of the discipline, is not done in a theoretical vacuum. Indeed, the task involves more than simply finding a ball game in progress somewhere, climbing into the bleachers, and jotting down observations on the back of a scorecard.

The theory underlying sport anthropology fieldwork and analysis, like theory in general, is best understood in terms of what it *does* rather than what it *is*. As Kaplan and Manners (1972:12) have presented the issue:

A precise definition of theory has so far eluded even those scientists and philosophers of science who are directly concerned with the clarification of such matters. But while there may be some disagreement about what theory *is*, there seems to be a considerable agreement about what theories may *do*. In general, if a proposition or a body of propositions explains, predicts, retrodicts or leads us to "new" facts or "new" avenues of research it is likely to be called a theory. In short, theories are defined pragmatically rather than strictly in terms of their formal properties.

Theory is constructed rather than discovered, the latter being a characteristic of laws (e.g., the law of gravity). A theory's ultimate validity is to be found in its testability and resulting empirical consistency. In this sense, a theory can be viewed as a methodological concept that provides a perspective for structuring observable data. Its reliability hinges on its continued utility. In anthropology, then, a theory at its simplest level is a way of looking at human behavior and is prerequisite to any fieldwork and analysis.

I have chosen to employ a modified ethnoscientific model of cultural reality as a way of viewing Choctaw team sport behavior. The primary assumption of ethnoscience is that culture is knowledge, specifically, the information shared by an individual with other members of his group about their world and relationships with it and each other. At the same time, what a person knows is not simply a mass of undifferentiated data. Rather, it is structured in a way that is consistent among members of the same group, each person sharing similar concepts, categories, and perceptions. The cultural experience is the process of reacting to sensory stimuli and sorting them out by means of the structured knowledge that one has internalized as a result of the enculturation or socialization process unique to his particular historical circumstances.

This being the case, the primary data for the ethnoscientist in cultural description is the native's perception of his own world. This is communicated to the fieldworker primarily through spoken language, the assumption being that cultural knowledge is structured linguistically. However, individual responses to external stimuli other than verbal are also significant sources of information about culture.

In the interpretation of the cultural experience, it is further assumed that the native's point of view (the emic perspective) is a legitimate method of explaining process and event in a particular system. For example, if the Dani tribesmen of New Guinea, the subjects of the classic anthropology film "Dead Birds," tell the anthropologist that they fight with their neighbors on the other side of the valley in order to appease the ghosts, that is a significant piece of information and an important explanation (Heider 1970:132). This "inside view" (Kaplan and Manners, 1972:22) provides not only humanistic understanding, but also a degree of scientific predicta- bility. Technically, such emic models of culture are the final products of ethnoscience. (For a thorough discussion of ethnoscientific tech- nique, see Spradley, 1972.)

However, an emic analysis left to stand on its own merit has obvious limitations. As Pitt-Rivers (1967:31–32) notes: "The models of the native differ from those of the anthropologist in that they are centered on his own place in society, inevitably, since they are models-for-action rather than models-for-comparison. They partake of his knowledge of his society, but they also represent his aspira- tions. They are not only the world as he knows it, they are also the world as he would like it to be."

The tendency of the individual culture-bearer to rationalize, legit- imize, and speak of ideal categories rather than actual behavior sug- gests that the pure ethnoscience model must be tempered with an objective, outside view (the etic perspective).

Treating culture from an outside as well as an inside perspective does not negate the utility of ethnoscientific technique, for "actual behavior can be treated in both an emic and an etic fashion" (Harris, 1968:581). In fact, by integrating both the native's and the anthro- pologist's perception of the same event(s), a much more valuable description evolves. For example, if it can be demonstrated that Dani warfare functions to keep population and supportive capacities in balance, the anthropologist can deal with the problem of conflict and ecology more thoroughly than if he is limited to the ghost-appease- ment explanation.

The simultaneous use of both emic and etic models of particular cultures is especially convenient in analyzing function. Philosopher Denis Dutton (1977) has argued for the combination of these two perspectives in an attempt to avoid the ambiguities of Merton's (1968:105) classic distinction between "latent" and "manifest" func- tion. Instead of focusing on the consequences of cultural action, Dutton (1977:388) turns to "intention," both explicit and implicit. Explicit intentions are "those recognized by an actor in connection with his activity." Implicit intentions are part of the whole activity, not "consciously contemplated" but still intentional. Because all hu- man cultural activities are part of that overall strategy of group ad- aptation and survival, they are intended, whether they are recog- nized or not.

This being the case, the problem, then, is the way that these intentions are phrased. For example, ecological explanations requiring the isolation of adaptive functions can be phrased in terms of both explicit and implicit intentions. On the one hand, the emic model provides a means by which the native can express in his own categories those dimensions and consequences of the total cultural experience that he recognizes as significant. On the other, the anthropologist can, as a result of his access to vast amounts of demographic, nutritional, climatological, and historical data, construct an etic model by which to render explicit those implicit intentions not immediately recognized or verbalized by the untrained layman. The two perspectives should be seen as complementary in the description of the realm of intentions and consequences basic to the adaptive system.

Such an approach does not violate the basic ethnoscientific view of culture. Intentions, whether explicit or implicit, are part of the cognitive focus of the cultural experience. Emic descriptions emanate from within the framework provided by native symbols and classificatory devices, while etic models approach the same reality from an external perspective. The final product is a workable description of culture that balances the ideal with the real and yet does not sacrifice humanistic sensitivity for scientific objectivity.

Concepts: Work and Play

In the attempt to describe the serious side of Choctaw leisure, I am assuming that I can isolate "work" and "play" as separate phenomena or states of being. Also, I am taking for granted the notion that in such a description I can use the language and concepts of the industrialized West, although the fact that the distinction between play and work may be "itself an artifact of the Industrial Revolution" suggests caution at this point (Turner, 1973:14).

According to de Grazia (1962:14), the ancient Greeks perfected the idea of the leisurely life. The most noble pursuits, for example education (schole), were those requiring freedom from both temporal and spatial restraints: "The classical Greeks wanted to be wise. To be wise one had to have leisure. Not everyone could have leisure. The body needs food and shelter and to get them requires work [therefore, slave labor was a necessity]. All animals seek food and shelter. Man alone can think, reason, and invent. If some men at least could be freed from mundane occupations, they might soar to remarkable heights . . ." (de Grazia, 1962:35).

One of the words the Greeks used for "work" was *ascholia*, literally, "un-leisure." As opposed to the thinkers of the post-industrialized European world, the early Hellenistic educated elite saw work as a temporary state interrupting an otherwise perpetual, unbounded life of leisure.

With the advent of the Roman world, the rise of Christianity, and the later development of industrialization and Western capitalism, the work ethic evolved, and leisure was replaced by labor as the ideal. In less than 2,000 years, labor had become the norm, and leisure, un-work.

The problem of treating "work" in a non-Western setting is further complicated by the fact that some societies have "no generic word for play, and thus seemingly do not distinguish work from play" (Norbeck, 1974:1). In such systems, daily activities are graded by degree of seriousness or element of oughtness.

Dumazedier (1968:248) also argues that leisure has not always been an element in all cultures at all times. In fact, among tribal societies, "work and play alike formed part of the ritual by which men sought communion with the ancestral spirits. Religious festivals embodied both work and play."

Regardless of the possible historical peculiarity of the distinction, the work-play contrast of the contemporary Western world can be useful in analyzing human behavior in any cultural setting. As Turner (1973:28) suggests, "it often happens that the historically *later* can throw light on the *earlier*, especially when there is a demonstrable sociogenetic connection between them." Also, leisure and labor, despite the absence of a universal system of classification, are readily recognized and identified even in those societies lacking comparable linguistic categories. In fact, even nonhuman primates play in a way that provokes immediate recognition by human observers (Norbeck, 1974:1–3).

For these reasons, I am assuming that the Western experience is instructive in analyzing work and play in any cultural context. Likewise, the reverse should be true; work and play realities seen from within the emic framework of a particular non-Western society are of heuristic value in understanding life in the Western world.

Concepts: Sport and Recreation

In the analyzing patterns of Choctaw leisure behavior it is also important to define the terms "sport" and "recreation." Unfortunately, cross-cultural definitions of these two behaviors, which appear to have obvious meanings in Western society, remain problematic in the literature and are too often used inappropriately with reference to activities in other cultural settings (Tindall, 1976:3).

The term "sport" is perhaps the more difficult of these to universalize. In a much-quoted work, *Sociology of Sport*, Harry Edwards (1973:57–58) defines the phenomenon as referring to any "activities having formally recorded histories and traditions, stressing physical exertion through competition within limits set in explicit and formal rules governing role and position relationships, and carried out by actors who represent or who are part of formally organized associations having the goal of achieving valued tangibles or intangibles through defeating opposing groups."

For Edwards, "sports" and "athletics" are synonymous. As Sack (1977:194) has noted, however, a distinction should be made between "athletic and nonathletic sport," a distinction he makes on the basis of the amount of physical exertion expended in a particular activity. Playing golf with friends, for example, is nonathletic sport, while professional football is at the other end of the athletic continuum. For Sack as for Loy (1969:62), sport is simply "an institutionalized game, dependent on physical prowess." "Game" is defined as "any form of competition, staged for the enjoyment of either participants or spectators, whose outcome is determined by physical skill, strategy, or chance employed singly or in combination" (Sack, 1977:194).

Sport, viewed from this perspective, can have both work and play dimensions. For example, compare the activities of the professional during a regularly scheduled major league baseball game with those of the teen-aged amateur enjoying an afternoon of "pick-up" baseball on a local sandlot. The former is dealing with the phenomenon as primarily vocational and the latter as avocational, yet in both cases the activity is still sport.

The anthropologist is normally wary of such general definitions of human behavior, because of the reality of cultural variation. In the first place, physically combative sports (i.e., athletic sports) do not occur at all in many societies (Sipes, 1973:65). Second, in those in which these activities do take place, their structures may vary from one cultural setting to another. Even when the game being played is formally identical to a particular game being played in another social context, the observable behavior may be so different as to obscure similarities. Take, for example, basketball among the Rimrock Navajos. Adopting the game from their Anglo-Mormon neighbors during the 1920s and '30s, the Navajos over the years have developed a distinctive style of basketball.

In general, Rimrock Navajo basketball behavior tends to be more individualistic run-and-shoot, kin-oriented, pure good times, and less morally educative and principle-centered than that played by the town's Anglo-Mormon faction. This observation is reinforced by the behavior of Navajo fans who appear to enjoy the continuing play of the game more and get involved in the final outcome possibilities less than do their Mormon counterparts. Even from the most nonscholarly perspective, Navajo basketball must be seen as a different game [Blanchard, 1973:7].

Tindall (1975) has made a similar observation among the Utes in northeastern Utah. Ute perceptions of basketball behavior were found to vary significantly from those of their Anglo-Mormon peers within the same general social setting.

Despite the reality of cultural variability, I find the definition of sport suggested by Sack (1977:194) and Loy (1969:62), in which the phenomenon is understood as an institutionalized game utilizing physical skills, convenient to cross-cultural analysis. At the same time, I admit that the meaning of the terms contained in the above definition of "game"—competition, skill, strategy, and chance (see p. 20)—may vary between human groups, as may the perception of particular sports. For this reason, the definition is employed with a degree of flexibility.

Like the Rimrock Navajos, the Mississippi Choctaws have unique ways of playing and talking about particular games like basketball, but in all cases, actual behavior patterns are consistent with the aforementioned definition of "sport." For example, while the Choctaw word *itibbi* can be used for both "fight" and "sport contest," Choctaw sport is primarily institutionalized gaming, although it may be defined in more explicit conflict terms (Blanchard, 1975:169).

In this work, the primary focus is on Choctaw team sports, athletic events pitting groups, rather than individuals, against each other. The most popular team sports among the Choctaws are stickball, baseball, basketball, and softball.

"Recreation," on the other hand, is a more inclusive term than "sport." While an explicit, transcultural definition is difficult, there are several observable characteristics of such activity. Kraus (1971: 261–62) and Kando (1975:27-28) discuss the concept of recreation in terms of existing definitions and arrive at six elements implicit in the activity. Recreation is (1) based on freedom of choice, (2) rewarded intrinsically, as opposed to extrinsically, (3) potentially applicable to any human activity, (4) actual rather than ideal behavior, (5) defined in opposition to work, and (6) only infrequently intellectually strenuous. Defined from this perspective, I view recreation as a form of leisure available to all, which includes many forms of play, both individual and group, sport and nonsport, athletic and nonathletic, formal and informal.

The traditional Choctaw term for recreation (*foah*) suggested passive activities such as "rest" and "relaxation," but the word *okča*, meaning "wakefulness," "viligence," or "refreshment," could also be used to translate the concept.

Today, the Choctaws use several expressions to communicate the idea of recreation, including *na okla wašoha* ("to play anything"), which puts the focus on the active, playing dimensions of recreation. When the Native Mississippians use the English term "recreation," however, they are usually referring to a formal, organizational structure, a program defining and governing team sport activities.

Summarizing the conceptual framework, using both English and Choctaw categories as well as considerations of logical consistency, when I use the word "sport" in this volume I am referring to a form of institutionalized gaming that involves physical skill. This phenomenon can be viewed as involving either play or conflict or both. By "recreation" I mean a particular type of leisure-time activity that usually entails some form of play and sometimes participation in a sporting event, organized or informal, athletic or nonathletic. It is assumed that each of these activities, sport, play, recreation, leisure, as well as work, has both an identifiable structure and a characteristic flavor or milieu. In other words, one can observe one of these activities in progress and immediately recognize it structurally (e.g., play, recreation, leisure, work, sport). On the other hand, he can also see that participants in that event are manifesting at the same time attitudes characteristic of any other of these phenomena. For example, the structure "work" can suggest a "play" milieu; likewise, recreation can have observable work dimensions.

Choctaw team sport behavior in this setting is, by definition, primarily a form of play. When the Choctaws talk about sport they call it "play," in the sense that they "play basketball or stickball" or "play a tournament game." However, they also see sport as conflict, and the attitude underlying their approach to and participation in many recreation league games or high school athletic contests is often more than simply a playful one. In these cases, sport often assumes a seriousness and engenders a commitment among its participants that reflect attitudes not unlike those that characterize work in the Choctaw world.

What follows is an attempt to describe the Choctaw passion for team sport, isolate the sources of that passion, and defend the viability of a work attitude toward play as a rational adaptation to the economic uncertainties of the twentieth century.

CHAPTER 2

Choctaw Sport in Historical Perspective

The Mississippi Choctaws have long taken their sport life very seriously. This avid interest in group names, however, is difficult to
document for the period preceding the early 1700s. Anthropologists
and historians can only speculate about the nature of such events
in Choctaw prehistory.

In general, American archeology has failed to treat the sport and
recreation phenomena. The paucity of references to these behaviors
in the archeological literature is explained by Fox (1977:66):

> First, few archeologists appear to be willing to confront these as
> cultural phenomena worthy of scholarly investigation. Second,
> these individuals who have acknowledged the respective roles of
> sport and recreation in prehistory have often used it as a means
> of classifying data that cannot be readily inserted into a more
> conventional category of cultural behavior. . . . Third, a converse
> of the above is the misrepresentation of material evidences of
> sporting and other forms of recreation as manifestations of eco-
> nomic, ritual, or other cultural behaviors. Finally, the archeologist
> is confronted with the very real problem of actually gathering the
> material data of sporting and recreation activities, which are, for
> the most part, few.

The problem of sport prehistory is particularly acute when one
approaches the Choctaw situation, for the archeological record is
virtually blank regarding the problem of that group's past in general.
A specialized area such as game behavior is predictably even more
difficult to reconstruct.

Although it is generally agreed among archeologists that the Choctaws are historical remnants of the widespread Mississippian phase
of southeastern prehistory, there is no existing data affording insight
into the nature of that period's sport behavior nor that of the early
historic era: no balls, no ball courts, no related representational art.

Choctaw legends themselves suggest that the group migrated
within only the past 400 or 500 years from out of the West into what
is now Mississippi. One story that some Choctaws tell, for example,
claims that the tribe is related historically to the Flatheads of
Montana.

According to Choctaw origin myth, this west-to-east migration terminated at Nanih Waiya mound, about twenty-five miles north of Philadelphia, Mississippi. At that point, the previously undifferentiated group split into two factions, Choctaw and Chickasaw, and went their separate ways. In no origin legend is there any mention of ball games.

The earliest historical references to the Choctaw people are found in the chronicles of de Soto, whose party apparently encountered them in southeastern Mississippi during their exploratory invasion of the area during the 1540s, labeling them as "Long Hairs." It was not until the late 1600s and 1700s that any significant descriptions of Choctaw recreation were recorded. For this reason, it is necessary to date the first period of Choctaw sport history from the beginning of the eighteenth century, even though it is reasonable to suspect that team sports were a vital part of community life among these people long before their first encounter with the written word.

Therefore, in treating the history of Mississippi Choctaw sport I have structured existing data and records within the following three periods: (1) the stickball or early historical period (1700–1917), (2) the rise of modern sports or late historical period (1918–63), and (3) formal recreation and athletics or recent historical period (1964–present).

The Stickball Period (1700–1917)

Early historical accounts of the Southeast often include references to several varieties of team sports and games among the native populations in the area. The most common of these activities included shinny, chunkey, double ball, traditional types of football and handball, as well as stickball (see Culin, 1907:36–43).

One of the earliest descriptions of a southeastern ball game is of a Timucuan handball game witnessed by Laudonniere in 1562 (p. 171): "They play at ball in this manner: they set up a tree in the midst of a place, which is eight or nine fathoms high, in the top whereof there is set a square mat, made of reeds or bullrushes, which whosoever hitteth in playing thereat winneth the game."

A similar game that involved hitting the ball with the foot was described by Father Juan de Paina (1676:4), who watched the Apalachee play during the seventeenth century.

It is assumed that the Choctaws were playing a variety of games similar to those of their southeastern neighbors during this same time period. However, explicit historical references are so limited that it is impossible to talk about Choctaw sport and games until the eighteenth century. After 1700, there are many accounts that describe the Choctaws at play.

One Choctaw game popular in the eighteenth and nineteenth centuries was chunkey (*čąki*), the southeastern variant of the widespread hoop-and-pole game. Romans (1775:80) has provided a description of this event in his *Concise Natural History of East and West Florida*:

> The manner of playing the game is thus: They [the Choctaws] make an alley of about two hundred feet in length, where a very smooth clay ground is laid, which when dry is very hard; they play two together having each a straight pole of about fifteen feet long: one holds a stone, which is in shape of a truck, which he throws before him over his alley, and the instant of its departure, they set off and run; in running they cast their poles after the stone, he that did not throw it endeavors to hit it, and the other strives to strike the pole of his antagonist in its flight so as to prevent its hitting the stone; if the first should strike the stone he counts one for it, and if the other by the dexterity of his cast should prevent the pole of his opponent hitting the stone, he counts one, but should both miss their aim the throw is renewed; and in case a score is won the winner casts the stone and eleven is up; they hurl this stone and pole with wonderful dexterity and violence, and fatigue themselves much at it.

Other early descriptions of the chunkey contest suggest that it was played in several different ways. For example, Adair (1775:401), in describing the Choctaws playing the game, observed that the poles were only eight feet in length, though several inches in diameter, and were prepared with bear oil in order to facilitate their propulsion along the hard ground of the chunkey yard. In the contests he witnessed, one of the contestants would begin play by hurling the chunkey stone, the *ačahpi*, down the middle of the well-worn field. The two combatants would then attempt to slide their respective poles in front of the rolling object so that the cumbersome shafts would come to rest at a point which they calculated would be directly adjacent to the ultimate disposition of the *ačahpi*. The contestant whose resting pole was positioned closer to the immobile chunkey stone was then declared the winner of that particular toss. Points were accumulated, and the game could go on indefinitely.

Chunkey not only provided recreation and a means for improving manual skills basic to the hunt, but it also was the focus of much gambling. The stakes often reached ridiculous proportions. Romans (1775:80) relates an incident in 1771 in which a Choctaw chunkey player lost everything he owned during a game and went home, borrowed a gun, and shot himself.

The chunkey contest and its associated betting, though viewed as recreational, was often approached with an attitude approaching boredom. Halbert (1888:284) tells of an informant who complained to him that the game was "very tedious," expressing "some surprise that his ancestors should have taken any pleasure in such a dull, uninteresting pastime."

Though some modern imitations can be witnessed periodically, the Choctaws no longer play chunkey. The original game disappeared during the last century. Halbert (1888:284) claims that the sport's demise resulted from the failure to manufacture new chunkey stones, which at one time were passed from one generation to the next as precious heirlooms: "As they began to come into contact with the civilization of the white man, implements of iron, new ideas, habits and industries were introduced. No new *achahpih* stones were then made to supply the place of those that were lost or destroyed, and in consequence the play gradually passed out of use; and now [1888] there are few living persons whose eyes have looked upon this ancient pastime of the Southern Indians."

Another sport, a handball game, was once played by Choctaw men and women alike. According to Romans (1775:79), the game, a type of racketless stickball, was played with a large ball of woolen rags. Contestants were divided into two opposing teams and attempted to move the ball the length of the field, using their hands to throw the ball through goals at opposite ends of the playing area, approximately 150 feet apart.

The Choctaws also engaged in other, less physical forms of play such as the corn and moccasin games, as well as something very similar to modern jacks (see Swanton, 1931:158–60). Romans (1775:81) describes the latter as a women's contest in which the participants "take a small stick, or something else off the ground after having thrown up a small ball which they are to catch again, having picked up the other."

The most important and consequential game in Choctaw history is undoubtedly stickball. Called *toli* by the Choctaws, and ball play, match game, racketball game, or baggataway in other contexts, the phenomenon is the original version of lacrosse.

Toli is a very physical and often dangerous sport that involves the confrontation of two teams on a large, open field. Both sides attempt to move a small ball (*towa*) toward the goal of the opponent, using only their rackets (*kapoča*) to carry and throw the ball. The first team striking the opposition's goal a predetermined number of times, usually twelve, wins the match.

Stickball was common to most of the Native American tribes of the historic Southeast (e.g., Chickasaw, Creek, Cherokee, Yuchi, Seminole). While the rules and actual patterns of play varied from one cultural setting to another, it was essentially the same game and appears to have diffused into the different parts of the region from a single source.

Existing archeological evidence suggests that the general ball game concept underlying the development of stickball was part of an integral pattern of cultural items emanating from Mesoamerica and diffusing, either directly or indirectly, into the Southeast. Stern (1948:93) has concluded that the game is one of several "diversified, wide-spread descendants of a ball-and-stick game that was ancestral as well to the competitive rubber ball game" of Mexico and the Southwest.

Apparently the racket game, as it has been played in recent centuries among Native Americans in the Southeast, developed originally in the Northeast. Ethnohistorical data supports the notion that it was played first among one of the eastern tribes and diffused later into the south via the influence of the Iroquoian-speaking Cherokees (Hoffman, 1896:130).

As to the probable date of this event, the historical record is ambiguous almost to the point of impossibility. However, when one studies the accounts written by the earlier explorers and travelers in the Southeast, he is struck by the detail of ethnographic description on practically every area of Native American life, including games and athletic activities. Still, there is no mention of stickball in the region until the early 1700s, although it had been witnessed and described by persons traveling in the Northeast several decades earlier (de Brébeuf, 1636:185; du Peron, 1639:155). As I have suggested in another context, "since the game is obviously so much more dramatic, brutal, and ritualized in the historic Southeast than in the North . . . , why were travelers so slow to mention it? The most logical answer is that while there were certainly ball games in the Southeast at an early date, it was not until the eighteenth century that stickball became the predominant sport form in the area. . . . Stickball was most visible during the 200 years after the advent of the eighteenth century" (Blanchard, 1979:194).

The first historical reference to the game in the Southeast is Father Pierre François Charlevoix's (1721:134–35) description of Creek stickball. The earliest mention of the Choctaw version of racketball is in a brief French manuscript translated by Swanton (1918:68), *Relation de La Louisiane*, written by an anonymous Jesuit priest around 1755 but referring to events in the period between 1729 and 1731. Calling it "a ballgame which is like the long racket," the original writer described only the betting that accompanied the sport, not the game itself.

The many descriptions that followed in subsequent decades lead one to assume that stickball, though often played intracommunally, was the most popular Choctaw recreational activity and a very effective device for stimulating social interaction between the many communities.

Previous to removal in the 1830s, the Choctaw world was divided into towns or villages that were scattered across what is now southern and central Mississippi. Swanton (1931:55–75) lists 115 such communities as they existed in the early 1700s, but adds that

> the places designated were probably not all occupied at the same time and there is reason to suspect that, on moving to a new site a Choctaw community sometimes changed its name. Moreover, certain of these names no doubt belonged to villages never permanently detached from some larger town. Making all due allowances, however, there were probably at one time from 40 to 50 communities constituting small States, each with its chief, war chief, two lieutenants of the war chief, or Taskaminkochi, and an assistant to or speak for the town chief, the Tishuminko [Swanton, 1931:95].

Relations between these different communities during this period ranged from constructive cooperation on the one hand to open warfare on the other, and it was against this political backdrop that the formal stickball match developed.

In the first place, the reasons for scheduling a stickball contest between two Choctaw communities varied with the season, political situation, or general inclination of the townspeople.

According to contemporary Native Mississippians, the most important of such athletic confrontations were scheduled by the chiefs of the two communities when other sources of conflict threatened to involve their respective towns in a war against each other. In such cases, the planning was a political matter, as community leaders, in conjunction with team captains or managers, determined the date and location of the game. Runners were then sent into the surrounding areas to announce the game. Often, small bundles of sticks would be distributed by the messengers with instructions that on each successive day one stick was to be removed until there were none remaining, signifying that the day of the festivities had arrived. At this same time, community leaders would select players and appoint their respective ritual specialists to act as officials, all of this occurring some three to four months before the actual event.

While the formal stickball match was often deliberately used to resolve intercommunal conflict, on many other occasions a contest would be scheduled merely for the enjoyment of the participants and spectators. In these situations, political boundaries might be ignored, two managers simply selecting players from a broad area to compete purely "for the fun of it." For example, during the late 1800s it was common for a local coach or team captain to announce that on a certain day everyone interested in playing should bring his stickball equipment to a specified site and be prepared to play. After the group had assembled, players were matched according to ability so that ultimately two equally talented teams evolved, and the game commenced.

Even though they are aware of the frequency of the informal, often intracommunal, match, today's Mississippi Choctaws argue consistently that the real stickball match of the past was that of pitting two towns against each other. Ideally, such a contest was initiated as a deliberate effort to avoid a more dangerous conflict or encounter. In any case, the formal game was a serious matter involving literally all persons residing in the towns affected by the event.

Once a *toli* game had been announced, the ensuing preparations were extensive. The players, exclusively male, spent many hours practicing, either individually or as a group. They were expected to observe strenuous ritual restrictions and they could eat no pork or any type of grease. Neither were they to participate in any sexual activities in the thirty days before the game. During the forty-eight hours prior to the contest itself, they ate and drank only minimally.

The women of the communities were also actively involved. Preparing food and gifts for the festivities and generating enthusiasm through their many hours of singing and dancing, they encouraged their respective teams and created a preliminary spirit of victory.

Local leaders were faced with the daily problems of directing the event, supervising all necessary arrangements. Often they would have to resolve conflicts that might arise between two teams or managers over an issue like unfair training practices or illegal player recruitment. For example, two opposing team officials might claim the same player if there was some question as to his primary community identity and affiliation. At that point the *miko* would have to make a final, mutually acceptable decision, which might ultimately mean that the player in question could not compete for either team.

The Choctaw ritual specialists (medicine men, witch doctors,

prophets, rainmakers) were also involved in the advance preparations for the formal stickball match. They administered special medicine to the players, treated equipment, manipulated weather conditions for the day of the planned event, and appealed to the
supernatural world for assistance in their village's effort toward victory. (See Chapter 6 for a more complete discussion of the roles of
medicine and magic in Choctaw sport.)

On the day of the stickball game itself, the respective teams and
their entourage of fans and officials would move en masse toward
the playing field. As Baxter York, the late Choctaw statesman and
unofficial tribal historian, once told me:

> In coming to the game, the teams would march down the trail,
> one-by-one, sometimes for as much as fifteen miles. . . . They
> would travel down the trail, the drum would beat, and the people
> would hear them coming. The leader of the group would lead in
> a chant, and the rest of the group would answer with a "Yoo!"
> The other group that was their competition for the match would
> meet them about half way, and there would be much shouting
> back and forth. Sometimes there would be wrestling. . . . Every-
> one was getting ready.

On the night before the actual game, preparatory activities took
on a greater frenzy and included everything from body-painting and
stickball practice to dancing and witching. One of the songs that was
sung on these occasions was the "Song for Success in the Ball Game"
that is recorded in Frances Densmore's *Choctaw Music* (1943:131).
Players carefully applied their paints, stroking symbolic designs on
the more visible parts of their bodies, and donned their brief but
flashy uniforms that, according to Catlin (1841:32), had to conform
to certain regulations: "No man shall wear moccasins on his feet,
or any other dress than his breech-cloth around his waist with a
beautiful bead belt, and a "tail," made of white horsehair or quills,
and a *"mane"*, on the neck, of horsehair dyed of various colours"
(see Figure 2).

Because of the very rigid routine and the anxiety generated by the
anticipation of the impending game, most of the players remained
awake all night.

The religious-ritual personnel moved through the group that had
congregated in anticipation of the following day's events and exercised their respective skills. They appealed to the other world for
strength to benefit both players and fans as well as for help for the
game's officials, that they might use only the wisest judgment in on-
field decisions.

Figure 2. Catlin's Ball Player, *Tullock-chish-ko*, "He who drinks the juice of the stone," (from Catlin, 1844:124) (Courtesy of National Collection of Fine Arts, Smithsonian Institution)

When most of the other details had been properly disposed of, the serious preliminary dancing and singing began. Henry S. Halbert (n.d.:148–49) describes the ball game dance which took place around one of the two goalposts on the playing field: "The painted ball-players with their ball sticks in hand . . . come forward, dance and shout around their post, then form a circle at the outer end of the line of women where they clash their ball sticks overhead, then hold them poised erect for a few moments. While they are thus standing in silence, the women, prompted by the mingo, dance and chant a song in a low tone, keeping time with their feet. The song generally was: '*Onnakma, abi hoke*' (To-morrow we will win it)."

On the following morning, preceding the actual clash of sticks and bodies, similar dancing took place again. This time the women sang: " '*Onnakma, abi hoke*' (To-day is good, we will win it). '*Towa itonla achumka abi hoke*' (The ball lies so handy, we will win it)" (Halbert, n.d.:149).

The early morning hours before the contest also witnessed the extensive betting that characterized the classic stickball game, as both sides wagered on the outcome: "The parties betting articles with each other tie the articles together and deposit them on the scaffold [specially constructed for the ball game wagering]. The women are as great bettors as the men. One woman, for instance, bets a dress against a blanket. The articles at once are tied together and placed on the scaffold. . . . Nothing was considered too sacred for a bet" (Halbert, n.d.:149).

Indeed, everything imaginable was used as stakes: horses, guns, clothes, skins, chickens, furs, trinkets, blankets, knives, whiskey, pots and pans, dogs, money, packaged food and produce: "When they are very much excited they wager all that they have, and, when they have lost all, they wager their wives for a certain time, and after that wager themselves for a limited time" (Swanton, 1918:68).

The bets were made between individuals, but the process actually amounted to one group collectively wagering their goods and services against those of their opponents. Bets were automatically placed on the team representing the betting party; there was no speculation as to relative strengths or possible outcomes, nor any odds. The winning party simply took all the spoils, and sometimes these were extensive.

The basic item of equipment in the stickball game was the racket (*kapoča*), carved from hickory, roughly squared at the handle end, but flattened, bent around, and tied to the main shaft at the other end, leaving a large loop shaped like the eye of a needle (see Figure 3). Across the space within the loop were laced several strands of

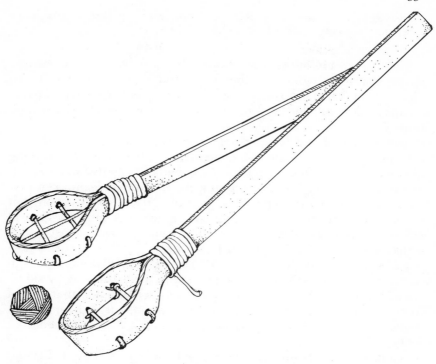

Figure 3. *Toli* Rackets (*kapoča*) and Ball (*towa*)

leather that formed a net or pocket, within which the ball was caught and carried. Sticks were usually made in pairs so that the pocket of one would interlock and fit snugly within the loop of the other. This made it possible for a player to "put the ball away," securing it between the webbed facings of the two rackets and wrapping both hands tightly around the handles of the sticks. Such interlocking decreased the possibility that one would either drop or have the ball dislodged from his racket by an opponent.

The length of the racket was variable, depending on the position and personal preferences of the individual player. Baxter York once recounted:

On the stickball team there were three types of positions: guards, forwards, and centers, with different sticks for each position. The forward stick was longer so that the ball could be thrown straighter. The center stick had a longer and narrower cup for more playing and huddling. You can shove it in there much easier. The guard stick had a long cup with holes drilled about midway in the cup. The guards protected the goals. You can throw it as hard as you can; still, they can catch it. Then they want to throw it back as far as they can; a hundred yards, if they can.

The ball used in the stickball match, the *towa*, was made of narrow strips of leather wound in the shape and size of a golf ball (see Figure 3). If it were properly made, the ball was surprisingly heavy, compact, and capable of inflicting pain if it hit a player with any force.

The nature of the playing field was never strictly defined. The only boundaries were the two goalposts at either end of the playing area, and these could be anywhere from 100 feet to five miles apart, as apparently was the case in one game in the nineteenth century.

The poles (*fabossa*) themselves were of variable construction, but frequently were made by placing two large posts into the ground side by side so as to create a broad striking surface against which a player threw the ball in order to score.

Halbert (n.d.:148) describes these as being "about twenty feet high and . . . the split halves of a log planted in the earth, side by side." Culin (1907:602) observed goalposts in another situation that looked like "two trees, lashed together with ropes, about eight inches in diameter and cut flat on one side, presenting a face of about 12 inches."

There were no boundaries on the sides of the playing field, and the game's action simply followed the ball. Many times spectators were rousted from comfortable vantage points as the fleet-footed, fast-swinging, and hard-breathing athletes scrambled after a far-flung pass. Occasionally, a slower fan was overrun by the action and sustained severe bodily injury.

The rules, like the layout of the playing field, were ambiguous and limited to only three or four stipulations. Of primary importance was the restriction that no player was to touch the ball with his hands, using instead only his rackets to carry and throw the small ball. At no time were spectators allowed to interfere in the game's process. If they did, a penalty was assessed against their team. This usually meant that one or more points were deducted from their current total.

While players could tackle, block, or use any reasonable method to interfere with the other team's movement of the ball, there were implicit limits to acceptable violence. A stickballer who displayed excessive amounts of hostile aggression was usually reprimanded and withdrawn by his manager.

Culin (1907:604) tells of one game staged in the nineteenth century in which the teams were prohibited from butting with their heads, a rule whose violation cost the culprits a five-goal penalty. Other sources and contemporary informants, however, do not mention such a restriction.

The number of persons on the two teams in a stickball match was determined at the beginning of each event, the total controlled by a requirement that combatant units field an equal number of players. Before play was initiated, both sides would line up facing each other and pair off, individual contestants laying their sticks on the ground facing those of one of their opponents. If one team had more players than the other group, the surplus was forced to retire to the wings with the spectators, participating only when called upon as substitutes.

Because of this numerical flexibility, a game could be played with as few as 20 or 30 or as many as 200 or 300 players. Catlin (1841:321) observed a game among the Oklahoma Choctaws once in which 600 to 700 men participated.

The officials for the games were chosen for each match by the leaders of the respective communities as a part of their general preparations for the events. Usually those designated were religious/ritual personnel from the competing local groups. It was their job to throw the ball up at the onset of play and at each successive juncture in the match, and to watch for any rule infractions that might occur, often determining the nature of as well as administering the resulting penalty. Also, these *apisači*, as they were called, kept score, in most cases using some visible mnemonic device. The most popular technique was that of putting into the ground the number of sticks equaling half the total necessary to win and end the game. The scorekeeper then proceeded to withdraw a stick with each score until all had been extracted, at which point he began reinserting them into the ground. When all the sticks of one of the teams had been removed and replaced, the game was over.

Another important position in the stickball game was that of the drummer, who was active throughout the match and its assorted festivities. As Baxter York has told it: "Before the stickball game, the drum would begin to beat, and you would know they were going to have a game somewhere. . . . Drums were used to pep up the game and add excitement. They beat them with a certain rhythm. This would change when one of the teams scored. This way the message could be sent to people in surrounding areas. They could tell by the beat of the drum that one of the teams had scored a point."

Using a percussion instrument made by stretching a deerskin over a tree trunk, earthen pot, or kettle, the drummer beat no predetermined pattern but simply kept pace with the ball game. As the tempo of the game increased, so too did that of his rhythm. Contemporary Choctaws contend that the drumming itself had little ceremonial meaning, serving primarily as a means of generating spirit and maintaining excitement levels among players and spectators alike.

The Choctaw doctors were also active during the game as they moved among the spectators and the players, administering special medicine to help their particular teams. One common practice was scratching the legs of players with sharp pieces of metal or glass until blood was drawn, ostensibly to prevent cramps during play.

The witch doctors moved up and down the field during the game's proceedings, going through a broad repertoire of gestures and verbal incantations. Halbert (n.d.:149) refers to the antics of these "prophets": "Each carries a small looking-glass. He turns to the sun, holds his glass towards it with a gyratory motion then turns and throws the rays upon the bodies of the players of his side. . . . As all life and power comes from the sun, the prophet flatters himself that he can infuse a portion into his own party; and if he can utilize more of it than the prophet of the opposite side, his side will win the day."

The singers (*italowa*) were responsible for the group chanting that characterized all stages of the *toli* festivities. During these activities, they would lead groups from their own communities in traditional Choctaw dances that were often designed for the particular, impending contest.

At some of the ancient stickball meets, clowns entertained by dressing and acting ridiculous. Also at some of those matches were men designated as stakeholders who supervised the betting: "The bets are made through the stakeholders—four or five Indians—who constantly ride about on horseback. Whatever is bet is put with what is bet against it. If handkerchiefs, they are knotted together and thrown over the stakeholder's shoulder; if money, the sums are put together in his pocketbook. His memory is remarkable, and he never fails to turn over the stakes correctly" (Culin, 1907:603).

The spectators or the fans (*okla yopísa*) were more than simply observers. Indeed, they played an active role in the classic stickball match. The game was an important community event; every member stood the chance of winning or losing great amounts of personal goods and prestige, so all made what constructive contributions they could to the winning effort. The women, for example, encouraged their men by shouting and pressuring them to keep the pace. Occasionally, they gave the players coffee or water to refresh them. On a more forceful level, they often carried small whips with which they lashed the naked legs of their athletes in order to increase their vigilance. Not infrequently the women would get very zealous in their participatory roles. Jackson Isaac told me: "Sometimes the women would get an ax and chop down little trees [about two inches by eighteen inches] and pile them up close to the goal by the center. Then, when they [the team] started a fight, that's when they [the women] started throwing those sticks. Just get those clubs and throw at you; just hit anybody and get into the fight."

The fans took great interest in the relative skills of individual players, and each of the athletes developed a reputation, particularly with reference to his speed. Fast players were referred to as *pałki* and the slow ones as *saláha wašoha*. Also, there were many nicknames for the contestants: *čanáša* (moccasin snake), *opa niškin* (owl or owl eyes), or *siti* (snake). The high level of fan participation made the classic stickball match the spectator sport par excellence.

The actual *toli* contest, as a part of the several days of festivities surrounding it, began in the morning of the second day, around nine o'clock. Both teams would take the field, and the players assumed their positions. A large contingent of the athletes would congregate at the point midway between the two goals with their sticks thrust high in the air to await the opening toss (see Figure 4). The official would then throw the ball up in the air, and amid much shoving and pushing the game would begin, as players swung their rackets and clutched frantically for the small deerskin sphere.

> Like a herd of stampeded buffaloes upon the western plains, they ran against and over each other, or anything else, man or beast, that stood in their way, and thus in wild confusion and crazed excitement they scrambled and tumbled, each player straining every nerve and muscle to its utmost tension, to get the ball or prevent his opponent, who held it firmly grasped between the cups of his trusty kapucha, from making a successful throw.
>   . . . a scene of wild confusion was seen—scuffling, pulling, pushing, butting—unsurpassed in any game ever engaged in by man [Cushman, 1899:127–28].

The classic stickball encounter, fast-moving, physically demanding, and usually brutal, was often marred by serious injuries. Broken arms and legs, cracked skulls, surface wounds, and a variety of minor sprains and abrasions were expected in the game. In fact, there have been cases in which so many players were injured and rendered unable to play that the game had to be called. Culin

Figure 4. Catlin's Choctaw Ball Game; Ball Up, (from Catlin, 1844:126). (Courtesy of National Collection of Fine Arts, Smithsonian Institution)

(1907:604) reported on a nineteenth-century contest in which two men were killed, such occurrences being not uncommon to the very aggressive and serious business of the racket game.

Some writers have suggested that the violence associated with the game was rarely provocation for outright fighting among the players. Bossu (1768:170), for example, claimed: "The players never become angry. The old men present at these games constitute themselves mediators and consider that the game is only a recreation and not something over which to fight."

On the other hand, most observers and informants admit to an almost predictable pattern of fighting that characterized the stickball event. Jim Gardner recalls the stories his grandfather used to tell him.

> They used to fight a lot at the stick games. The chief would set the game up and tell them not to fight, but they would fight anyhow. If two people started to fight, everybody would pretty soon be right in there fighting too.
>
> It was because of the fighting that they changed the way they played the stick game. The chiefs told the people not to fight. If they wanted to fight, he would make them wrestle; two falls. The first one to fall twice was the loser, and the wrestling was over. Then they stood up and shook hands, and the chief told them not to fight anymore.

In some cases, the fights that began at the stickball match were so serious that they carried over into future relations between the communities or families involved. In fact, several intratribal wars during the eighteenth and nineteenth centuries were aggravated initially by an altercation or injury at the *toli* game.

Fogelson (1962:151) has suggested with reference to the racket game played by the eastern Cherokees that "the ferocity of the contest was in direct proportion to the magnitude of the stakes." In some ways, the same thing can be said with reference to the classic Choctaw stickball match. As one contemporary stickball enthusiast has speculated:

> It probably would have been important as a team to win the whole thing [all the stakes that had been wagered]. . . . I think I would have tried harder if someone was betting that much on me. In a lot of cases, they even put up a woman too. And sometimes a man would think he was that good and he would put his kids up, too. And he had something to play for. I think he would have tried his best. If I had my wife and kids standing out there as my stakes, I would have played like hell.

The *toli* contest lasted until one of the two teams had scored a predetermined number of points. The number 12 is the most frequently mentioned figure when Choctaws talk about the way the game used to be played, but there are records of games that went to 100 points. Usually, the two teams would play ball from about 9:00 in the morning until 4:00 or 4:30 in the afternoon, and a game could go on for several days if the scoring was sporadic, if there were an excessive number of penalty assessments, or if many interruptions occurred because of injuries or fighting. During these several days, most of the activities focused on the events of the playing field, but there was much feasting and dancing in the evenings.

When the final point had been scored, and the outcome of the stickball match determined, the victors claimed their spoils and everyone headed for home. According to most descriptions, the Choctaws were generally stoical in dealing with the results. As Cushman (1899:130) observed: "In those ancient ball-plays, I have known villages to lose all their earthly possessions upon the issue of a single play. Yet, they bore their misfortune with becoming grace and philosophic indifference and appeared as gay and cheerful as if nothing had happened."

On the other hand, there are reports of matches in which the defeated contestants were not so generous. Jim Gardner once told me a story about a stickball game that was played in the late 1800s. The competition had been in progress most of the day when one team scored their eleventh point, needing only one more to win. Moments later, the same team regained control of the ball and was threatening to make that final tally. At that point, the rainmaker representing the team faced with imminent defeat pulled the last trick from his repertoire and caused it to rain with such suddenness and ferocity that the game had to be called, thereby saving his team from a demoralizing and expensive loss. Immediately, however, both parties broke for the scaffolds where the wagered items were being held. The almost-victorious team claimed that the stakes were all rightfully theirs, despite the unexpected early termination of the contest. Riotous fighting broke out as everyone got into the act and tried to salvage what he thought was legally his. Several hours of bloody rioting ensued.

In one sense, the violence often associated with the stickball experience was simply an expression of the basic seriousness of sport in general and *toli* in particular. Indeed, the racket game was an important part of Choctaw life in the 200 years prior to 1900.

Mississippi Choctaw stickball came under fire in the 1890s, and its popularity began to decline. During that period, there was growing concern among local whites as well as tribal leaders regarding the violence which characterized so many of the formal matches, although by this time there were few if any of the more traditional intercommunity contests. Increasingly, Anglo residents from surrounding areas began to participate as spectators. Gambling and liquor became more evident factors in the already heated competition, and many of the games ended in violent melees. The late Simpson Tubby (1975:36), Choctaw leader and Methodist clergyman, once wrote of those days: "I shall never forget those brutal ball games of my childhood days. The Indians always had whiskey on such occasions, and sometimes a number of them would get drunk and the Indians, women and children, would scatter in every direction. With battle axe, war hatchet or knife, these drunken demons would pursue their best friend, and while yet a child, I have run from 5 to 10 miles through the darkness to escape from them."

With the intrusion of whites into the spectator ranks, the betting took on new and broader proportions, and the problems of control increased. On one occasion, a local Anglo was selling peanuts during a stickball game at the Pearl River community and got into an argument with another white compatriot over a wager. Eventually there was gunplay, and an innocent Choctaw bystander was fatally shot.

One of H. S. Halbert's (1897:24–25) reports from the era reflects a typical concern:

> I wish here to state that the greatest obstacle in the way of the educational and religious progress of our Mississippi Choctaws is the Indian ball play, as it has been conducted for the past fifteen years. To put it mildly, the ball play is the most demoralizing institution in Mississippi. It is, in a great measure, now-a-days manipulated or controlled by a white swashbuckler element, and gambling, whisky drinking, fighting, and not infrequently bloodshed have become the regular concommitants of the play.

In this same context, Halbert (1897:25) recommended that the Mississippi legal code be amended to outlaw gambling at the ball games: "Legislate against betting at a ball play and the institution will soon die out, for hundreds of Indians would not go to a ball play if they were not permitted to bet or gamble there."

Shortly thereafter, in 1898, the State of Mississippi outlawed gambling at all Indian ball games. That year, Chapter 69 of the Mississippi General Laws was enacted to amend section 1122 of the Annotated

Code of 1892 in relation to gambling, "so as to include Indian Ball Plays." The amendment reads as follows:

> If any person shall encourage, promote or play at any game, play or amusement, for money or other valuable thing, or shall wager or bet, promote or encourage the wagering or betting any money or other valuable thing upon any game, play, amusement, cock fight, Indian ball play or duel, or upon the result of any election whatever, upon conviction thereof, he shall be fined in a sum not more than five hundred dollars; and, unless such fine and costs be immediately paid, shall be imprisoned for any period not more than twenty days nor less than five days.

Within a few years, Halbert's prediction had practically become a reality, as the large-scale stickball match disappeared. Although the Choctaws in Newton County had abandoned the sport as early as 1894 (Peterson, 1970:73), most of the Mississippi group continued to play. However, play was restricted to the local community setting and did not entail the festivities and elaborate trappings of previous years. Its limited visibility and gradual retreat to the backyard pushed the sport to the edge of complete obscurity. The church became the center of tribal life, and other athletic activities began to take the ball game's place as the important community events and mechanisms of social interaction.

It is interesting that the Oklahoma Choctaws also abandoned the classic racket game around the turn of the century. Unlike their Mississippi relatives, however, the western group simply quit playing because the sport had become too violent. In fact, players often came to the games with sticks specially prepared for use as personal weapons. A lead ball wrapped in leather thongs was hung from the handle end of the racket and used for clubbing opponents. One well-placed blow was easily capable of cracking a man's skull. Needless to say, games frequently degenerated into costly bloodbaths, and it soon became apparent that the gaming dimensions of the sport had been obliterated by its brutality (Garrick Bailey, personal communication, December 1, 1977).

In the past twenty-five years there has been a revival of interest in the sport among the Mississippi Choctaw people. When the Choctaw Fair was instituted in 1949, its activities were structured around stickball matches between teams representing the different local groups. In time, this new enthusiasm spread into areas outside the confines of the summer fair, even though it is still the focal point of annual stickball events.

This new interest in *toli* is manifested in many ways: a growing interest in the crafting and hand-manufacturing of rackets (*kapoča*) and balls (*towa*), the developing excitement of local groups about their representative stickball teams, the increase of games scheduled beyond the format of the fair, and the tendency for individual players to spend more time practicing and perfecting the basic skills of the sport.

The re-emergence of stickball's popularity is also evidenced by the advent of traveling teams and stickball clubs. Since the 1960s, many of the southeastern Native American tribes (e.g., Cherokee, Seminole, Coushatta) have developed stickball programs. Choctaw athletes have traveled to other reservations to compete with these groups, as well as to nonreservation areas where intrasquad games are played for the entertainment of non-Choctaw audiences. One such event took place at Gadsden, Alabama, in 1969. With support from notables like football coach Paul "Bear" Bryant, the exhibition attracted 6,000 persons despite the rain. The match itself was filmed professionally, with the assumption that ABC Television was going to buy and use the footage on its "Wide World of Sports," but according to the promoter of the show, "the film must have gotten lost in the mail."

Even though *toli* is no longer the constant preoccupation that it once was for the Mississippi Choctaws, it is still a significant factor in community life and is beginning to generate a commitment reminiscent of what it commanded in centuries past. (For a thorough description of the new racket game, see Chapter 3.)

The Introduction of Modern Sport (1918–63)

During the time that the stickball phenomenon was fading from the scene, baseball was beginning to make its presence felt among the Mississippi Choctaws. Exposed to the sport as a result of contact with white and black teams in the area, the Choctaws began to learn the rules and develop the skills of the Western game just after the turn of the century. For several years, most of their baseball playing was done in backyards and cow pastures, using makeshift equipment and competing among themselves.

Around 1910, the Choctaws organized a team in Pearl River and began ordering "real" equipment from a supply house in St. Louis. Soon, other Choctaw communities followed suit, and a league was created, composed of four or five teams that played either each other or against teams representing black communities in the surrounding area.

Jim Gardner played in that first league.

> When I was fifteen [about 1911] I played league ball. I played with my relatives in Dixon. There was a group of us there, families and sharecroppers, that lived in a bunch of houses that were together. It was like a community. We had a pretty good baseball team. We played teams from Tucker, Connehatta, Bogue Chitto, Red Water. . . .
>
> Tucker had the best team in those days. Jimmie MacMillan played for them. He was real good . . . never played any pro ball, though.
>
> In those days the manager and the team captain planned the games. They would get together with the other managers and decide on a time and place, and just tell us to be there. . . . We didn't have any cars then. We just walked. I used to walk twenty miles to go to a game in Beat Five [north of Philadelphia]. Then, the man I worked for got a car, in 1926, and he used to bring me over here [Pearl River] and let me off by the swamp, and I would walk the rest of the way. Usually, after the game I would just stay and walk back on Sunday.

Perhaps the single most significant event underlying the introduction of modern team sports in Choctaw society was the advent of the Bureau of Indian Affairs Choctaw Agency in 1918 and the subsequent opening of government schools in the area. Prior to this date, formal Choctaw education had been limited to a mission school that had been established in the Tucker community and to Choctaw public schools for a brief period during the 1890s.

Under the first federal program for the Choctaws, the Pearl River and Standing Pine schools opened their doors in 1920. These were followed by Tucker in 1921, and by 1930 there were schools in all the Choctaw villages offering at least six years of education. The Pearl River School added a ninth grade in 1945.

From the beginning, the schools had programs in baseball and basketball, pupils were taught the fundamentals of the sports, and competition was arranged between teams representing the different educational institutions. In many ways, these interscholastic contests were modeled after older intercommunity stickball matches and reflected some of the same solemnity.

By the 1930s, baseball had replaced stickball as the most popular Choctaw sport. The men's teams and leagues had become more sophisticated, there were more good players, and the elementary schools offered at least recreational periods in which the children, specifically the boys, could play the game and master its skills.

At the adult level, most of the intercommunity competition remained largely informal. The manager of the individual team was the key to league organization. He was chosen not only for his knowledge of the game and coaching ability, but also because he had some form of transportation by which the team could make the often lengthy trip to scheduled games. At the beginning of the season (as early as March), the managers of the teams got together and worked out a rough schedule of games. It was then up to each manager to contact the players on his team and inform them as to when the first game was going to be played and where and when to meet on that day in order to ride with him to the ball field. While communication was solely by word of mouth, enthusiasm and anticipation were high, so communication problems rarely developed, and players were seldom absent or even tardy when a game or practice session had been planned.

During the '30s and '40s communities developed tremendous pride in their respective baseball teams, and intertown competition began to achieve levels comparable to that characterizing nineteenth-century stickball.

During this period it was an honor to be on the local baseball team, and usually only the best players were asked to join. As a Choctaw boy was growing up, he often devoted large segments of time practicing and playing baseball with his age-mates, dreaming of the day he might be recruited by the manager of the community squad. Albert Farve recounts his own experience:

One day I was playing out in the yard. . . . We used to have a lot of this little gravel, with little round rocks. I would get a broomstick, cut it, and go out there and just hit. I learned to hit that way. . . .

I was out there, and my Mama hollered at me, and there was old Willie Solomon. He was managing the baseball team and had been for a long time. He was standing in the yard, and Mama was sitting on the porch.

"Willie wants to know if you'll join up with him. He wants you on his team."

At that time I asked Mama, "What do you think?"

She said, "It's really up to you. If you want to play; it's up to you."

We sat there and talked for a few minutes; finally Willie said, "I'll take care of him; see that he gets to the ball games and all."

So I agreed to it, and he said, "Be there Saturday."

I was ready at nine o'clock in the morning. I was there at twelve o'clock. . . . The manager just got his ballplayers together and brought up the changes he had in mind. . . .

So he told them, "Here's a guy that you were talking about that you wanted to train. He wants to be a ball-player, so I got him on the team last Wednesday."

So they picked on me a little bit. They told me about all the dangers. "You could get hit by a fast pitch," and things like that.

One of them took me up to the batter's box, and the pitcher was throwing. . . . They tried to give me a feeling of what it was like standing up there at the plate holding that bat and getting ready for that pitch. . . .

They didn't start me off. I just warmed up with them. I didn't get to play that game and I didn't get to play the next game, but gradually, I got the feeling of playing the outfield.

Finally, one game he stuck me in there. . . . That was the biggest day of my life.

In the early days of Choctaw baseball, the expense of maintaining the individuals, the teams, and the league itself was handled primarily by the players. Occasionally, the manager would have to buy some new equipment, a new bat for example, and at the next game squad members would be asked to contribute from their own pockets. No records were kept, but everyone apparently assumed an equitable responsibility so that no additional pressures were required.

By the mid-'40s costs had increased, but at the same time new sources of income were being generated. Sometimes a Choctaw league team would play an off-reservation team and get a flat fee for transportation and also a cut of the gate receipts. For example, they might play a team from Jackson that would advance them forty-five dollars for transportation and later give them an additional 60 percent of the money from ticket sales if they won and 40 percent if they lost.

Still, baseball always ended up costing its participants, but they rarely complained. One player who was active during the late '40s speculates that he spent an average of fifteen dollars a season on league baseball, not including the initial expenditures for a glove and other basic equipment. Most of this money he gave to the manager to help cover weekly transportation costs. Also, there were the occasional dimes and quarters placed in the team collection to cover the purchase of new balls and bats. Finally, his uniform would require a cash outlay of about three dollars a year. According to this same player's calculations, that fifteen dollars then represented the equivalent of over a hundred dollars in 1977.

Because of the novelty of the sport during the early part of the century, young boys had few opportunities outside the schools to play baseball or perfect its fundamental skills. Most parents were not familiar with the details of the game and children were rarely encouraged, much less instructed, by their fathers or mothers. Older brothers and uncles were the most important persons in the baseball socialization process during this period—where, when, and if it took place.

Another limitation to the development of baseball expertise among Choctaw youth at that time was the lack of good equipment, particularly balls, bats, and gloves. Many of a boy's first experiments with the sport were conducted with homemade equipment.

Generally, a Mississippi Choctaw athlete's initiation into the world of baseball was a situational, almost haphazard process. Albert Farve once told me about his first exposure to baseball:

> I guess I was about ten years old when I had my first experience with baseball. My father . . . had never played any ball in his life . . . and never taught us anything about ball-playing. My brother was already playing on an independent baseball team. . . . He used to take me to the games, the local games. We used to walk up to the field. I would just sit back and just watch them play. I was not so interested at that time. While the ball game was going on, kids my age would get together and chase some butterflies and grasshoppers. A couple hundred people would be there, but we would go into the woods . . . chase lizards. We could care less what was going on.
> Later on, the following year, I began to watch the ball game a little bit more. My friends and I used to do the same things; just chase each other around. But one time, I was sitting beside my brother, and a foul ball came rolling by me. I picked it up and threw it back to the ball-players. Somehow or other, I felt the ball inside of me. It was something I can't describe. I just wanted to feel the ball more and more. So every time there was a foul ball, I used to go after it. The next thing I knew, the kids I hung around with stopped chasing butterflies and started chasing balls.

Later, after expressing an interest in the game, Farve and his brother had several discussions about the basics of sport.

> One time, Mama, while this conversation was going on, stepped in and said, "If you really want to play, why don't I make you a ball?"
> I asked her if she could make a baseball.
> She said, "No. Baseballs are made somewhere else, but I can make you a ragball."
> A few days later she wound me a ball about the size of a baseball; rags and what-have-you, put together. So I went out by myself and played. . . . I cut me a piece of wood, about this long and this big around [the size of a baseball bat] and started hitting. I had watched ballplayers enough so that at least one of them was my idol. I would hit it and catch it before it hit the ground. I started running and hitting by doing that.

During the '40s and early '50s, ragball, a game common throughout the rural South in this period, was the principal mechanism whereby many Choctaw children were introduced to baseball and developed its fundamental skills. Carl Tubby remembers his early years:

> Sometimes our cousins would just come over so we could play ball on Saturday or Sunday afternoon. Just playing ball, all afternoon, ragball.
> The ball was made out of rag. We just found a good, strong piece of wood, light, that we used. Sometimes we would go out and cut a pine tree just to make a bat. We'd select a certain size and get the bark off and let it dry out a little bit. Then we'd use it for a bat. . . .
> We used to make gloves out of some kind of cloth; just sew it together and put it over our hand like a glove. We used to have a lot of ingenious ways of doing things. Our parents may have been able to buy us one, but we didn't need it. Even when we had a rubber ball, which could go very far, we never hardly used it. We had a softball, but we didn't play with it; just the homemade stuff.

The rules as well as the equipment were not always consistent with written regulation when Choctaw children played their ragball brand of baseball. As Albert Farve admits: "I don't know where we got the idea, but we did not play exactly like the real ball-players. We didn't play regular put-outs. You just hit the guy with the ball, and he was out. That was a lot of fun. If a guy is on first base heading toward second, and the ball comes to the second baseman, he's not going to tag the runner. He's just going to wait on him until he's about five feet away and just throw the ball at him. If he hits him, the guy is out."

During the late '30s and early '40s the public media began to affect levels of both enthusiasm and baseball knowledge among the Mississippi Choctaws. The radio and newspaper, novel items in the Choctaw world at that time, were valuable to the ball-diamond education of both young and old members of the tribe. One budding athlete of the 1940s recalls:

> One time I turned the radio on. . . . It was run by batteries; we didn't have electricity then. A baseball game was on. It was the New York Yankees at that time. So, I listened, and began to get interested more and more. I began to imagine that I was in Yankee Stadium watching the Yankees play. I listened to all their games, and by the end of the season I knew the names of the whole Yankee team. . . . At the time, Mickey Mantle was there, Hank Bauer, Gene Woodling, Yogi Berra, Phil Rizzuto, Dr. Bobby Brown. . . . I always imagined being there when I listened to the game.

I finally said to myself, "One of these days I'm going to be a ball-player."

That was at the end of my thirteenth year.

The late '40s witnessed the return of the World War II veterans, and many of them brought home a new baseball sophistication and training. While few participated in World War I because of their lack of citizenship status prior to 1924, 136 Mississippi Choctaws served in the second international conflict. Of the 125 who returned, many were athletes and had both learned and developed new ball-playing skills while in uniform. Their freshly acquired abilities and knowledge were a boon to the general refinement of Choctaw sport behavior.

During the years that baseball was the king of Choctaw team sports, one of the occasional highlights of the season, which lasted from March to often as late as October, was the picnic. In many ways comparable to the festive stickball match of centuries past, the picnic was a combination of sporting events, dancing, singing, and eating. Unlike its stickball model, however, the picnic was usually only a one-day event.

During the early 1900s, the picnic was the stage for two major athletic activities. According to Jim Gardner, "They would get together on Friday and play baseball, then dance all night, and then play stickball the next day."

Later, however, stickball was dropped, and baseball became the focal point of the picnic, as several communities came together at the invitation of the host village to participate in a day-long tournament, eat, and then spend the evening doing traditional dances. Beginning early on the morning of the picnic, usually held on a Saturday, the women of the entertaining local group would begin preparing the food that had been brought for the occasion: a pig, chickens, corn, beans, bread, and squash. They would cook all morning while the baseball tournament was under way. The teams would play until the food was ready at lunchtime, after which they would resume their competition until supper, when once again all would stop to eat. After dark the traditional dancing would begin and go on all night. By early evening, most of the persons left in attendance were those of the host group, the others having gone home after their particular teams were eliminated from the tournament.

One who has many fond memories of the picnic recalls the typical evening's activities: "The dancing was led by the chanter, the *talowa*. He was usually an old man in the community that everybody liked and respected. In those days, the chanter, the singer would dance with everybody else, and everybody would join in the singing. That made it more fun, more interesting" (than his standing off to the side and chanting, with or without a public address system, as is usually the case in the contemporary Choctaw situation).

The picnic was an important meeting for community interaction, as distant tribesmen came together to re-establish old ties and talk of new group concerns as well as to play baseball and indulge large appetites. In some instances, it also served to provide a setting within which courtship might take place. Despite controls limiting such liaisons, Choctaw boys and girls often took advantage of the situation to make new acquaintances or reaffirm old relationships.

On the other hand, the picnic was not a completely congenial event. Like its stickball forebear, the baseball contest was highly competitive and, because community and individual prides were at stake, sometimes led to violence. While the open hostility was not consistently expressed, occasionally fights would erupt between representatives of different communities over a game or a long-standing disagreement between the two areas. Certain of the several Choctaw local groups were more likely to provoke physical confrontation than others. Even though none of these incidents were of any really serious nature, the chronic troublemakers were generally not invited to picnics.

Some older Choctaw raconteurs contend that it was drinking that led to the ultimate demise of the picnic, sometime during the late '50s. However, for several decades the picnic was a red-letter day on the local social calender.

Another important occasion in the annual round of sporting events in the Choctaw world during the 1930s and '40s was the Gala Day, held once a year on the first Friday and Saturday in July at the grade school in the Tucker community. The activities included a festive meal on Friday night and softball and baseball games on Saturday. In many ways, the Gala Day festivities can be viewed as the forerunner of the annual Choctaw Fair.

Of greater consequence relative to local standings than the picnic and Gala Day celebrations were the annual play-offs, during which the league championship was determined. This grand finale brought to a head all of the efforts and community enthusiasm generated during the long season.

Each year, on the basis of regular season play, the top four teams were selected to enter the final tournament. Entry fees were charged, and this money along with that made from concessions was divided primarily among the victors, although every team got some share of the income. The winners would get 50 percent, the runners-up 25, and the others 15 and 10, respectively. A now-retired baseball player from Tucker once told me that his team won the play-offs at the end of the old Choctaw Independent League's last season. That year the winners made a total of about $100 and used the money to finance a big potluck supper for the whole community. To the end, baseball remained a community enterprise.

During the years that baseball was the most popular sport among the Choctaws, it was viewed as more than entertainment. It was a serious part of community and personal life. Choctaw men and boys spent many hours practicing in an attempt to improve individual skills and game performance. Albert Farve recounts a period when most of his teammates were hardworking sharecroppers who would head for the ball diamond as soon as they finished work each afternoon during the baseball season. On Monday, Thursday, Saturday, and Sunday afternoons, if no formal game were scheduled, this group would congregate and compete in a rotational variety of the sport. Three players would form a team and take the bat, while the rest covered the positions in the field. They would bat until they had made three outs, at which point three other players would step to the plate, retiring the batters to the defense until their turn arose again. They would continue at this game for several hours, usually until darkness made further play impossible.

Besides time spent practicing or scrimmaging, many additional hours were spent repairing or cleaning the local ballfields. Each team, under the supervision of its representive manager, was responsible for maintaining its own diamond. This meant that from time to time, members of the local team would meet at their ball park and spend a large portion of the day picking up trash, cutting the grass, repairing the backstop, and raking the base paths. Again, however, this was assumed to be simply part of the price one had to pay for the privilege of swinging a bat and wearing a glove for the hometown baseball team.

Baseball players during these years were anxious to develop a complete knowledge of the game, and they appreciated the instruction of managers and older athletes. They learned to read defenses and hit to the weak side of the field. They developed an encyclopedic knowledge of the special strengths and characteristics of each of their regular opponents. They knew individual batting averages, pitching percentages, and the nuances of each field on which they played. Baseball was mental as well as physical exercise.

Choctaw baseball players were also expected to observe certain pre-game restrictions, similar to those characterizing the traditional stickball match, in order to be prepared physically and emotionally for each contest. As one of the older players told me,

> Many times when an important game was scheduled the following day, for example a Sunday, the night before the game the coach would sit his players down and preach to them. Getting everyone together in a group, he would tell them, "Tomorrow's game is very important. This team has some good players."
>
> Then he would give them instructions about how they should play that team and what they should know about each player on that team, their hitting, pitching, fielding. He would also tell them not to drink any that night, and in those days the team respected their coach and would not touch that alcohol before an important game.
>
> It was also important before a game that a man not have sex with his wife . . . if a man's wife was pregnant, he would not play for the whole time that she was pregnant. . . .
>
> . . . any kind of contact with women was prohibited; holding hands, or anything like that. In fact, riding to the ball games in the flatbed trucks like we used to do, we couldn't even sit next to any female. They said that it would weaken us or take our minds off the ball game.

Players often appealed to medicine or magic to assist them in their quest for success on the ball diamond. The services of a Choctaw doctor, black witch doctor, or local sorcerer might be solicited by an athlete for a special treatment that would work to give him special powers, defend him against the magic of the opponents, or otherwise affect the outcome of the ball game. (See Chapter 6 for greater detail regarding the role of magic and medicine in Choctaw sports.)

For the forty years that baseball was the dominant team sport among the Mississippi Choctaws, it was an important focal point of community life.

Basketball began to assume a significant role in the Choctaw sport repertoire in the early 1920s. Like its summertime counterpart, the winter event had diffused across cultural lines as a result of contacts between the Native- and both Afro- and Anglo-American communities in east central Mississippi.

Unlike baseball, however, basketball in its early years among the Choctaws tended to have its greatest impact on the youth, only later affecting the adults. This pattern of differential diffusion was due to the fact that during the 1920s, the principals of the Bureau of Indian Affairs' elementary schools introduced the sport as a recreational option, supervised the construction of outdoor basketball courts, and encouraged student participation.

According to Beckett (1949:70), the Choctaw school squads often played off-reservation groups. For example, during the 1940s they competed with several 4-H teams composed of local Whites in one of the school gymnasiums in Philadelphia.

Most of the basketball competition was interscholastic, however, as the boys' and the girls' teams from one school in the Choctaw system played against those from another.

During the late '40s, the Choctaws organized several adult basketball teams. However, they could not participate in any of the independent leagues in Philadelphia because of racially exclusive policies. Nevertheless, when the Bureau of Indian Affairs organized a basketball league on the reservation in the early '50s, any team—white, black, or otherwise—was allowed to participate, and many did, both Choctaw and non-Choctaw.

By the end of the '50s there were both Choctaw men's and women's basketball leagues. Enthusiasm for the sport reached new highs. The development of intercommunity rivalries, the improvement of individual player skills in ball-handling and shooting, and the emergence of well-polished teams led eventually to a sophisticated seriousness that had characterized both stickball and baseball during the heights of their respective popularities. Night after night, league teams would play before standing-room-only crowds in the community gymnasium in Pearl River. Players practiced and trained with great sincerity, and along with the fans, manifested a basic commitment to their respective teams and their success.

Besides the community independent leagues, church basketball teams were organized, and interdenominational competition was instituted. One of the continuing rivalries was between the Baptists and the Methodists in Pearl River.

The popularity of the sport and the many opportunities for play at both adolescent and adult levels led to the gradual extension of basketball's seasonal limits until it completely filled that part of the year when baseball was in hibernation, from October until April.

Similar to the process by which Choctaws learned to play baseball, basketball socialization in the first five decades of the twentieth century was apparently incidental and only ambiguously structured. Most of the Choctaw youngsters developed their basketball skills with rough, homemade equipment on improvised backyard courts. One ambitious boy who later became a reputable athlete in local competition claims that he first learned to play basketball in a large vacant room in his older sister's house. Having seen the game played by local Whites and some of his schoolmates, he tacked a small wagon-wheel ring to the wall and, buying a small rubber ball, spent many hours developing the ability to throw the ball through the hoop.

Another Choctaw basketball player remembers his first attempts at the sport:

> Some of us got together; we got tired of playing ragball or just rolling tires down the road or fishing in the creek. We found a rubber ball and just learned to play. We'd seen a lot of basketball before.
>
> What we'd do, we'd find some kind of round thing that had a hole in it. We'd hang it up on a tree or something. Sometimes we'd cut out both ends of a fruit can and hang it up. . . . We set up a pole, put the can on the pole, got a small rubber ball [from the dimestore] and just started playing.
>
> We used to play basketball out there all the time. Just rough-and-tumble kind of basketball; no referee, no rules, just shoot and make points. Nobody knew what a foul was.

Another limitation on a Choctaw youth's ability to fully develop his basketball playing skills was the fact that in order to complete a high school education, he had to matriculate to schools in either North Carolina or Oklahoma. The Choctaw schools in the area offered nothing beyond the ninth grade until 1950, when Pearl River added a tenth. As a result, there were no real opportunities for participation and training in a solid secondary scholastic program except for those few who opted to make the long trek across state lines to get a diploma. Of those who did go, some played basketball, and often quite well. Hamilton Farve and Luke Jimmy, for example, were outstanding athletes in the school-away-from-home environment who came back to Mississippi after graduation and had a significant influence on the basketball skills of their age-mates without real high school experience.

Basketball's reign over the Choctaw sport world, which peaked during the 1960s, was different from those of its earlier counterparts—stickball and baseball—in their primes. Basketball never became the focal point for broader community celebrations and festivities. However, basketball did provide an opportunity for women to compete seriously with each other and develop their own contingent of faithful fans. In this sense, basketball was the first real community-wide participation sport engaged in by Choctaw athletes.

While basketball never provided a focus for community events like the picnic or Gala Day, it did make possible the "marathon tournament." This special competition, sponsored by the recreation department or an off-reservation group, recently the United Southeastern Tribes, was designed to get a complete double-elimination basketball tournament involving as many as sixteen teams in a single weekend. Play would begin on a Friday and continue without interruption until the final championship game on Sunday. This meant that games had to be scheduled at all hours of the day and night, some teams were forced to play two games in succession, players slept and ate only when it was convenient between contests, and the winning squad might play as many as six or seven games in the short span of the three-day festivity. Marathon basketball created the need for a new, comfort-defying commitment, but the Choctaws relished the experience and would drive hundreds of miles to compete in such a tournament.

Softball initially worked its way into the world of the Native Mississippians during the 1920s, but was largely ignored because of the great fascination with baseball and basketball. Also, in its early years on the reservation, softball was seen purely as a women's sport, "sissy baseball," even though for many seasons only the fast-pitch variety was played. Slow-pitch softball was not introduced in the area until the 1960s.

During the period between 1920 and 1960, softball remained primarily a women's game among the Choctaws. Certainly, female participation in the activity was an important element in the sport socialization process and aided significantly in the development of healthy attitudes toward the idea of women competing and becoming athletically skillful.

Choctaw women, as compared to their Anglo-American counterparts, are generally more sophisticated and enlightened in their conception of female roles vis-à-vis athletic competition. Young girls are encouraged by their parents to develop physical coordination and ability, Choctaw men view athletic accomplishment as an attractive attribute among members of the opposite sex, and females themselves select certain athletes of their own gender as role models very early in life. Choctaw women are not intimidated by male athletes, and girls grow up learning to compete with and defeat their masculine peers without fear of rejection or social ostracism. Fathers and mothers take great pride in a daughter's beating a boy in a footrace or throwing him to the ground in a wrestling match. In school, girls stand their ground in fistfights with their fellow male students, and as they grow older, the best female athletes tend to be the most popular members of their sex among the high school population.

The healthy female athlete self-concept is reflected in the language. The Choctaw term for a masculine girl (*alla nakni iklanna*, "half boy") reflects essentially the same meaning as that for a feminine boy (*alla tik iklanna,* "half girl"). Neither has stigmatizing overtones. If anything, there is something rather wholesome about being "tomboy" in Choctaw society.

The equality of men's and women's sports among the Choctaws is reflected in the female's primary commitment to the athletic activities of the "fair" sex. Gloria York has expressed this sentiment:

> I remember going to women's games when I was young. They played fast-pitch then. I used to watch my sisters—Dessie and Shirley—play. I used to sit and wonder if when I got as big as they were I could play too. . . .
> The women's teams always made a bigger impression on me than the men's. Why do you think I'd be impressed by the men? . . . I don't think my nephews or cousins would want to play like me at softball; why should I want to play like them?
> Men's games were to me boring. Maybe I just couldn't identify with that. Whereas with women's games, I knew eventually I would be part of that.

No area of Choctaw athletic life is too sacred. Even stickball, which has always been primarily a man's game, although women have been known to play in informal matches, is now being threatened by female invasion. Though I have yet to see or hear about an actual women's stickball match, there was at least one such activity planned during the summer of 1977. Only a conflict with the softball schedule prevented it from taking place.

Despite its effect on and popularity among Choctaw women, softball did not really capture community-wide imagination nor instill in its participants the kind of commitment generated by basketball and baseball until the late '60s.

Another game that became popular during this era of Choctaw history was an event referred to locally as "rings." Equipment for this amusement consisted only of four sets of large metal washers, which could be purchased at one of the hardware stores in Philadelphia. Ideally, in the game of rings, four contestants stood in a circle facing a small hole that had been dug in the ground some ten to fifteen feet from the circumference and alternately attempted to toss one ring at a time into the hole. If one of the combatants managed to loop one of the washers into the goal, he scored four points. However, if on the next toss the opponent to his left likewise sank a shot, the previous score was canceled. When one of the players ran out of rings, they were retrieved, and play continued until someone scored a predetermined number of points.

Rings were generally viewed as a pastime game requiring limited skill. However, many men would spend hours looping washers to-ward the little hole and frequently betting on the outcome of indi-vidual games. In these cases, stakes were usually very small and won or lost with relative indifference.

Men also played horseshoes in backyards and shot pool in area taverns. Choctaw children played well-known favorites like kick-the-can, hide-and-seek, and other time-filling pleasures of their own invention. For example, Carl Tubby tells of a golf-like game he and his brothers developed in the front yard of his parents' home. With no previous exposure to golf, they dug eight small holes in various places around the house and, with sticks cut especially for this pur-pose, hit small rubber balls from one hole to the next.

Among the variety of skill games that were played during this period, however, baseball, basketball, and softball were the premier sport activities of the Choctaw, and each in its own way and time commanded the serious attention of participants and spectators alike.

The Recent Historical Period (1964–Present)

In 1964, the new Choctaw Central High School facilities were opened, the first senior class was graduated, and a new era in local history began. For the first time, Choctaw students could complete their secondary education locally.

The high school afforded novel opportunities for local athletes. In the 1950s, the Pearl River School had had a sports program, but it featured limited activities and schedules. Explicit racial bias, resulting from the segregation policy of white schools and their refusal to associate or compete with non-Whites, as well as inadequate staffing and facilities, kept the institution barred from the Mississippi Athletic Association. As a result, Choctaw high school athletes were forced to compete among themselves or with other private schools. In other cases, they were pitted against informal teams with adult-aged players.

In the late '50s, the Pearl River School basketball team did compete against a few other public institutions, but with the verbal under-standing that the Choctaw school's lack of MAA affiliation would not affect the status of those scholastic teams choosing to compete with them.

Between 1960 and 1964, however, there were no athletic programs at the Pearl River School at all. According to staff members from that period, there were simply not sufficient personnel to handle the necessary planning, scheduling, and coaching responsibilities.

The opening of the new high school symbolized the beginning of a new sense of tribal unity, as Choctaw life increasingly focused on events in Pearl River. When children from the several communities came to Pearl River in order to go to school and lived in the dormitories with students from other areas, high school activities often created the need for intercommunity cooperation. This, coupled with the development of new programs and employment opportunities in Pearl River, caused many tribesmen from other communities to move from their traditional homes and settle in the more progressive environment. As a result, many old local group rivalries were altered, and migrating families developed new community identifications. The athletic events at the high school served to channel this new sense of community.

High school basketball came to Choctaw Central in 1965. Limited to a small schedule because of their exclusion from the Mississippi Athletic Association, they fielded men's and women's teams, both faring well that first season. With their eventual entry into the MAA in 1968, the level of competition increased as did their own competency, and Choctaw basketballers developed regional reputations. In 1970, for example, the boys' team won fifteen of their twenty-four games and went to the state tournament. Several of their players that year were named to all-star teams, including Thurman Sam, who won all-state honors.

Football was added to the program in 1966. Previously, few of the students at the Choctaw high school had had any exposure to the game. Some of the boys had footballs and they had played a rough, sandlot variety of the game, but with only a limited understanding of the sport and its fundamentals. Carl Tubby recalls his first experience with the game:

> It was around when I was in the third grade. We just picked it up from the other kids who had played before. . . . We didn't know what a quarterback was. All we knew was that we lined up at one end after someone scored, then kicked off the ball, and that was it. After that, it was free-for-all; no rules or regulations on how you were supposed to play. The only thing that mattered was to get the ball to the other side and score. We could only score by touching a pole, maybe a telephone pole, an electric pole, or some kind of pole, as a goal post. We had to touch it with the ball. If we threw it, it didn't count.
> There were no rules, and we played anywhere when we got a bunch of boys together. Girls would never play. They thought it was too rough. As a matter of fact, sometimes kids would almost get their leg broken or their arm broken. Somebody might crack their head on a concrete sidewalk, be dragged all over the ground,

getting scraped. No matter how rough the ground was, we played on it.

With the advent of the first football season at Choctaw Central, the new coach persuaded about thirty boys to come out and participate. He put together a small schedule of five games against parochial schools in the area and worked for several weeks, teaching his inexperienced team the fundamentals and trying to get them in physical condition for the sport. One of the major problems faced by the novel sports program was the fact that the high school had no pads, helmets, or uniforms of any kind. Despite the equipment shortage, the first game went as scheduled. The Catholic school that they were to play was gracious enough to bring along additional outfits, so minutes before the game, the Choctaw Central gridsters donned the protective paraphernalia of the sport for the first times in their lives and trotted out onto the field. Surprisingly enough, they lost that first football contest by only two touchdowns.

They went on to lose all five games they played that year, but the following year the Choctaw Central football team acquired a new coach, and the entire sports program became a part of the Mississippi Activities Association. Three years later they were admitted to the Cherokee Conference, and since that time Choctaw Central has been quite successful on the gridiron. Three times they have won the northern division conference title, and several of their outstanding ball-players have had brief stints as college athletes.

In 1966, the Choctaw community was admitted to the Mississippi Recreation Program, making its boys' team eligible to participate in the state's Dixie Youth Basketball Association. In subsequent years, several of the villages fielded squads, and on many occasions they have had good showings in the Dixie Youth play-offs. In the early years of their participation in the program, however, there was open opposition from white teams in the area. In 1968, for example, the manager of a Philadelphia team threatened to take all the local groups out of the league if their all-stars had to compete with a Choctaw team in the championship tournament. Their protest was overruled by Dixie Youth officials, and as threatened, Philadelphia withdrew from the competition.

More recently, though, most of the old prejudices have been shoved to one side, and Choctaw teams have encountered little adverse reaction from local Anglo groups. Now, Little League, girls' softball, men's and women's basketball and baseball teams compete freely with non-Choctaw units, and friction is rare.

During the late '60s, softball began to come into its own among the Mississippi Choctaws. Slow-pitch teams were organized for men and women, leagues were formed, and a new intercommunity excitement over summer softball developed. An all-star team, selected from the women's league, helped to put the Choctaw world on the sports map of the Southeast at this time, winning several area and regional championships in tournaments as far away as Atlanta, Chattanooga, and Memphis. By the mid-1970s, softball had become so popular among Choctaws that it was beginning to threaten the decade-long domination of basketball. In a survey conducted among the several Choctaw communities in the summer of 1975, 31 percent of the total sample queried claimed that softball was their "favorite sport." Baseball and basketball polled 22 and 16 percent, respectively. In defense of the latter, however, it is probably significant that the questionnaire was administered during the softball-baseball season, and results may not reflect overall popularity.

In 1973, the Choctaw Recreation Board was created to supervise tribal sporting activities. The board is composed of ten regular (seven community and three at-large representatives) and three ex-officio (non-voting) members who are appointed by the tribal council. Under this administrative structure, recreation was given a new emphasis, and more Choctaw athletic aspirants began to participate in one of the several activities directed by the group.

Previously, many of the community recreation programs (e.g., basketball) had begun to be dominated by the white teams and their managers, who had been allowed, in fact invited, to join the league. At one point, the Anglo faction in the Choctaw Independent Basketball League, even though they were playing on reservation land and in tribal facilities, attempted, albeit unsuccessfully, to reorganize and virtually take over the program. Because of the manipulation and domination by outside groups, many Choctaws had begun to lose their excitement over league competition. With tribal reorganization, however, this changed; the Anglo terms were quieted, and simultaneously, Choctaw participation and enthusiasm increased dramatically.

For several years since its creation, the Choctaw Recreation Board, with a director and three local coordinators, has administered programs in basketball, softball, baseball, and swimming. Most of the activities have been geared to the adult population. On the other hand, the high school, local Little League, and Dixie Youth organizations have provided many sport options for the school-aged faction of the community. In order to avoid overlap or conflict of interest, the board ruled in 1974 that no athlete, male or female, playing on a Choctaw Central High School team could participate in a recreation league activity at the same time.

In recent years, the Choctaws have also participated in the functions of the National Indian Activities Association. Headquartered in Seattle, Washington, this organization annually sponsors basketball tournaments, rodeos, boxing matches, and other sporting events in which Native Americans from all over the country compete. While they have yet to win a major NIAA championship, the Mississippi Choctaws have sent several teams to the regional finals.

In 1976, a total of 815 persons participated in tribal-sponsored recreation activities (Mississippi Band of Choctaw Indians, 1977:6). The following year, 120 Choctaw adults played on basketball and 250 on softball teams in a total of more than 475 games under the authority of the tribal program. Baseball teams were organized that summer, but operated outside the jurisdiction of the board because regulations prohibited certain forms of non-league competition players deemed essential.

Nonetheless, the program had an obvious impact on the daily lives of most local Choctaws who participated as either player or spectator. In many ways, the formal recreation activities had become symbolic of that basic passion for sports characteristic of this group. The large contingent of sport enthusiasts among the Choctaws in 1977 took very seriously and were vitally committed to their respective athletic activities and teams.

This obsession with intercommunity athletic events may not be unique to the Mississsippi Choctaws, but certainly it would be difficult for any other group to top their general excitement over or investment in such team sport activities. Outsiders often observe and comment on this obvious fascination and commitment, and the Choctaw people themselves are quick to admit that such observations are generally justified.

Many times members of the community who play on a league team will miss work for several days because of an illness. Yet during that time they may show up for a ball game and play, despite the fact that they are not well and should be home in bed. Ball games can be more important than one's health. One can afford to miss work for health reasons, but not a scheduled ball game.

Choctaw league athletes, though normally soft-spoken and even-tempered, can often get very agitated if for some reason a game is canceled. A political rally, a church-sponsored revival, or the threat of bad weather often provokes such cancellation and, simultaneously, the wrath of the sport enthusiasts. Even in cases where a death in one of the communities has forced the rescheduling of a recreation event, a practice consistent with the traditional respect accorded to the recently dead, some will protest.

Expense is generally of limited importance where athletic activities are concerned. Costly shoes and gloves, color-coordinated uniforms, sweat bands, special batting gloves, ankle and knee supports, and warm-up jackets are all simply part of the particular sport, be it baseball, softball, or basketball. Choctaws generally do not question the amount of money spent for such items relative to income and other normal household needs. The proprietor of a sporting goods store in nearby Philadelphia claims that it is not unusual to see a Choctaw couple spend $100 or $200 on any given day, simply to equip several members of their family for the sport currently in season. As he put it, "Those Choctaws really put a lot into their gloves. They might need other things, household items, clothes for the kids, but that expensive glove comes first. They might owe money all over the place, but they'll spend what they've got on that new glove if they need it. It doesn't matter what their financial state is."

Recreation activities can also be more important than other vital economic concerns. Often, planting will be delayed and garden work left undone if these activities conflict with a sporting event. Money that might be needed for farming equipment is sometimes spent on sporting goods. Occasionally, athletic priorities override agricultural ones completely. On a day in June, 1977, when league softball tournament play was scheduled, one of the men who was to officiate at the evening's contest commented on what appeared to be the likelihood of rain. Even though it had been an extremely dry month, he told me, "I know we need the rain around here, but the people really need those games more."

Distance is also a negligible factor from the perspective of a Choctaw recreation league devotee. Choctaw communities are at significant distances from one another (e.g., from twenty to seventy-five miles). Under normal conditions, most games require significant amounts of travel. There are many other situations in which people make special trips just to play in a single ball game. College students in school as far away as Jackson, about eighty-five miles from Pearl River, will regularly drive back and forth on week nights for a few quarters of basketball or several innings of softball. During the 1975–76 recreation league basketball season, one team had enlisted the services of a talented young man attending Wood Junior College in Mathiston, about eighty miles from tribal headquarters. Since he had no car, the manager of the league team took it upon himself to drive the eighty miles to pick him up and bring him back to Pearl River for the game, making the return trip later that same evening. Apparently, such 320-mile trips are considered reasonable investments of time and money where basketball is concerned.

Tribal leaders often complain that recreation too often conflicts with programs they feel are more important. For example, if a ball game is scheduled on a particular evening, it is difficult to hold a committee meeting that same night. In the late spring of 1975, the chairman of the tribal school board called a meeting on three consecutive evenings, and each time he failed to get a quorum because most of the members were at softball games in the various communities. The softball schedule was finally altered, and the school board meeting was held as planned.

Team sports have been and continue to be a very important part of Mississippi Choctaw life. And, whether one is devoting a month of his time to preparing for a stickball match or driving 100 miles to a softball game, the seriousness of the athletic event is obvious.

This high-priority will-to-sport is an old and vital element in Choctaw culture. The Choctaws' serious commitment to recreation and athletic activity can be viewed as a functional cultural trait. While obviously important in today's Choctaw world, this work-ethic approach to play may also have a valuable message for twentieth-century man. A life devoted to serious play can be a very meaningful and satisfying one.

One way of measuring the relative seriousness and importance of team sports among the Choctaws is by analyzing the functions that such behaviors play within the total Choctaw cultural context. As several years of research have demonstrated, recreational activities among this group manifest significant economic, social, political, and ritual dimensions. It is my contention that these functions are of such an essential nature in Choctaw society that the seriousness characterizing their sport behavior is not only justified but demanded and has become fundamentally important as a means of asserting one's identity as Choctaw.

CHAPTER 3

Sport and Choctaw Identity

Many people work very hard at play and take such activities very seriously. In this sense, it could be said that the Mississippi Choctaws are not unlike many other groups who view games such as basketball and softball as important parts of their social lives.

In fact, in ways that go well beyond the realm of sport behavior, the Mississippi Choctaws can be viewed simply as rural Southerners. Thompson and Peterson (1975:179–80) have noted that

> as a result of living in the rural South, the Southeastern Indians have adopted many cultural traits which are often attributed to rural Southerners, both white and black. This is especially true for the Mississippi Choctaws. The Southern Baptist Church is the largest and most active religious denomination among the Choctaws. Corn bread and pork form important parts of the Choctaw diet. Choctaw women make quilts and, until recently, most Choctaw men wore bib overalls. Even the spoken English of most Choctaws bears a heavy Southern accent. A few years ago, a western Indian visitor to Mississippi asked jokingly, "Are you sure you guys aren't red-necks instead of redskins?"

Yet, there is a distinct Choctaw identity that is obvious to both Choctaws and non-Choctaws alike. "There is little that is clearer to a Choctaw in Mississippi than that he is a Choctaw, neither white nor black, not a Mississippian or a Southerner, but a Choctaw" (Thompson and Peterson, 1975:180).

This distinctive "Choctawness" is the product of a unique language, a strong sense of community, reservation life, and a new self-determination in Choctaw political life. It is manifested in all areas of Choctaw cultural behavior, including sport. Choctaw sport is uniquely Choctaw.

Sport and Identity

The idea that sport and games reflect the basic values of a culture is not new in anthropology. As far back as the turn of the century, Stewart Culin, who has been called the "major game scholar of the past 100 years . . . in the field of anthropology" (Avedon and Sutton-Smith, 1971:55), stressed the importance of the relationship between sport and its particular cultural context. This is reflected in much of his work, including his famous *Games of the North American Indians* (1907). Later, anthropologists like Firth (1931:95–96) and Roberts (in Roberts, Arth, and Bush, 1959) reiterated and specified the nature of sport and games as integral features and expressions of specific cultural patterns.

This integral relationship between sport and culture is characteristic not only of preliterate societies, but also of more complex, modern systems. In his 1964 presidential address to the American Anthropological Association, Leslie White (1965:633–34) developed the idea that professional baseball could be seen as a meaningful expression of the American cultural system itself.

The interrelationship between sport and culture is obvious in those situations in which particular sport forms have crossed cultural lines. In these cases, the sport (e.g., basketball, soccer) tends to be revised in the adoption process, so that the resulting sport behavior fits very conveniently in its novel cultural setting and becomes a part of the process by which cultural lines are drawn and maintained.

This phenomenon has been witnessed in many situations. British missionaries introduced the game of cricket into the Trobriand Islands during the early years of this century. Gradually, as the sport became more a part of everyday life among the Trobriands, it took on new characteristics that made it a unique form of the game, specifically, "Trobriand Cricket." By the 1970s, the Trobriands were playing a brand of cricket that involved rules, symbols, procedures, and ritual accoutrements that made the sport something related to but quite different from the activity originally introduced by the British (Leach, 1976).

To study this process of sport change in greater detail, I analyzed Rimrock Navajo basketball during the 1970–71 season (Blanchard, 1974). Basketball had been a popular sport among the Anglo-Mormons in this small New Mexico community since the 1920s. By the 1940s, it had become an important element in the lives of the Navajos in the area, who had been taught to play by their white neighbors. By 1970, the game had developed a distinctive Navajo flavor, quite different from that of their white Mormon counterparts. In a comparison of Navajo and Anglo-Morman basketball in the area, the following significant differences were evident.

1. In strategy of play, the Navajos tended to be less deliberate and pattern-oriented, choosing a more wide-open, run-and-shoot style

that placed a premium on individual speed and ability while underplaying the importance of teamwork.

2. Defensively, the Navajos were less aggressive than the Whites, and relied on man-to-man more often than on zone techniques.

3. The Navajos were less concerned with the "proper" administration of rules and were not as offended by "bad calls" on the part of officials.

4. The Navajos were less likely to engage in intrateam chatter, banter, and outward physical demonstration on the court than their white Mormon counterpart.

5. Navajo basketball was more informal, and authority in that context was more diffuse, often leading to managerial problems and confusion.

6. Kinship was a significant factor in Navajo, on-court decision-making.

7. Navajos viewed basketball as purely a pleasurable pastime and put a greater emphasis on having a good time than on winning. On the other hand, the Anglo-Mormons tended to perceive the game as a serious, though recreational, contest within which one received an important moral education.

In general, Navajo basketball is a different game than that played by the Anglo-Mormons in Rimrock. The sport can be viewed as a basic expression of Navajo values and is probably more important as a mechanism of enculturation than one of acculturation. Navajo basketball serves to underscore the uniqueness of that group and preserve its identity in a setting where they are in frequent contact with other cultural patterns (e.g., Spanish-American, Zuni, Anglo).

Stickball and Choctaw Identity

Choctaw sport in similar ways reflects characteristics that set that group apart from other racial and cultural groups in east central Mississippi. In this sense it serves as a cultural maintenance device.

The most distinctive Choctaw sport is the classic ball game or stickball. The revival of interest in this sport in the past three decades has provided an opportunity for analyzing the new version of the game, comparing it with ethnohistorical records of the older parent game, considering its significantly Choctaw dimensions and its role as a means of reinforcing a sense of Choctaw identity, and suggesting ways that stickball may have influenced the style of play in other sports engaged in by today's Mississippi Choctaws.

The most visible version of contemporary stickball occurs during the annual Choctaw Indian Fair every July. Because players are reimbursed for their participation and because of its formality, it is viewed by participants as the most important stickball event of the year, even though there are other matches and exhibition games.

Billed as the "World Series of Stickball," the Choctaw Indian Fair event pits four or five teams against each other in a single-elimination tournament. Teams representing Choctaw communities, specifically, Pearl River, Connehatta, Bogue Chitto, and Nanih Waiya, compete in games scheduled in either the early afternoon or late evening during the fair, so as not to conflict with prime-time entertainment events. On the final day of the fair, the championship game is played, and upon its conclusion a world's champion is declared, a designation that does not sit well with other Native American groups in the Southeast, such as the Cherokee, who also play the racket game with some degree of seriousness.

During the fair, stickball games are played on the football field of Choctaw Central High School in the Pearl River community. For purposes of the *toli* matches, pieces of decoratively painted one-by-six lumber, approximately ten feet in length, are wired to the center posts of the goals at each end of the field. Points are scored by striking these vertical boards with the small ball, either as it is held tightly between or thrown with the rackets.

Prior to each game, the two teams assemble near the tribal offices, some 200 yards from the playing field. From here they parade to the ball field in single file, as a drummer leads the way, ceremoniously pounding a small, commercially made drum in a slow but steady rhythm.

The players are generally dressed in colorful uniforms, a pair of pants hemmed at the calves and a pullover shirt with an open neck and three-quarter-length sleeves. Made of a bright satin sheen by Choctaw seamstresses, the uniforms are of solid colors, loose-fitting, and modeled after early twentieth-century styles of Choctaw dress, even though they do not reflect the styles characteristic of the traditional ball play itself (see Figure 2). However, consistent with tradition, today's stickball contestants often play in their bare feet. Also, in 1978 and 1979, some teams discontinued using the colorful uniforms, playing instead in gym shorts without shirts and shoes.

The rackets and balls are still made in essentially the same way as in the nineteenth century (see Figure 3). Several older artisans in the community, such as Laymon Shumake of the Connehatta community, make and sell these pieces of equipment to tourists and *toli* players alike.

As the players move out onto the field to begin play, they position themselves strategically, either near one of the goalposts, at the center of the field, or at a point midway between the goalposts and the fifty-yard line. In some ways, the positions of the stickball match parallel those of basketball, with guards, forwards, and centers or goalies. However, each team has many more than the five players characteristic of the basketball team, and positions are less constraining in ball play than they are on the basketball court.

Similar to the stickball of tradition, contemporary *toli* rules do not regulate the number of players that any one team may field during any particular game. The only stipulation is that opposing teams use an equal number of players in any one contest, and at times this may mean as many as thirty players on a side. In recent years, the Choctaw Fair Board has limited the number of players to fifteen per team as a means of holding down the expense of paying players for their participation.

The stickball game itself begins as the designated official, one of three or four working the game, calls the teams together at the midpoint of the field and tosses the ball into the air. The clock is started at that point and runs for twelve minutes, being stopped by the timekeeper only when the ball goes out of bounds or after a point is scored. On these occasions, the official comes on the field again to toss the ball into the air for the competitive jump, at which point the clock is started again and play resumed.

Once the ball is in play, the action begins. The men joust to gain control of the ball by catching it between their two rackets as it is tossed into the air. Once a player establishes control, he attempts to break away from the aggregate of pushing and shoving ball-players and move toward the open field and the opponent's goal. As long as he has an open field he generally continues to hold the ball and run. However, if threatened by a member of the opposing team he throws the ball down the field rather than be hit with a racket or tackled and ultimately have the ball dislodged.

When the ball is thrown down the field, players in the vicinity of the goalpost scramble for its possession. Although deliberate passes from one player to another member of his team are attempted, successful exchanges are less frequent than in the related game of lacrosse. Therefore, the movement of the ball through the air is generally characterized by misdirection, confusion, and scrambles for control.

When in the immediate vicinity of the goal, the ball is often carried in clutched rackets as a member of the offensive team attempts to power it against the goalpost, while players of the opposition use any means at their disposal to dislodge the ball and throw it back toward the other goal.

Frequently, a player will break free with the ball within a ten- to fifteen-yard radius of the goal and have the opportunity for a shot. Slinging the ball in the direction of the goal, he attempts to strike the upraised post and score. Accuracy in this particular tactic is rare, even if the player is left unhindered, so predictably, many more shots are taken than actually hit the goal.

However, eventually a player will successfully throw or strike the ball against the post, scoring a point. The ball is then declared "dead," returned to the official at the center of the field, and play is resumed with another center toss.

As the game proceeds, players begin to tire from the incessant running, shoving, pushing, tackling, and throwing. The heat and humidity of a Mississippi summer afternoon or evening also take their toll, and after two or three quarters, game events slow down noticeably; in many cases players simply stop to relax and catch their breath.

The game consists of four twelve- or fifteen-minute quarters, and at the end of the regulation playing time, the team with the most points is declared the winner. In the event of a tie, a sudden-death play-off takes place, the game ending on the event of the first score in the extra period. One of the longest games on record is the 1977 championship match between Pearl River and Bogue Chitto that went into overtime and lasted for a total of two hours and forty-five minutes before the former scored the decisive, winning goal of a four-to-three contest.

After the game is over, the teams move ceremoniously off the field amidst some display of excitement and gradually disperse, putting on additional clothes and mingling with crowds of friends and family.

Overall, the modern stickball match is marked by the following characteristics.

1. The Choctaw stickball players have adopted a wide-open style of play. In other words, there is an apparent lack of any integrated strategy. Rather, players simply run up and down the field in pursuit of the ball or the ball carrier, using whatever means is available to them to either move the ball toward their own goal or impede its movement toward that of the opponent. This general flow with the movement of the ball is the only apparent order in the game that otherwise often strikes the observer as a hopeless array of confusion.

2. While ostensibly there are formal positions and some organi-

zation in the new *toli* contest, these are of seemingly limited importance in the game itself. Guards and forwards move at will into various areas of the field, and periodically a player will simply drop his sticks and relax. The goalies are the most consistent in maintaining their positions. While this is necessary in order to prevent the other team from scoring, it is also significant that that goalie is usually larger, older, and less mobile than other members of the team.

3. The stickball match is marked by a relaxed and pleasurable atmosphere. Players generally appear to be having a good time, despite the physically demanding nature of the game.

4. The ball-players in the new racket game generally manifest a strong desire to win, yet this is not viewed as the overriding purpose of the event. Having fun and enjoying oneself is more important. In fact, some Choctaws argue that since stickball is a traditional sport it should reflect more of that enjoyment of participation and less of the will-to-win characteristic of modern sports like softball or basketball.

5. Stickball, as it has been played in recent years among the Mississippi Choctaws, is a very physical game. The shoving, tripping, tackling, and jousting with the sticks are unavoidable dimensions of the contest, yet rarely do these contacts lead to disruptive conflict or violence. It is to the credit of the organizers of the Choctaw Fair, the team managers, and the stickball players themselves that very few injuries have been incurred in the games played in the area during the past thirty years.

6. Coaching and managerial styles characteristic of the typical stickball matches reflect the political norms of tradition. The ball-play manager is generally an older member of the community whose role is primarily one of assuming the title and making substitutions when warranted. He rarely makes an authoritative or forceful decision about either an individual's or the team's play.

7. The kinship factor is obvious in the composition of the stickball teams, since they generally represent the highly endogamous Choctaw communities, but it seems to have little if any influence on the actual style of play. However, because of the open, flexible nature of stickball strategy, it is unlikely that there would be any logic at all to a style of play that involved the deliberate controlling of the ball by individual kin groups within particular teams.

8. The contemporary racket game is marked by the presence of a degree of traditional ritual. Not only does the event reflect many specifically Choctaw norms and values, but ritual personnel are also involved either directly or indirectly. The only visible role is that of

the drummer, who, by virtue of the steady, rhythmic pounding of his instrument, brings a certain order to the hodgepodge of activities characterizing the game. However, behind the scenes the Choctaw doctors and witches continue to affect the stickball game. (For additional treatment of the sport and ritual phenomenon, see Chapter 6.)

9. Stickball, as it has been played during the annual Choctaw Fair, has had only a limited amount of fan participation. During the late '60s, the games were generally scheduled in the afternoons and mid-evenings. Sometimes as many as 1,500 to 2,000 persons were seated in the stands and scattered around the football field at Choctaw Central, but most were non-Indian observers and had no emotional attachment to the game or its outcome, viewing the event more as spectacle than as contest. On the other hand, Choctaw fans who might have been interested in the actual flow and total meaning of the game found themselves at a significant distance from the action, intimidated by the presence of the non-Choctaw crowd and irritated by the constant chatter of the announcer making "instructive" comments about the game over the public address system.

Within the past few years, stickball games have been scheduled more frequently during the late evenings of the annual fair's daily activities. By this hour, most of the non-Choctaws have left the grandstand area, and the majority of the remaining spectators are Choctaw. As a result, Choctaws have had a greater opportunity in recent years to get involved in games and their outcomes. However, even within this context, the enthusiasm and emotional commitment appear less pronounced than those characteristic of many other Choctaw sporting events.

The racket game played during the past thirty years in the Mississippi Choctaw community, though modeled after its ancestral form, is different from the game of tradition in the following ways.

1. The new stickball is not the community-wide event of previous eras. In some ways, modern sports like baseball and basketball have taken over that particular function of traditional ball play. Stickball today does not involve the extensive preparation, explicit ritual performance, and comprehensive festiveness that once made the formal match a major part of every Choctaw's life. Also, betting is not a visible element in the contemporary stickball event. In fact, it has not been part of the game since it was outlawed by the state. Nevertheless, reference to the "Indian ball play" was included in the 1972 Mississippi state law against gambling (Chapter 33, 97-33-1).

2. According to older informants, the play of today's stickball

enthusiasts is less skillful than that of centuries past. No longer do young men develop the ability to catch and throw the ball with the long hickory rackets as a consistent part of socialization, nor do players practice these techniques throughout the year. Traditionally, Choctaw boys were trained in the art of the racket game when very young. In many ways, the sport was viewed as simulated war, and the skills one developed in this context were important to becoming an effective warrior. Though young men were encouraged to learn the fundamentals of the activity and master its skills at an early age, they were not actually allowed to compete in a real contest until they were well into their teens, for fear that they might suffer severe injury.

Despite the exclusion from the games of their fathers and older brothers, Choctaw boys would devise stickball games of their own, improvising equipment and using a front yard for a playing field. By the time they were old enough to compete with the men, they had become fairly proficient at catching and throwing the small ball with their rackets. In some ways, the first real match in which a Choctaw adolescent participated symbolized his movement into manhood. If a boy could play stickball, he was no longer a boy; he was a man.

Most of the contemporary stickball players have not been subjected to this type of socialization. Few of them put as much effort into skill development as did their ancestral counterparts. Today, practice is generally limited to a few days of preparation for the annual fair and special exhibition matches that might be scheduled at other times of the year. There are simply not as many opportunities to play stickball as were once available to the Choctaw athlete, at neither formal nor informal levels.

3. Some of the more obvious differences between the new and the old versions of the stickball matches are the novel physical accoutrements surrounding the game: the boundaries, the uniforms, the lights, the use of three or four officials, the scoreboard, and the use of the time clock. These in turn have necessitated new rules and new strategies which have had a significant impact on the style of play.

4. The traditional version of the stickball game was more physically punishing than its contemporary counterpart, if one can believe informant descriptions and ethnohistorical accounts. In previous centuries, a formal stickball match might generate violence that would lead to open warfare between the competing communities. The ag-

gressiveness associated with today's ball play is quite mild when viewed from the perspective of tradition.

The modern stickball match is a different game from its parent game. While the basic mechanics and equipment of the game have been revived, and while there are some obvious parallels between the two phenomena, the new version is only a distant imitation of the older sport. Just as Choctaw culture in general has changed, so too has the basic art of the racket game.

Many of the Choctaws themselves, particularly the older men, argue that the new racket game is just a fad and radically different from the old version of the game. As one member of the community explained,

> A lot of times they [the old men] talk about how the players today don't even compare with some of the players they had in those days [nineteenth century], in terms of stamina, strength, and how smart they play, how well they play with their sticks and ball. . . .
> That's how my father used to put it. He hasn't seen good ball-players in a long time. . . . The old men say the players these days are not as strong as they were in the old days. They couldn't take the punishment they did. . . .
> It was a man's game then. If you weren't man enough, they wouldn't let you play. They said, "If you're man enough to get out there and play, you're man enough to take it."

These observations regarding the relative skills of the old and new racket-game players aside, stickball is still an important part of Choctaw life. Also, it can still be seen as an expression of that basic need to assert one's Choctaw identity. Stickball, though not the *toli* of centuries past, is still a uniquely Choctaw sport, and participation therein is an expression of that will to define ethnic boundaries and reiterate the cultural pride evinced by the phrase *"Chahta sia hokat"* ("I am a Choctaw").

Modern Sport and Choctaw Identity

The new sport activities that have been added to the Choctaw recreational repertoire, such as baseball, basketball, and softball, function in much the same way as the revived stickball, albeit more subtly. However, unlike stickball, these new sports are played by other cultural and racial groups in Mississippi and offer the anthropologist the opportunity to compare their characteristics across social lines and more aptly illustrate their distinctively Choctaw dimensions.

BASKETBALL

Basketball is *the* winter sport for the Mississippi Choctaws. The season begins in October, as recreational league teams are formed, new tennis shoes and uniforms purchased, officials contacted, and talented players recruited. By the time the first games are played, both the men's and women's leagues have anywhere from eight to fifteen teams each, with names like Outlaws, Hawks, Rebelettes, Marvellettes, Deputies, Rangers, Royals, Natives, and others.

Most of the players in the Choctaw Recreational League Independent Basketball Program are Choctaw, though the league is not closed to outsiders. Each team is allowed to use two non-Indians. Also, in some years (e.g., 1976) non-Choctaw teams have been admitted to the league.

However, most of the teams represent Choctaw communities, and some simply use the community name (e.g., Connehatta, Standing Pine). Teams are composed predominantly of individuals who either live or have strong family ties in the communities they represent. As a result, many of the basketball teams each year are made up largely of kinsmen.

The games are played in the community centers that have basketball facilities, and the officials and the equipment are furnished by the recreation department subsidized by the tribe. Additional money to operate recreational programs is also received in the form of entry fees and other special collections.

Actual play in the basketball league is governed by the "High School rules as sanctioned by the National Basketball Committees of the United States and Canada" (Choctaw Recreation League, n.d.:7). Men's games are played in four ten-minute quarters. Women play four eight-minute quarters and are subject to the formal rules of high school girls' basketball.

In addition to standard rules of the game, special regulations are imposed by the recreation department. Misconduct, physical or verbal abuse of officials, and alcohol or drugs are prohibited. Also, players are required to wear "clean tennis shoes," and all "teams must be in similarly colored, numbered uniforms" (Choctaw Recreation League, n.d.:8).

At the same time, spectators are expected to abide by the general rules governing player behavior. For example, they are prohibited from bringing alcohol into the gym, attending games under the influence of alcohol or drugs, or engaging in unnecessary horseplay. Also, "children accompanying players to the gym must remain seated and properly supervised" (Choctaw Recreation League, n.d.:6).

The responsibility for enforcing the rules is left to the officials, recreation department employees, and members of the recreation board.

I first attended a Choctaw Recreation League basketball game in March 1974 at the Pearl River community center. What follows is a description of the setting and major characteristics of that experience.

The Pearl River gymnasium is an aging, Quonset-shaped building that occupies a large portion of the community center. The main area is a regulation-sized basketball court with a tile floor, glass backboards, and bleachers on both sides of the playing floor that can seat as many as 450 people during a basketball game. At one end of the gymnasium is the main entrance, the recreation office, and a kitchen-concession stand. On the other end of the court, behind the east backboard, is a large stage with adjacent storage rooms in the wings. Midway on the south side of the court is a scorer's bench with electronic equipment controlling the electric scoreboard on the west end of the court.

On the night described, three games had been scheduled, two men's and one women's. When I arrived, the women's game had been completed, and the 7:30 men's game, pitting Union against the Black Hawks, was about to begin.

There were two Choctaw officials, both of whom wore the standard black-and-white striped shirts. One had a matching pair of black trousers while the other wore a pair of blue jeans. Both wore standard basketball shoes as opposed to the regulation official's shoes.

After some pregame banter and confusion, the more officially dressed referee blew his whistle, made reference to the time, called the two teams to the center circle, lined them up, and threw the ball into the air to begin the game.

The game itself appeared at first to be like most recreation league basketball games, Choctaw or otherwise. However, as the game progressed, interesting features emerged. I was struck by the highly informal nature of the affair. Both teams seemed primarily intent on enjoying themselves. No one appeared to be too concerned with the game's final outcome. Rule infractions were taken seriously by only one official; neither the players nor the referee in blue jeans seemed to worry much about typical violations, such as fouling, double-dribble, three seconds in the foul lane, or walking with the ball. Most of the shooting was done from outside, fifteen or more feet from the basket, and there appeared to be few attempts to maneuver the ball to the inside for the higher percentage shots.

While winning did not seem to be vital to most of the players, they did put a great deal of effort into the contest. There was much running and scrambling for the ball. Certainly, no one could accuse either team of "slacking off." However, while players were on the bench, either as a result of substitution, time-out, or break between quarters, they often smoked cigarettes or sipped wine from one of several bottles conspicuously camouflaged in brown bags and kept in the stands behind the player bench.

During the game some eighty persons were in the gym at one time or another. Many others were milling around outside and in the lobby. The ones actually seated in the stands tended to be clustered at various points, usually by age and sometimes by sex. About four groups of high school students talked, clowned, and laughed during most of the game, only infrequently giving any indication that they were aware of the events on the playing floor. One group of young adult males sat in a cluster behind the scorer's bench and carried on a constant chatter among themselves and with the players seated on the sidelines. Other factions included groups of women and children, families, and occasional individuals who simply sat quietly and watched the game.

Generally, the spectators did not appear to be very interested in the game itself. Occasionally there was some interaction between the persons in the stands and the players or officials, as wisecracks or infrequent words of encouragement were shouted in the general direction of the basketball action. However, most fan activity was oriented to events external to the game. They made frequent trips to the concession stand, wandered back and forth from the parking lot and the lobby, and created novel forms of entertainment. For example, one small boy, about five years old and grossly overweight, began running in and out of the curtains on the stage at the end of the gymnasium, about midway in the first half of the game. Each time he would emerge from behind a curtain, often falling down, the spectators would break into raucous laughter. Admittedly, it was amusing, but it illustrated the rather casual attitude of the fans to the basketball game and the sense in which the total entertainment was much broader than the sport itself. When any real interest was shown in the events on the court, it was normally with reference to some unusual occurrence. On this particular evening, the Union team was fielding a rather obese forward who inadvertently continued to collide with members of the opposition, in most cases knocking them to the floor. Again, the Choctaw fans found this quite amusing, and as the game progressed the robust player took a great deal of ribbing from the spectators.

Overall, the basketball game, eventually won by the Black Hawks, seemed to be simply a focal point for a larger community social event in which everyone, players and spectators alike, was entertained.

As a result of that experience, I began to collect data relative to Choctaw bsketball that would allow me to compare the phenomenon with the same sport as it was played by non-Choctaw teams in the Choctaw league or in other leagues in the east central Mississippi area. Over the next three years, I watched many ball games, interviewed many players, administered several tests, and collected data relative to basketball behavior. As a result of these efforts, I offer the following observations about the distinctiveness of Choctaw basketball.

1. Choctaw basketball tends to be more highly individualized than that of other racial groups in the area, particularly when compared to Anglo basketball. There seems to be a premium on individual rather than on team styles of play. In this context, "hotdogging," a deprecating adjective when used by white players in Mississippi, becomes a positive attribute. In many cases, Choctaw players have admitted to me that it is more important to look good and play well than to win, an attitude quite foreign to their Anglo counterparts, although apparently shared by some black athletes in the area. This tendency to individualize is evident on the playing floor as Choctaw players are more likely to risk losing control of the ball or taking low percentage shots rather than passing the ball to a teammate. Also, the pre-game warming-up process becomes an individualized ritual for the Choctaws as each player shoots and retrieves a ball before he shoots again, unlike the typical Anglo procedure in which individuals take turns standing under the board, rebounding, and throwing the ball back to persons warming up from the outside, several yards away from the basket.

2. Choctaw basketball is generally characterized by a de-emphasis on the necessity to win. Losing is not as fatal to the typical Choctaw basketball player as it is for his non-Choctaw counterparts in the area. While the competition is important, and playing is a serious business in the sense that each participant has important responsibilities relative to the total event, winning and losing are generally viewed as simply necessary by-products of the game.

At the same time, Choctaw athletes openly admit that one of the primary benefits of their team sport involvement is the pride that comes from community recognition. In this sense, personal success in a particular athletic event is as important as winning, if not more so. One's teammates may not fare well during the basketball game, and it might be lost, but if he scores thirty points and makes a good showing defensively, the contest has been personally beneficial, and he has had a good time. In other words, among the Mississippi Choctaws it is possible for both teams to win in any given sporting activity.

This attitude has frustrated Anglo coaches who have worked with Choctaw athletes. Lonus Hucks, a former coach at Choctaw Central High School, once related to me the difficulties he had in trying to instill a "winning philosophy" into his teams. He told me that once, after losing a crucial game, one of his players noticed his disconsolate demeanor and approached him.

"Coach, you really want to win, don't you?"
Well, that's the name of the game. That's what we were out there for.
"Well, why win? What does winning mean? We had a good time. What do you prove if you win? All we want to do is have a good time."
They were more joyful after the game; you couldn't tell if they won or lost.

While the coach found it difficult to deal with that approach, the Choctaw conception of competition appears to be a humane one. It allows the athlete to take the game seriously, both in terms of his own performance and his team's, without seeing his own success only at the expense of his opponent. In fact, the emphasis on individual play may temper the perception and maintenance of aggression in the typical Choctaw ball game, especially in those pitting Choctaws against non-Choctaws.

3. Choctaw basketball is characterized by a limited concern for the propriety of rules and of rule enforcement. Consistent with their highly informal approach to the game, Choctaw players rarely get too excited about missed calls or mistakes made by the officials. Occasionally, an individual player will express some unhappiness and initiate a complaint, but generally the sentiment is not shared by teammates. In fact, those who complain too much soon develop a reputation as "soreheads."

At the same time, referees are expected to take their job rather casually. They get paid three dollars for every game they call, and they are expected to enforce the rules, but not too conscientiously. The late Leonard Jimmie was perhaps the best known among Choctaw basketball officials. Licensed by the state of Mississippi, he officiated at many high school and junior college games in the region and took his position very seriously. A hardworking and ambitious young man, Leonard prided himself on his ability to call close ball games. For example, he once told me that he held the record in the state for the most fouls called by an official at a high school basketball game. Leonard brought this same seriousness to his referee assignments in the Choctaw Recreation League, and while his fellow Choctaws appreciated his skills, they often joked about his tendency to over-dramatize and kidded him about his many "unnecessary" calls.

4. Kinship is an obvious factor in team composition but negligible in actual team play. Since Choctaw communities tend to be highly interrelated, and basketball teams generally represent individual communities, it is to be expected that teams will be made up largely of kinsman. On the other hand, when I conducted an analysis of on-court exchanges in a series of recreation league games, I did not discover a pattern similar to that which I found in Navajo basketball, where the kinship factor tended to affect the nature of decision-making in the basketball process. (For additional information regarding sport and social organization, see Chapter 5.)

5. Female basketball is both legitimate and important in Choctaw sports. While women only rarely compete or play with men, they do have their own basketball-playing opportunities, both in the schools and the recreation program. Women take these opportunities seriously, are aggressively active in their basketball playing, and view the game as an important social activity and means of getting community-wide recognition. In fact, many of the young adult women who are active community leaders are also consistent participants in the recreation league basketball program.

While Choctaw women tend to be more excited than their male counterparts about female basketball participation, the men also view it as important. They encourage their daughters and wives to participate, attend games, and get excited about the women's league standings and special tournament outcomes. The fact that women's recreation league basketball games are generally as well attended as the men's suggests the comparable importance of the two divisions. It is also significant that, over the years, Choctaw women's teams have apparently tended to be more successful against non-Choctaw teams in the area than have their men's teams. While I do not have the statistics to verify this assertion, this is reported by amateur sport historians among the Choctaws and it may be an important factor underlying the relative importance of women's basketball among the Choctaws.

6. Choctaw basketball is characterized by a managerial style that is consistent with traditional political process. While some are more

direct and forceful than others, most basketball team managers in the recreation league are hesitant to command or reprimand, choosing rather to make suggestions and to be as democratic as possible. This style of leadership is consistent with the traditional model of the Choctaw politician, who led by example and mediation rather than by coercion, and is also similar to the Navajo pattern. (See Chapter 5 on sport and political organization.)

7. Choctaw basketball is characterized by less crowding and playing directly under the basket and more shooting from the periphery or the outside than is typical of non-Choctaw basketball in Mississippi. This is reflected in the statistics regarding personal fouls and body contact at the point of the ball. In 1974 and 1975, I did an intensive analysis of the number of contacts that occurred at the point of the ball during the time that it was actually in play in both Choctaw and Anglo men's recreation league games in Pearl River and Philadelphia, Mississippi. Though these are difficult to measure precisely, the range of error corrects itself if one takes these data in enough games. Collecting these figures in a total of twelve basketball games, I discovered that the Choctaw teams averaged a total of 1.38 contacts, both incidental and deliberate, at the point of the ball (i.e., involving the person controlling th ball) during each minute of play. The Anglo teams, on the other hand, averaged 2.36 contacts per minute of play during the ten basketball games in which I collected that data. The difference between the two groups was a significant 71 percent, but has an obvious explanation. The white teams tended to use their hands more, touching and shoving their opponents more deliberately than the Choctaw teams, despite the rules prohibiting such behavior. That, coupled with a greater amount of inside play and scuffle under the backboards, led to the significantly greater amount of physical contact in the non-Choctaw basketball games.

The reasons for this tendency to shoot from the outside and to avoid physical contact may be related to the fact that the Choctaws tend to be shorter than their Anglo counterparts and are therefore less effective when close to the basket, either shooting or rebounding. However, this comparative height difference is not a factor in games pitting one Choctaw team against another, yet the same tendency to stay outside is still evident. It may be that among Choctaws there is simply a greater respect for one's personal space and a related disapproval of unnecessary physical contact, something that is reflected in their general attitude toward aggression. (See p. 97 and the section on the Choctaw concept of conflict.)

9. Related to the tendency to shoot from outside, Choctaw basketball teams generally employ a run-and-shoot style of play. There are only infrequent attempts to "work the ball" into a central position and take the "better shot," although some of the more successful and bigger teams, such as the Outlaws, have tended to adopt this style in recent years. Still, the wide-open, run-and-shoot strategy is the norm, and in many ways parallels the free style of contemporary stickball play among the Mississippi Choctaws.

10. The spectators at the typical Choctaw recreation league basketball game are different from those attending a similar contest in the local white community. In the first place, there are more of them, they represent a broader spectrum of the total community, and they view the contest as a more important social event. On the other hand, the smaller audiences at the Anglo basketball games tend to concentrate more on the events of the games themselves and get involved less in peripheral activities. While there are many possible explanations for differences here, one of the obvious factors is the greater range of entertainment options open to the Anglo population. By their own admission, many Choctaws show up at a recreation league basketball game on a given night during the winter months simply "for a lack of anything better to do."

11. Choctaw basketball is different from that played by other cultural groups in Mississippi for the simple reason that it, like Choctaw sport in general, reflects some basic values and premises of Choctaw tradition. In this sense, Choctaw basketball is a distinctly Choctaw ritual. Subsequent chapters will elaborate on the distinctive cultural dimensions of Choctaw sport.

In general, Choctaw basketball is different from that engaged in by the white and black communities in east central Mississippi, by virtue of the game's style, strategy, involvement of fans, structure of rule enforcement, general social significance, openness to female participation, and manifestations of the distinctive qualities of Choctaw culture.

SOFTBALL

The Choctaw Recreation Department also administers a slow-pitch softball league, with both men's and women's divisions, every summer. Increasingly, this brand of softball has become more popular than either the fast-pitch variety or baseball among the Choctaws. Each summer, as many as twenty-eight teams are formed. Similar to the basketball teams, they represent particular communities, use many of the same nicknames (i.e., Deputies, Bravettes), and are composed largely of Choctaw players, although league rules allow a team to have as many as five non-Indian players.

Governed by official slow-pitch softball rules and beginning in April, the games are played at the several ball fields located in the Choctaw communities. The same special regulations that constrict both player and spectator behavior at basketball games are in effect at the softball games, and again, enforcement is up to officials, recreation department employees, and recreation board members.

One typical softball contest that I attended took place in June 1977 at the Tucker community softball field. The field is located at the intersection of two gravel roads on the south side of the community. Well lighted, the field features a large, metal-screen-on-wood backstop, bleacher seats with an approximate capacity of 150, two player benches, and a concrete block concession stand and storage room. The field itself has a well-contoured red sandy clay infield, grassy but uneven outfield, and borders a baseball diamond in left field and a heavily forested area in right and center fields. While there is no home-run fence, generally any hit that gets past the outfielders, especially if it goes into the woods, is a "round tripper."

This softball game in the summer of 1977 was marked by obvious informality typical of most Choctaw Recreation League events. This was particularly evident among members of the offensive team, the team at bat. During this phase of the game, players awaiting their turn at the plate would wander around the ball park and circulate among the spectators, sometimes sitting with family, playing with the many children running unchecked in the area behind the bleachers, or simply standing under one of the trees between the road and the ball field and chatting with friends.

On this occasion, there was no evidence of alcohol, but at least one of the players, by his own admission, had been drinking heavily prior to the game, and it was obviously affecting his behavior.

While a team was on defense (i.e., in the field), players tended to concentrate more on the events of the game, and at the same time they were less likely to clown or let distractions remove their attention from the game than when awaiting their turns at bat.

One of the things an observer notes when watching the Choctaws play softball is that while perhaps the Choctaws pay less attention to the propriety of right and wrong calls by the umpire than area Whites might in a comparable game, Choctaw athletes are more intent on the rules in this context than when they play basketball. In particular, the team in the field and the batter tend to take the official's decisions seriously, and are quick to express some concern if they feel that an incorrect call has been made. At the same time, with the exception of the manager, players on the bench are less likely to involve themselves in the discourse over the proprieties of a particular decision by the umpire.

In this particular contest between Tucker and Connehatta, the softball game, like the typical basketball game, was a festive occasion for spectators and players alike. That night, in addition to the thirty players and the two managers, about seventy persons were scattered around the ball field, in the bleachers, drinking soda pop or snow cones and eating popcorn, playing catch behind the concession stand or along the south road, sitting on cars, of which there were about thirty parked in the area, watching babies crawl in the dust and climb through the stands, or loitering behind the backstop conversing with friends. For the most part, some of these would-be fans, did not express much enthusiasm for the softball game itself. Some laughed at bobbled balls, aimed joking remarks at an unsuccessful batter, encouraged the pitcher or a hitter, and occasionally questioned the umpire's decision on a particular pitch. However, these expressions were limited. Spectators only infrequently injected themselves into the game and only rarely showed any interest in its final outcome.

When the last out had been made and the game was over, Connehatta having won, everyone was smiling, winners and losers alike, and players mingled with the rest of the crowd as one of the teams to play in the 9:00 game came onto the field to begin its infield warm-up. Had I not been familiar with Choctaw softball, at that point I might have had some question as to whether or not the game had been completed. Things just came to a stop with the same limited hoopla and bravado which had characterized the contest throughout its entire seven innings.

While I have not studied Choctaw softball as extensively as I have this group's special brand of basketball, I have analyzed it in comparison with the game played in the adult slow-pitch softball league in Philadelphia, Mississippi. This league, in which I played during two summers, is composed of both black and white teams, and gives one another perspective by which to isolate the distinctive features of Choctaw softball. The slow-pitch softball played in the Choctaw Recreation Department Independent League is distinguished by the following characteristics.

1. Similar to Choctaw basketball, kinship is a team factor in team composition, but of little significance in actual playing behavior.

Unlike basketball, softball provides few options from which a player may choose in deciding which teammate to involve in a particular play. For example, if you are playing shortstop and a ground ball is hit sharply toward your position, with no other runners on base, you have only one alternative; you must throw the ball to first base. In basketball there are many options, so a wider range of factors can enter into the decision-making process.

2. Similar to basketball, the managerial style typical of Choctaw softball tends to be more subdued than that of non-Choctaw softball in the area. Most managers are slow to be assertive. However, softball managers, especially some of the older, more experienced ones, tend to be more forceful than their basketball counterparts. Possibly the openness of the softball playing field as opposed to the basketball court allows for a greater expressiveness on the part of coaches and managers. Their actions are less conspicuous in the outdoor setting than in the enclosed gymnasium.

3. Though it is not as pronounced as it is in basketball, Choctaw softball players tend to express less concern over the rules and regulations governing the game than do their Anglo counterparts. As suggested earlier, the typical Choctaw softball player appears to devote a greater amount of attention to the decisions made by officials than does the Choctaw basketball player. This is especially true of the batting and pitching roles. When an umpire decides that a questionable pitch is a strike, the batter will often express dissatisfaction in ways not at all typical of his behavior on the basketball court. In some cases, this has led to violence, and, in one, a killing. I would suggest that the factors underlying this more intense preoccupation with official decisions characterisitic of softball is a product of the game itself. The one-on-one relationship between a player and the official that is created by the umpire-batter and umpire-pitcher confrontations makes decisions more individual and personal. Most of the official calls made during a basketball game involve more than one player and are less conspicuous; the offender is less likely to be the focus of attention.

4. While winning is obviously important, it does not seem to be the primary purpose of Choctaw softball in the same way as in the Anglo version of the game. At some of the ball fields on the reservation there are no scoreboards, and persons interested in knowing the score must check with the scorekeeper, a recreation department official or one of the team managers, who is recording the official score in the record book. Again, as in basketball, for most of the

Choctaw softball players having a good time is more important than defeating an opponent.

5. Spectators view the softball match as an important social event which is both productive and entertaining. The game provides a reason for getting together with friends, especially those from other communities, exchanging information, and having an enjoyable afternoon or evening. Because of the openness of the softball field and the season, the game allows for an even more festive air than that created by basketball.

6. Female involvement in softball is an important part of Choctaw sport and community life. In fact, slow-pitch softball, as suggested earlier, was initially seen as a women's game, and though Choctaw men have now adopted the sport with great enthusiasm, they still appreciate the female's equal right to facilities, recognition, and opportunities to play. It is significant that the coverage afforded women's softball in the *Choctaw Community News* is generally equal or superior to that devoted to men's softball (e.g., August 30, 1976:30).

Perhaps for reasons similar to those underlying the greater aggressiveness of males in a softball- as opposed to a basketball-playing context, women tend to be more assertive and outspoken when they are playing outdoors on the ball diamond than when they are in the gymnasium. Though women who are too forceful or aggressive during softball games often become the subjects of gossip and ridicule, that type of behavior is still regarded as more legitimate here than in a basketball game.

7. One interesting feature unique to Choctaw softball in comparison with that of the Anglo counterpart is the way in which the pitcher's role is defined. Among the Choctaws, one's ability to throw and master the slow pitch is viewed as critical. Therefore, older, more seasoned persons tend to pitch, the logic being simply that experience and knowledge are more valuable than strength and youthful coordination when one is on the mound. At the same time, there is a greater likelihood among the Choctaws that the pitcher will be a team leader than is true in the white and black leagues in east central Mississippi. In many cases, it appears that the game revolves around the pitcher in a Choctaw softball game, while it centers on the batter for the non-Indian ball team, reflecting what may be simply a relative difference between the respective emphases on offense and defense.

In some ways, this behavior conflicts with the tendency of the

Choctaws to de-emphasize central positions in other sports, such as they do in the wide-open stickball match or in basketball. This focus on the role of the pitcher is less a factor in strategy and more a simple attitude which has little, if any, effect on the total process of the game. It does underscore the Choctaw athlete's tendency to stress the importance of the cognitive dimensions of a ballgame and a player's ability.

The good Choctaw athlete is one who is knowledgeable about the game as well as physically skillful. Since knowledge comes with age, the softball pitcher, frequently older than the other members of the team, is often viewed as an expert.

In general, Choctaw softball, manifesting many of the features characteristic of Choctaw basketball, is a special community event that is entertaining, part of a broader social activity, more informal, open to females, and less geared to the importance of winning than the similar game played by non-Choctaws in east central Mississippi.

Choctaw Sport and Identity: General Observations

Since those characteristics of Choctaw basketball and slow-pitch softball that make these activities distinctive in the multicultural world of the rural South have been noted, it is legitimate to suggest that these two sports are part of Choctaw identity in the 1970s. At the same time, many features common to all or most Choctaw sports allow for a characterization of Choctaw sport behavior in general, a culturally significant pattern that can be viewed as a factor in this group's ability to maintain a distinctively Choctaw identity.

1. Choctaw sport and recreation activities are characterized by a greater penchant for team rather than individual activities. For example, softball is much more popular than track, in many ways because the latter is a "lonely" sport and does not allow for as much camaraderie and playfulness. On the other hand, in a team context, individual excellence is of primary importance, often overriding team welfare as a purpose. "Hotdogging" and "showing off" are not necessarily improper on the ball field, and it is of great importance that the participant feel good about his or her performance. This does not negate the importance of the team. It is necessary to the social definition of entertainment and recreation that the Choctaws espouse a positive attitude toward the idea of group participation in sport. However, a certain balance must be maintained between group and individual interests when one engages in sport activities.

2. Related to the first characteristic, Choctaws compete yet they tend to de-emphasize the importance of winning as the primary purpose underlying participation in formal athletic activities. It is fun to win, but it is more vital to enjoy playing, have a good time, and go away feeling that one played as skillfully as possible. At the same time, a winning team must be careful that it does not win by too great a margin, thereby humiliating its opponents. One recreation league basketball game that I attended in 1975 illustrated the negative reaction that is engendered by a lopsided victory. The Outlaws played IHS (Indian Health Service) at the Red Water community center, and consistent with the former team's domination of the league that year, they easily defeated the small IHS squad. During the last few minutes of the game, the winners continued to run the score up, and though it did not appear deliberate to me, the Choctaw spectators, even some of those supporting the Outlaws, were fuming. As one young woman expressed it to me, "Why do they have to rub it in? Isn't winning enough?"

The emphasis on "having fun" as a primary motivation for participating in formal sporting events is illustrated by the difficulty most Choctaw athletes have in rationalizing practice that cannot be conducted playfully. When practice becomes hard work, it ceases to be enjoyable and detracts from the event for which it is viewed as preparation. A football coach at Choctaw Central High School once told me that one of biggest problems was getting his team to take practice sessions seriously. He blamed his players' frequent failures to attend practice on their parents, who he claimed did not support or cooperate with the high school athletic program. However, I would argue that the causes of this rather casual attitude toward intensive preparation and training is rooted much more deeply, in the very nature of Choctaw attitudes toward play in general. It is serious business, but it is also supposed to be fun, and to the Choctaw it is not necessary to work hard in order to have a good time.

3. Sporting events are community-wide social occasions among the Mississippi Choctaws. Players, spectators, and officials are all part of a larger event that functions to facilitate interaction between members of different communities, reinforce traditional Choctaw values, create a sense of community, and, most of all, provide an important form of entertainment for participants. Sports are invariably tied to good times, in the Choctaw world view. For this same reason, officials are slow to enforce recreation department rules gov-

erning player and spectator behavior. Only rarely are persons reprimanded for drunken behavior, bringing alcohol into the playing area, or failing to control their children.

4. Female athletics play an important role in Choctaw recreation. Sportswomen among the Choctaws tend to have wholesome self-concepts and men respect them for their talents and encourage their active participation. The women enjoy competing among themselves, and the rest of the community supports them by attending their games as frequently and expressing as much enthusiasm for these contests as it does for those of the males. They view sport participation as an important part of both physical and emotional well-being, and their male counterparts concur. As Choctaw women frequently point out, "It is important that a woman be strong and healthy."

5. Choctaw sport is characterized by a distinctive sense of competition or conflict. In this context, I am treating sport as a specialized form of social conflict, by which I mean "a struggle over values and claims to scarce status, power and resources in which the aims of the opponents are to neutralize, injure, or eliminate their rivals" (Coser, 1956:8). Even the mildest forms of sport competition can be viewed as such struggles over scarce status (e.g., the winner) in which one opponent simply aims to neutralize the claim of the other to that status.

Employing such a definition of sport competition as a type of social conflict, I have attempted to analyze the distinctive characteristics of the Choctaw concept of conflict as it applies to their sport behavior. Using a set of five nonstandard projective pictures roughly depicting events occurring in a hypothetical gridiron contest, informants were asked to respond by describing the activity they assumed to be projected by these drawings and then asked specific questions about each (Appendix B). Responses were elicited from thirty-four juniors and seniors at Choctaw Central High School and the entire discussion recorded and analyzed. These results were later compared with those from the same test administered to a similar group of twenty-nine Anglo students at Riverdale High School in Murfreesboro, Tennessee. The comparison of the results from four of the five plates was significant and instructive.

Plate 1 (see Figure 5) depicts two football players involved in a negative exchange. When I asked if the athletes were on the same team, 31 percent of the Anglo sample responded in the affirmative, as opposed to only 9 percent of the Choctaws, the others assuming the combatants were on different teams (see Table 3). The infrequency with which the Choctaws perceived the conflict as intrasquad in nature may be a product of the fact that kinship is a regulating factor in relationships between members of the same team in their sport world. In the same sense that a man is hesitant to raise his hand against his kinsman, so too against his teammate (see pp. 117–18 on Choctaw intra-team relationships).

Although all the informants agreed that the type of behavior represented in Plate 1 was disruptive and of negative value in the game, 62 percent of the Whites saw the event as normal in football while only 15 percent of the Choctaws were willing to brush off the picture's implications so lightly (see Table 4).

Plate 2 (see Figure 6) portrays a group of persons in the bleachers expressing themselves with apparent emotional excesses. When I queried my informants as to the subject of the fans' displeasure, 45 percent of the Murfreesboro group, as opposed to only 18 percent of the Native Mississippians, suggested that the spectators were directing their fury toward the officials (see Table 5). Likewise, when I asked the specific nature of their concern, the same pattern was reinforced; the Anglos generally claimed that the referees had made a bad call, while the Choctaws suggested they were simply upset because their team was losing. In both of these cases, the results reinforce the notion that Choctaws are little concerned with rules and their rigid enforcement and likewise slow to berate athlete officials, unless they become too zealous in the administration of their duties.

In Plate 3 (see Figure 7), a runner carrying the ball is depicted as he encounters what all respondents saw as a would-be tackler. When I asked if they thought anyone in the picture was mad or angry, the Choctaws appeared less likely to see the tackler-runner confrontation as having negative conflict dimensions. More pointedly, I then asked whether or not anyone was trying to hurt the other party in the projected contact. Here, 73 percent of the Anglos concluded that someone in the picture was trying to inflict pain on his opponent, while only 6 percent of the Choctaw sample believed that any such malicious intent was implied (see Table 6).

Plate 4 (see Figure 8) is a football field sidelines scene with a man standing and facing seated players, addressing them animatedly. Most of the respondents in both groups described the situation as a coach addressing his players ("talking," "cussing them out," "jumping on their case," "getting on their ass"), and the general feeling was that the mentor was unhappy and scolding his team for their apparent shortcomings on the gridiron. Ninety-four percent of the Choctaws saw the situation as "bad," while 93 percent of the Whites viewed it as "good" (see Table 7). The Choctaws felt that the coach was being excessively dictatorial and harsh, while their counterparts saw the behavior as "the way a coach is supposed to act." When asked if they thought they would like the coach in real life, the Anglos generally responded affirmatively, while without exception the Native Mississippians responded negatively (see Table 8). In many ways, the reaction to this plate can be seen as consistent with traditional Choctaw values. For example, the effective Choctaw leader is more an adviser or mediator who instructs by setting a good example than one who commands or coerces (see pp. 136–37).

Overall, the results of the projective test outline a distinctively Choctaw model of conflict in general and sport conflict in particular. In comparison with the members of the Anglo-American sample, the Choctaws were less likely to envision fighting between members of the same team, quicker to attach negative labels to scenes of obvious violence, and slower to express concern over rule infraction. Where brutality was evident, the Choctaws expressed strong disapproval; the Anglos generally voiced approval. Where the reality of excessive violence was not clear, the Choctaws interpreted the event as having only competitive overtones; the Anglos tended to deal with these same events as violence. In general, while witnessing the same event, the Choctaw spectator would be likely to perceive less deliberate conflict than would his Anglo counterpart.

A comparison of specific Choctaw and English language categories reinforces the findings of the analysis of the projective picture and the idea that conflict is culturally defined. Choctaw has no equivalent for the English "conflict," and appears to have a less elaborate and specialized conflict vocabulary than does English. There are fewer words that refer to specific forms of social conflict. In most cases, the term *itibbi* ("fighting") is used, but this word technically refers only to a particular category of explicitly physical conflict. The phrases *ittįkano kiyo* (literally, "not peace"), one of several special constructions that can be used to translate the more generic "conflict," is likewise limited.

The term *itibbi* can be used to translate the noun "contest" (i.e., a sporting event) as well as "fighting," suggesting the implicit understanding of sport as conflictual in nature. However, this is not unique to the Choctaw language. In fact, the Old English word for play, *plegan* ("to exercise oneself" or "move briskly") is derived from the Anglo-Saxon term *plega*, which meant not only "game" or "sport," but also "fight" or "battle" (Skeat, 1911:397).

Table 3. Football Projective Plate 1 (responses as to identification of players): Choctaw versus Anglo, 1974[a]

	Same Team	Not Same Team	Total
Choctaw	3	31	34
Anglo	9	20	29
Total	12	51	63
Chi-square = 3.71 (p < .10)			

[a]Chi-square test for two independent samples employed, using Yates correction for continuity to compensate for small cell frequencies.

Table 4. Football Projective Plate 1 (responses as to perceived normality of event): Choctaw versus Anglo, 1974[a]

	Normal	Not Normal	Total
Choctaw	5	29	34
Anglo	18	11	29
Total	23	40	63
Chi-square = 14.91 (p < .001)			

[a]Chi-square test for two independent samples employed, using Yates correction for continuity to compensate for small cell frequencies.

Table 5. Football Projective Plate 2 (responses as to identity of recipient of spectator attitudes): Choctaw versus Anglo, 1974[a]

	Officials	Not Officials	Total
Choctaw	5	23	28
Anglo	13	16	29
Total	18	39	57
Chi-square = 3.54 (p < .10)			

[a]Chi-square test for two independent samples employed, using Yates correction for continuity to compensate for small cell frequencies.

Table 6. Football Projective Plate 3 (responses as to intention of participants): Choctaw versus Anglo, 1974[a]

	No Intent to Hurt	Actual or Possible Intent to Hurt	Total
Choctaw	30	2	32
Anglo	7	19	26
Total	37	21	58

Chi-square = 24.92 (p < .001)

[a]Chi-square test for two independent samples employed, using Yates correction for continuity to compensate for small cell frequencies.

Table 7. Football Projective Plate 4 (responses as to valuation of perceived coaching style): Choctaw versus Anglo, 1974[a]

	Good	Bad	Total
Choctaw	2	25	27
Anglo	13	1	14
Total	15	26	41

Chi-square = 52.23 (p < .001)

[a]Chi-square test for two independent samples employed, using Yates correction for continuity to compensate for small cell frequencies.

Table 8. Football Projective Plate 4 (responses as to presumed affection for primary subject): Choctaw versus Anglo, 1974[a]

	Would Like	Would Not Like	Total
Choctaw	0	34	34
Anglo	17	11	28
Total	17	45	62

Chi-square = 27.17 (p < .001)

[a]Chi-square test for two independent samples employed, using Yates correction for continuity to compensate for small cell frequencies.

Figure 5. Football Projective Plate 1

Figure 6. Football Projective Plate 2

Figure 7. Football Projective Plate 3

Figure 8. Football Projective Plate 4

When the Mississippi Choctaws borrow English conflict language in the team sport context, they tend to temper its actual usage so that the implicit intention is less severe than in a typical Anglo-American athletic setting (Blanchard, 1975:171). For example, when a Choctaw basketball player says he feels "mean" or "aggressive" he is speaking of a self-contained state of mind rather than an attitude directed toward an opponent, at least to a greater extent than his non-Choctaw counterpart.

Overall, while conflict in its many forms is a continuing reality in the Choctaw world, it is perceived on ways both distinctive to and consistent with the cultural system of the Native Mississippians. It appears that, even though they deal with physical confrontation and competition as expected elements in their daily lives, the Choctaws abhor explicitly destructive and demeaning conflict and attempt to avoid any and all forms of aggressive behavior that presuppose obvious violence. This is evident in their sport behavior and helps to reinforce the distinctive nature of Choctaw play.

6. The Mississippi Choctaws approach sport and recreation with a purpose that has distinctive Choctaw dimensions. This is best illustrated by a recent study in which I attempted to isolate the motivations and concepts underlying participation in physical fitness activities (Blanchard, 1977).

In the summer of 1975, I conducted a physical fitness program at Pearl River through the tribal recreation department and in cooperation with the Public Health Service. Over 100 persons enrolled in the program, and sessions were conducted daily, using the track, exercise machines, and sauna at Choctaw Central High School. However, the Choctaw joggers' enthusiasm waned rapidly, and in three weeks only a handful of persons were still participating.

In the ensuing attempt to determine why the activity had failed to sustain community interest, it was decided that a workable physical fitness program in the area would have to be built around a consistently Choctaw concept of health.

While little published information on traditional Choctaw ethnomedicine is available, it is apparent that the Native Mississippians have long placed a premium on health maintenance, the development of physical skills, stamina, strength, and endurance (see Swanton, 1931:212–241). In the past, the tribe dealt with the matter of personal health within the broader frameworks of social organization and religion. There is still a sense in which the issue has these same dimensions, but the concept of health has obviously been influenced by the semantic categories of English and the scientific world view.

While there is no immediate Choctaw translation for the notion of "physical fitness," the term for health, *ačokma*, is basic in the language's vocabulary. The classic greeting, *Halito! Čimačokma?* ("Hello! Are you fine?"), actually inquires as to one's physical well-being. To be fine is to be healthy, and one can wish nothing better for a friend or kinsman.

In an attempt to elicit an emic model of Choctaw physical fitness, I developed and administered two projective techniques; one using a word list, the other a battery of pictures.

The first of these schedules, a "word-association check list," was divided into two sections. In the first, informants were asked to respond to a list of thirty-one adjectives as these were perceived to apply to what a healthy person should *be* (e.g., big, fast, happy, old, thin). The second, composed of thirteen verbs, elicited information regarding what a healthy person should *do* (e.g., sleep, work, sweat, ache). Results from this test were generally inconclusive, but the responses did suggest that the Choctaws are more concerned with process and ability than with form. For example, if one views being fat as an undesirable state it is because of the things a fat person cannot do (e.g., run, play ball), not because obesity is disproportioned, unsightly, or difficult to clothe.

The projective plate technique proved to be more valuable. Using the nine drawings of the ideal female somatotypes from Sheldon's (1940:291–99) *The Varieties of Human Physique*, I removed the figure enumeration and copied them individually. I then asked a sample of Choctaw informants to place the drawings (nude, front, and side views) in sequential order, from best to worst, in terms of the way they perceived the ideal female body. After the initial sorting, I went back through the pictures with each respondent and asked him or her to comment critically on each one. Both ranking and comments were recorded. This process was repeated with a sample of Anglo residents in Murfreesboro, Tennessee, and in Philadelphia, Mississippi, of similar age, sex, and educational background.

The drawings, which were numbered according to standard somatotyping procedures (1 to 7 in each of the three categories: endomorphy, mesomorphy, and ectomorphy), were ranked with reasonable consistency between the two groups (see Table 9). Both the Choctaws and the Anglos felt that somatotype 136 (i.e., endomorphy = 1, mesomorphy = 3, ectomorphy = 6) most closely approached the feminine ideal. After that the figures were ordered from thinnest to fattest with almost predictable regularity.

When I asked each of the respondents to comment on his or her

Table 9. Responses to Ideal Female Somatotypes: Rankings of Choctaw
and Anglo Samples Compared, 1976[a]

Somatotype	Choctaw		Anglo	
	Rank	Ave. Score	Rank	Ave. Score
136	1	(1.90)	1	(1.93)
117	2	(2.00)	3	(3.23)
127	3	(2.14)	2	(2.07)
172	4	(4.71)	4	(4.43)
171	6	(5.33)	5	(4.47)
362	5	(5.00)	6	(5.17)
632	7	(6.86)	7	(6.83)
731	8	(8.48)	8	(8.63)
711	9	(8.52)	9	(8.37)
	n = 21		n = 30	
	males: 12		males: 24	
	females: 9		females: 6	
	average age: 24.9		average age: 23.7	

[a]The data have been cross-checked to test for possible sex bias, but male/female
differences have proved to be of no significant consequence.

selections upon completing the ranking procedure, the differences
between the two groups were much more pronounced. For example,
the Choctaws were much less likely to berate obesity (see Table 10).
On the other hand, they were more likely to criticize the other
extreme (e.g., "She's too skinny," or "She's too boney,") (see Table
11). The most significant evaluations were those of the mesomorphic
types (i.e., 171, 172, 362). When the Anglos commented on these,
with few exceptions, remarks would be made regarding an apparent
muscularity ("She's too masculine," or "She's too butchy."). But
when the Choctaws looked at the same drawings, they rarely expressed similar concerns. In fact, in several cases, they suggested
that, on the basis of the second appraisal, they should have rated
these further up the scale than they had in the initial ranking (see
Table 12).

I pursued this Choctaw tendency to value muscularity as a female
physical characteristic further. Men admitted that there was something sexually attractive about strong women. Women themselves
claimed that it was important for a woman to develop her physical
potential to its maximum, whether for everyday household responsibilities, managing her children, or handling a belligerent, drinking

Table 10. Somatotype Projective Test (responses relative to perceived curvilinearity): Choctaw versus Anglo, 1976[a]

	Negative	Positive	Total
Choctaw	71	26	97
Anglo	102	4	106
Total	173	30	203

Chi-square = 19.64 (p < .001)

[a]Chi-square test for two independent samples employed, using Yates correction for continuity to compensate for small cell frequencies.

Table 11. Somatotype Projective Test (responses relative to perceived linearity): Choctaw versus Anglo, 1976[a]

	Negative	Positive	Total
Choctaw	24	6	30
Anglo	7	7	14
Total	31	13	44

Chi-square = 4.24 (p < .05)

[a]Chi-square test for two independent samples employed, using Yates correction for continuity to compensate for small cell frequencies.

Table 12. Somatotype Projective Test (responses relative to perceived muscularity): Choctaw versus Anglo, 1976[a]

	Negative	Positive	Total
Choctaw	1	6	7
Anglo	27	7	34
Total	28	13	41

Chi-square = 8.08 (p < .01)

[a]Chi-square test for two independent samples employed, using Yates correction for continuity to compensate for small cell frequencies.

husband. This insight helped me to understand in retrospect why, during the physical fitness program of 1975, the women consistently ignored my advice and spent a great deal of time on the weight machine doing strenuous arm and upper body exercises.

The results of the analysis of this data, coupled with the other aspects of the study, yielded the following conclusions relative to the Mississippi Choctaw concept of physical fitness.

a. Fitness is rarely correlated with being "thin" or "lean." Conversely, being overweight does not necessarily mean that one is "unhealthy" or "unfit."

b. The Choctaws, as opposed to urbanized southern Whites, are less likely to correlate fitness and masculinity, making the male athlete model less viable in this context.

c. Muscularity is not a negative quality in females. Men find the quality sexually attractive, while women view it as a desirable trait.

d. Physical fitness is a social process to be achieved through community activity rather than individually.

The Choctaw approach to physical fitness or health-maintaining forms of recreation is thus distinctively Choctaw in nature. This conclusion suggests that behind all specialized forms of Choctaw sport behavior there probably exists an equally specialized set of values that affects both their reasons for participating and the exact nature of that participation.

7. Choctaw sports tend to have distinctive styles and strategies that set them apart from similar activities among their non-Indian neighbors. The outside shooting in basketball, the wide-open style of both stickball and basketball, and the centrality of the pitcher's role in slow-pitch softball are just three of the better-documented illustrations of differences in this category.

8. Finally, Choctaw sport behavior is distinctively Choctaw by virtue of the fact that it functions as a vehicle for the expression of traditional norms and values. Economically, socially, politically, and ideologically, these activities reflect the many principles that are fundamental to Choctaw identity in the twentieth century, and this phenomenon is the principal subject of the next three chapters.

CHAPTER 4

The Economics of Choctaw Sport

When de Soto and his men first encountered the "Long Hairs" in the sixteenth century, the Choctaws were settled horticulturalists. Growing several types of corn, beans, and pumpkins, they supplemented their domesticated fare with plants, nuts, and fruits gathered in the forest and game taken in the hunt.

By the mid-eighteenth century, the Choctaw economy had been altered slightly by the introduction of some European crops and agricultural techniques. According to reports from this period, the Native Mississippians were cultivating three or four varieties of maize, two types of guinea corn (one of which they used for popping), beans, sunflowers, leeks, garlic, sweet potatoes, melons, squashes, cabbage, and some tobacco.

Farming small individual family plots and some larger communal fields of several acres each, the Choctaws developed a reputation as being among the most successful "toilers of the soil" among southeastern Native Americans, despite their relatively simple tools and techniques. Using a crude hoe, "made out of the shoulder blade of a bison, a stone, or on the coast a large shell" (Swanton, 1931:46), and a digging stick, the Choctaw farmer planted his seeds in specially prepared mounds or hills of dirt in a manner typical of prehistoric North America.

Men and women shared in the initial soil preparation and planting stages, but once in the ground, the growing plants became the responsibility of the women. However, the men often helped with weeding, while the children were assigned the time-consuming task of discouraging crows and other unwelcome pests.

Also important to Choctaw subsistence during the eighteenth century were domesticated animals, specifically chickens, hogs, and ducks. Cattle were only later introduced into the local barnyard.

Throughout their history and into the twentieth century, the Choctaw people depended heavily on the meat obtained by their hunters. Large game, such as deer, bear, and elk, were hunted in winter, while smaller mammals, like rabbit and squirrel, were exploited in the summer. According to Cushman (1899:130), "The Choctaw hunter was famous as a strategist when hunting alone in the woods, and was such an expert in the art of exactly imitating the cries of the various animals of the forests, that he would deceive the ear of the most experienced."

The deer was the principal game animal, and Choctaw hunters developed a range of skills to insure their success in locating, approaching, and killing the fleet-footed animal. Until the eighteenth century, the Choctaws used the bow and arrow, but then obtained rifles and ammunition from English traders. Still, each hunt was surrounded with extensive ritual observance, and on the occasion of a kill, the deer was usually shared among members of several related bands.

The blowgun, a ubiquitous device in the American Southeast, was primarily a boy's weapon among the Choctaws. Usually a hollow reed about seven feet in length, the instrument was used to propel a small arrow made of thistledown. Accurate and deadly within short ranges, the blowgun was used to kill small birds.

The rabbit stick was another important weapon in the early Choctaw arsenal. Cutting a short, hardwood tree limb about eighteen inches in length and three to four inches in diameter, the craftsman carved the piece so that on one end the stick could be held comfortably in the hand. The other end, the shorter segment (four to five inches), was left in its original condition so that the device looked like a primitive wooden hammer. Throwing the stick through the air, the hunter used it to fell small game, in most cases rabbits.

The Choctaws also took advantage of the fresh-water fish found in Mississippi. Using several types of poison (e.g., buckeyes), traps, snaring devices, and eventually metal hooks, they caught and ate perch, trout, suckers, and catfish.

In addition, much of the Choctaw diet was obtained from gathering wild edibles. Acorns, hickory nuts, chestnuts, wild sweet potatoes, persimmons, wild plums, and crabapples were some of the more important items collected. Much of this produce was preserved by drying or smoking.

By the early part of the nineteenth century, the introduction of Western farming equipment and technique had increased the agricultural efficiency of the Choctaws in some areas so that a few of the tribesmen had become very successful. According to local sources, many of them owned large tracts of valuable land, and in a few cases had small contingents of black slaves. Jim Gardner, who was born in 1895, claims that his great-grandfather on his mother's side of the family, Captain Isaacs, owned a large section of land in the vicinity of the Pearl River community. On this farm he maintained a handful of slaves, grew cotton and corn, and raised cattle. By local standards, both Anglo and Native American, Captain Isaacs was well-to-do and of considerable influence throughout the area.

As a result of the forced removal of the 1830s, the majority of the Choctaws in Mississippi emigrated to Oklahoma. Those choosing to stay behind were given land, much of which was located in Neshoba County. Under Article XIV of the Treaty of Dancing Rabbit Creek, each Choctaw head of family remaining in Mississippi was to be given a section of 640 acres, with an additional half-section for each unmarried child over ten and a quarter-section for each child under ten. Also, there were some cash settlements for lands expropriated under the treaty. However, the stipulation that all claimants had to file within one year in order to retain legal rights to the deeded land, coupled with unscrupulous and inept tactics of government agents, ultimately made the government's concessions seem much less generous. In the end, most of the Choctaws refusing to emigrate suffered economically in the wake of the removal.

As Beckett (1949:23) has noted, the "economic status of the Mississippi Choctaws during the nineteenth century varied from that of wealthy planter to poverty-stricken tenant farmer." However, the "wealthy planter" category was a very small one. In fact, Greenwood LeFlore was "the only wealthy Choctaw left in Mississippi after the removal" (Beckett, 1949:23). Living in one of the state's most spacious and beautiful mansions, LeFlore, who had been elected chief of the Northwest Choctaw District in 1824, owned 15,000 acres of land and more than 400 slaves.

With the advent of the 1840s, though, most of the Mississippi Choctaws had to struggle for survival. Living on either marginal land or white-owned farms as squatters, they were forced to eke out an existence by small-scale farming and hunting (Peterson, 1970:44). Some additional income was generated by the sale of herbs collected and baskets made by the women. The men also manufactured several handicraft items which were either sold or bartered to local Whites: rabbit sticks, blowguns, darts, and tool handles. Another source of income was provided by many local white farmers who used seasonal labor, especially during the cotton months of late fall and early winter. Nonetheless, this period was generally characterized by hard times. Peterson (1970:61) refers to the mid-1800s in Choctaw history as a time of "vagabond-like existence."

Around 1880, the Choctaws began to move from squatter status to that of sharecropper. Apparently, the postwar labor shortage in Mississippi had created a situation in which there was more farmland than farmers to work it. Many of the Choctaws moved onto these white-owned farms and worked the land in return for housing, some food, and basic farming supplies. In turn, they kept a percentage of the items harvested, either for sale or home consumption.

The so-called "second removal" of 1903, like its predecessor, adversely affected Choctaw standards of living, but unlike that of the 1830s, it was initiated by the Choctaw people themselves. In 1889, the Oklahoma Choctaw Tribal Council petitioned Congress to appropriate money to facilitate the emigration of Mississippi and Louisiana Choctaws to Oklahoma, where they could enjoy certain rights (e.g., citizenship) denied them in their home states. After Congress rejected the proposal, the Oklahoma Choctaws used their own money to fund the project, and over the next ten years many of the Mississippi group made the move. Then in 1903, under the Dawes Commission (Commission to the Five Civilized Tribes), the Choctaws were ruled ineligible for citizenship unless they moved to Oklahoma, so additional pressures toward emigration were put on the remaining Mississippi Choctaws. All together, over 1,500 Choctaws made the one-way trip from the southeastern state to Oklahoma during the fourteen or fifteen years after 1889, in this period of the second removal.

Depleted by the massive out-migration characterizing removal, the total Mississippi Choctaw population fell to approximately one-fourth of its pre-removal size. Of great significance was the fact that of those making the trek to Oklahoma, many were capable leaders and good farmers. Also, because of the legalities surrounding the 1903 removal, the Choctaws were without public schools, state funding having been terminated. Other services, such as those offered through area mission work, were either discontinued or severely curtailed. As a result, life for the Mississippi Choctaws in the early part of the twentieth century was difficult. Most of the tribe continued to rely on traditional sources of income and methods of subsistence, many families maintaining their sharecropping roles.

With the establishment of the Choctaw Agency in 1918, the federal government allocated $75,000 to provide tribal economic, educational, and health services. Under this program, Choctaw farmers were given long-term loans for the purchase of land in the immediate vicinity of established Choctaw communities as a means of improving economic stability and breaking the dependence of Choctaws on white landowners. While the program ultimately failed because of the inability of participants to repay the borrowed money, it did lay the foundation for the development of a significant Choctaw land base in east central Mississippi. The plan was eventually re-evaluated, and the lands on which payments had been defaulted were designated as trust lands held by the government for the Mississippi Choctaws. Also, in 1937, the Choctaw Agency instituted a program of land purchase under the guidelines of the Indian Reorganization Act (1934) which eventually added approximately 12,500 acres to Choctaw trust land.

With the establishment of the agency and the advent of direct government assistance to the Mississippi Choctaws came the schools (see p. 44). Not only did these institutions provide novel educational opportunities and hot lunches for school-age children, but also practical instruction and vocational training for adults. Until the 1960s, however, the administrative and teaching positions in the schools were staffed totally with local Whites.

Despite government involvement, economic change among the Mississippi Choctaws took place very slowly, and life continued to be difficult in the area.

Beckett (1949:68) describes a "typical" Choctaw home as he observed it in 1947:

> One Noxubee County family of three was . . . living in a small, poorly kept, windowless, one room house, without a bed or chair. A block sawed from a tree trunk was used as a dining table, and a small cook stove served as a means of keeping the house warm in winter. The family secured drinking water from a nearby stagnant slough. . . . The wife had no shoes, but wore a long clean dress. A six months old baby had on a clean diaper. Two dogs, two cats, one hen, and three baby chicks made up the worldly possessions of the family.

As late as the mid-'50s, Choctaw existence in east central Mississippi was one of marginality, basic rural subsistence, and economic dependence. By this time, the number of small farms in the area had declined significantly as a direct result of falling cotton prices. This led to the loss of many sharecropping jobs. Even for those Choctaws who managed to find work, wages were low. As recently as 1965, for example, some field hands were paid only ten cents an hour for "chopping" cotton. Increasingly, Choctaws in the region began to rely more heavily on nonagricultural jobs and welfare assistance.

With the passage of the Civil Rights Act in 1964 many employment opportunities in local industry were made available to the nonwhite sector of Mississippi workers. The results of this event are reflected in economic statistics. According to Peterson (1970:209), "the percentage of Choctaw heads of households engaged in non-agricultural wage jobs increased from 23.8 in 1962 to 44.6 in 1968."

The 1960s also witnessed the development of relocation and vocational training programs under the auspices of the tribe and the agency, which provided new job opportunities for many members of the Choctaw work force.

With the advent of the 1970s and the federal government's new emphasis on the Native American community's right to self-determination, the Choctaws began to move into the important tribal and agency jobs. Prior to this and subsequent to the creation of a tribal government among the Choctaws in 1945, many of these were held by area Whites (see the section on the history of Choctaw political organization, pp. 132–34). Also, the establishment of career education courses and the development of manpower programs, under which tribal members were prepared for professional positions, were significant factors in the gradual modernization and economic development of the Mississippi Choctaw community.

By 1977, the Choctaw labor force was employed predominantly in nonagricultural jobs as unskilled laborers, clerks, service workers, transport operators, teachers, teachers' aides, secretaries, craftsmen, health aides, social workers, program developers, and policemen. Many Choctaws still farmed, but primarily as a source of supplementary income or direct, household consumables. In some cases, Native Mississippians were continuing the traditional sharecropping pattern, while seasonal farm work provided occasional opportunity for others to make additional money.

Sport and Traditional Economics

Because of limited ethnohistorical data, it is difficult to understand the full economic impact of participation in sports like chunkey and stickball among the Mississippi Choctaws of centuries past. It is possible, however, to suggest costs that one might have incurred in something like the formal stickball match and to analyze the general relationship between such a match and the subsistence system of traditional Choctaw culture.

At an individual level, early historic Choctaws in Mississippi would have encountered the additional costs of playing equipment and uniforms, although until recently, most of these items were made by the participants themselves, therefore more time than actual material goods or money was expended. On the other hand, the additional cost of food was an expense for some participants during the festivities surrounding the formal stickball match. Also, there was the cost of employing the services of a Choctaw doctor or of other ritual personnel in the process of individual preparation for the intercommunity game.

At a group level, stickball matches also had some effect on the Choctaw economy in years past—the early nineteenth century, for example. To begin with, the ball game was a time-consuming enterprise and for this reason had to be fit conveniently into the total subsistence calendar in order to avoid conflicting with fundamental food-producing activities in an agricultural society. As a result, games were most frequently scheduled just before or immediately after the harvesting of the main crop. This was similar to the practice of other horticultural, ball-playing tribes in the Southeast. For example, the most significant game for the Yuchi was staged on the second day of the annual ceremony, "just as the corn ripens" (Speck, 1909:86). The "favorite time" for ball play among the Cherokees was "in the fall after the corn had ripened" (Mooney, 1890:110). Jones (1873:96) claims that all of the "Georgia tribes" that played stickball held their "principal matches in the fall of the year," after the harvest.

In another context, I have argued that the formal Choctaw ball-play matches were most frequent at these times of the year because these were the periods during which one would expect to witness some dietary stress and obvious intercommunity inequities and related pressures toward parity (Blanchard, 1979:199). The betting that went on in conjunction with the stickball games allowed for an exchange of produce between communities, thus helping to solve the inequities.

Others have argued that the Choctaws chose these times of the year to engage in the major stickball contests because it was simply convenient to the agricultural process (John Peterson, personal communication, November 1979). In other words, the periods just before and after the harvest were times in which there were a minimum of food-producing responsibilities and thus more free time in which to engage in leisurely activities. Also, people were together during the planting and harvesting seasons, so it was easier to get enough participants together to play stickball. In any case, the formal matches tended to be significantly correlated with important dates on the Choctaw subsistence calendar.

Perhaps more vital than that relationship was the impact of stickball betting on the economies of individual Choctaw communities. As mentioned in Chapter 2, gambling was an important element in the traditional stickball match. The two competing communities wagered literally every imaginable resource available, and the winning group took all.

Despite the volume of the turnover and the size of individual risks, the problem of winning or losing was reportedly viewed as insignificant, even though large amounts of energy were expended by players and spectators alike. While the Mississippi Choctaws were perhaps not always as "cheerful" about losing as some writers have reported (e.g., Cushman, 1899:130), it is obvious that the means were seen as more important than the ends.

Geertz (1973:440) has observed, with reference to the Balinese cockfight, in a valuable anthropological analysis of betting as a form of "deep play," that "so far as money is concerned, the explicitly expressed attitude toward it is that it is a secondary matter." The Choctaws similarly de-emphasized material gain or loss in the process. Even in the pregame betting, stickball match participants were only slightly concerned about value and parity. The Choctaws were said to "wager a new gun against an old one which is not worth anything, as readily as if it were good, and they give as a reason that if they are going to win they will win as well against a bad article as against a good one, and that they would rather bet against something than not bet at all" (Swanton, 1918:68).

In this type of gambling, like that engaged in by Geertz's (1973:433) cockfighters, "money is less a measure of utility, had or expected, than it is a symbol of moral import, perceived or imposed." Though the ultimate purpose of Choctaw stickball betting differed from that characterizing the Balinese event, it was serious business and for reasons that went beyond material value.

The unique moral import of the betting that pre-empted winning as the major concern of many stickball participants was incomprehensible to outsiders. This is probably one reason why the Whites who came to the Choctaw stickball contest in the 1800s became such a disruptive force. Death and injury were not new to Choctaw *toli* in Mississippi, but the preoccupation with the maximization of one's investment in the game's outcome was.

Over a long period of time, the economic impact of stickball gambling on a particular Choctaw community in the early nineteenth century was probably minimal. Reportedly, no one team or community dominated play over a period of time by consistently winning, so wins and losses were fairly evenly distributed, and the wagered resources could in effect be kept in circulation during the stickball season. On a short-term basis, however, a community that wagered heavily on the outcome of a game and lost could be severely affected and forced to deal with temporary shortages of certain material items, food, and livestock.

In general, stickball and other early Choctaw sporting activities had their costs, both short- and long-term, but only rarely did they seriously threaten resources in the many Native Mississippian communities or economic stability within the Choctaw tribe as a whole.

The Economics of Contemporary Choctaw Sport and Recreation

The fact that sport and recreation are important parts of Mississippi Choctaw life is reflected in the amount of money and resources invested in these activities.

In 1977, the tribe had over $2,000,000 either committed to or invesfed in land, facilities, and equipment that could be used, either completely or in part, for recreational purposes. This figure represented capital assets that included twelve ball fields, seven of which were lighted, four community centers, not including two under construction, and a large swimming pool. While the community centers are used for many nonathletic purposes (e.g., educational, religious, health, general administrative), large areas are devoted to basketball courts, bleachers, and other recreation-related space.

In addition to tribally controlled recreational facilities, the Choctaws have access to those located in or near the schools in several communities: playgrounds, outdoor basketball courts, and other game areas. At Pearl River there are tennis courts, an indoor gym, a track, and a football stadium.

About 1 percent of the total annual tribal budget goes to the recreation department. This figure of approximately $50,000 is used to pay the director's salary and those of two or three community coordinators as well as to fund other miscellaneous part-time positions (e.g., lifeguards, officials). In addition, some money is spent annually for equipment, facility upkeep, director travel, and uniforms. Besides the money earmarked specifically for recreation, another $15,000 to $20,000 is spent each year by the tribe for utilities, maintenance, and cleaning of the recreational facilities.

Some of the recreation costs are met by outside revenue generated by the program itself. Entry fees, concession stand profits, special film presentations, swimming pool admissions, and occasional grant monies bring in between $7,000 and $8,000 a year. However, this income falls far short of making the tribal recreation program self-sufficient, even though this is the goal expressed by the tribal chief in 1977. However, other community leaders see such a goal as unrealistic, arguing that recreation costs are a legitimate tribal expense to be underwritten by regular revenues. No one apologizes for the money that it costs to play. Playing is serious business.

Another economic dimension of traditional sport, betting, is no longer a significant element in Mississippi Choctaw play behavior. The preoccupation with betting on sporting events apparently died with the demise of the formal stickball match at the end of the last century. For example, very rarely does anyone wager on the outcome of a recreation league activity or a Choctaw Central High School athletic contest. While some gambling is reported in connection with backyard games like horseshoes and rings or with billiards at a local poolhall or tavern, the stakes are usually very small: a beer, a coke, a dollar. Apparently, the sport-betting phenomenon was an integral part of the formal stickball match rather than a general passion of the Choctaw people.

Nevertheless, many families still spend large amounts of money annually for equipment, uniforms, and other sport-related expenses. A middle-aged couple with four children, all of whom are involved in school and tribal athletic activities, could spend more than $1,000 a year to finance their sport habit: outfits, shoes, gloves, entry fees, travel costs, balls, bats, and other incidental items. One athletic Choctaw family estimated that in the 1976–77 fiscal year, they spent over $500 on recreation league and high school sporting activities, approximately 10 percent of their taxable income.

What possible economic rewards await the devoted Choctaw athlete? Participation in the sport program offers only limited material benefits. For example, some of the Choctaw stickball players make a few dollars playing exhibition games each year. In the past decade, some Choctaw athletic teams, in both the high school and tribal recreation programs, have had the opportunity to travel and play throughout the Southeast. Sport participation also provides some incentive for Choctaw youth to stay in school and complete their education, but, with two or three exceptions, few athletes have moved from Choctaw Central High School to the college ranks, and none successfully. No Choctaw ball-player from the area has ever played professionally, although there were several men who played "semi-pro" baseball in the '40s and '50s. Several counties in the east Mississippi area had a league composed of municipal teams, and the managers of these squads would recruit Choctaw players, furnish uniforms, and pay them approximately ten dollars a game, expenses being covered by gate receipts.

In general, the tangible benefits of serious play among the Mississippi Choctaws, despite the heavy investment of time and money, are limited. Where opportunities for any type of outside sport success, college or professional, have been made available, Choctaw athletes have shown little interest in pursuing them. They often fantasize about athletic stardom outside the community, but only as a model for their immediate sport activities, not as a long-term goal. The team sport activities of the tribal recreation and high school programs are satisfying and rewarding in themselves. They are not seen as "a way out" or as "avenues to bigger and better things."

In general, the immediate economic meaning of sport activity among contemporary Mississippi Choctaws must be defined primarily in terms of expense rather than income. A few additional jobs are created by the program, young people may earn a few extra dollars by officiating at games or maintaining the ball fields, and a service organization might make a small amount of money by selling concessions at important events. However, most of the funds expended move from tribal finances into off-reservation accounts. So, while sport and recreation stimulate some intratribal cash flow, the phenomena act primarily as drains on Choctaw resources.

1. Mississippi Choctaw stickball player, 1908

3. Man beating drum for dance at Choctaw stickball game, 1908

2. Mississippi Choctaw stickball player, 1908

M. R. Harrington, Museum of the American Indian

4. Choctaw group, 1908

Carl Tubby

5. Nanih Waiyah mound, Mississippi

6. Choctaw home, Pearl River

7. Choctaw home, Pearl River

Choctaw Community News

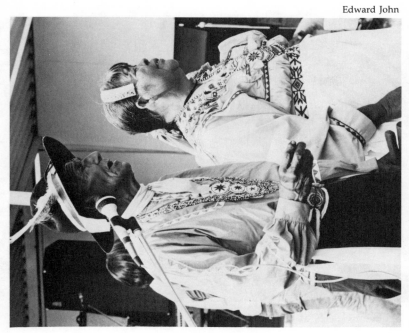

Edward John

9. Choctaw chanters

Edward John

8. Choctaw man and his stickball sticks

Carl Tubby

10. Between classes at Choctaw Central High School

11. Choctaw boys playing makeshift baseball

12. Choctaw social dancers

13. Stickball game action

Carl Tubby

15. The old and the new: stickball and the church

Edward John

14. Stickball game action, 1977 Choctaw Fair: Bogue Chitto versus Pearl River

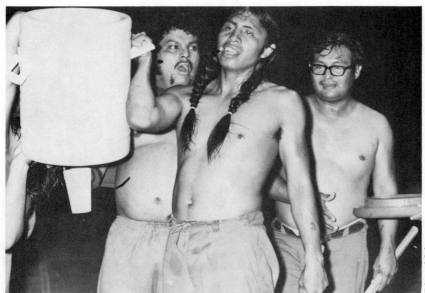

Edward John

16. Stickball game, water break, 1977 Choctaw Fair

17. Stickball team marching to game

18. Choctaw stickball player

19. Choctaw drummer

20. Choctaw Central High School band in Choctaw Fair parade, 1976

21. Bogue Chitto stickball team in Choctaw Fair parade, 1976

22. Making stickball sticks at the Choctaw Fair

23. Dinner on the grounds at Standing Pine

Edward John

24. Track season at Choctaw Central High School

25. Choctaw Central High School football team in action

26. Choctaw Central High School football team, 1974

27. Girls' basketball team, Choctaw Central High school, 1977

Edward John

28. Women's basketball, recreation league action

29. Men's basketball, recreation league action

30. Tucker baseball team, 1967

31. Men's softball, recreation league action

32. Women's softball, recreation league action

33. Choctaw Dixie Youth All-Star baseball team

34. Pumping iron during the recreation league physical fitness program, 1976

35. Practicing the art of self-defense at Choctaw Central High School

Choctaw Social Organization and Team Sports

Social organization is the process by which members of particular groups structure their relationships in order to cope more effectively with the problems of survival and adaptation. Sport and recreation behavior can be analyzed from a perspective of social organization. Team sports in particular are circumscribed by patterns of social relations and interactions in specific cultural settings. These patterns as they have been observed among the Mississippi Choctaws are the subject of this chapter.

Traditional Choctaw Social Organization and Change

The nature of traditional Choctaw social organization is only vaguely understood. Unlike some Native American systems (e.g., Navajo) that have been appraised as difficult to analyze because of their ambiguity (see Aberle, 1963:2), the Choctaw situation is complicated by the simple lack of ethnohistorical data. Traditional patterns of social organization are rendered even more elusive by the radical changes occurring in Choctaw life-styles over the past two centuries (Eggan, 1937).

Historically, it is apparent that the "Choctaws conspicuously lacked rigid, formal institutions" (Coe, 1960:4). Yet the entire group was at one time divided into two large matrilineal exogamous moieties. Choctaw origin myths claim that the people were actually divided into two large clans or families before they dispersed from Nanih Waiya, the tribe's legendary point of provenience, located in east central Mississippi.

Existing records suggest that these moieties were in turn composed of several totemic clans. However, the Choctaw term *iksa* is used for both "moiety" and "clan," and specific totemic names for the clans remain essentially a subject of speculation. According to early accounts, though, clan membership, which was inherited through the maternal line, was vital in the definition of marriage restrictions. Clan exogamy was strictly enforced.

113

The moiety division of Choctaw society, often illustrated in early formal stickball matches, gradually lost its significance in the eighteenth and early nineteenth centuries. According to Swanton (1931:81), "In the breakdown of an old exogamic system . . . among tribes having clans and moieties, it commonly happens that clan exogamy is maintained for a time after moiety exogamy has been abandoned."

However, clan identification was soon overshadowed by community or local group membership. Even though there is some evidence to support the notion that often several clans were represented in a particular community, these intracommunal distinctions were soon forgotten, and the term *iksa* was applied to the local, residential group.

Choctaw kinship terminology previous to removal illustrated the typical Crow pattern. With two different sets of terms for male and female egos, the system made a distinction between cross and parallel cousins, lumped parallel cousins with brothers and sisters, and made similar distinctions at the first ascending generation level. Also, father's sister and father's sister's daughter are referred to by a single term, *įhokni* (see Figure 9).

The customary marriage process among the Choctaws was initiated by the prospective groom. Having received a subtle indication of interest from the female he had selected, the male approached the family of his intended and offered them several small gifts (e.g., beads, clothing). If the parents accepted the tokens, it signified their approval. Subsequently, plans were made for the marriage ceremony, an elaborate event involving feasting, gift-giving, and ritualized exchange. The activities were presided over by an *anompa ištikiya* ("orator," or in this context "master of ceremonies").

Since the removal of the 1830s, Choctaw society has undergone drastic modifications, the family being the only intact and "continuous link between the Choctaws of today and the Choctaws before removal" (Peterson, 1970:144). Beyond the extended family, the most important social unit is the community. The local group has completely replaced the older clan designation. Choctaws are not aware of any clan membership, although as late as the early 1930s, according to Eggan (1937:42n), some members of the community were aware of former clan affiliations but defined them in terms of patrilineal rather than matrilineal descent. The term *iksa* is now used to refer to either religious sect or community identification. As Jim Gardner explains, "The *iksa* is like the name of your community; it's the group you belong to. In the old days you might say you belong to the Captain Jim group. He was your chief, and you were from

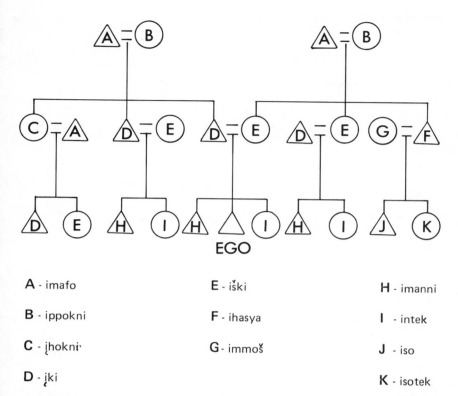

A - imafo	E - iški	H - imanni
B - ippokni	F - ihasya	I - intek
C - įhokni·	G - immoš	J - iso
D - įki		K - isotek

Figure 9. Choctaw Kinship Terminology (male ego) (adapted from Swanton, 1931:85)

the community where he lived. It was a way of saying where you were from and who you were."

The most critical changes in Choctaw kinship terminology apparently took place in the 1800s, resulting ultimately in a pattern one writer has described as "Crow-like with a patrilineal bias" (Coe, 1960:4). According to Eggan (1937:36–37), the older Choctaw pattern, relative to the Crow ideal type, has been "turned around" (see Figure 10). "Here the father's sister's son and *his* descendants through *males* are classed as "fathers," whereas the children of the father's sister's daughter (who is classed with the father's sister) become "brothers" and "sisters." . . . This is clearly something quite different from the typical Crow pattern of descent."

This reversal of the system is probably related to missionary, government, and other Anglo-American influences on Choctaw life during the nineteenth century. Peterson (personal communication, November 1979) has suggested that perhaps of even greater importance in effecting this shift was the fact that the male family member was

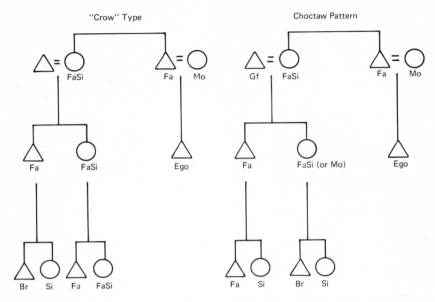

Figure 10. Choctaw Kinship Terminology Pattern Compared to Typical "Crow" Type (adapted from Eggan, 1937:37)

English equivalents are used for native terms: Fa, father; Mo, mother; Gf, grandfather; Gm, grandmother; Br, brother; Si, sister.

the person that "contracted" with the landowner in the sharecropping process.

At the same time, other related changes were taking place in the Choctaw kinship system. The role of the mother was being de-emphasized, and the position of the father as the head of the household was increasingly affirmed. As a result, a shift from a matrilineal to a patrilineal emphasis in the system occurred. Likewise, new patterns of political control led to the creation of leadership roles that were territorial rather than kin-based. Related to these changes, the old clan system became obsolete and soon dissolved.

By the 1970s, Choctaw kinship terminology had undergone additional changes in usage, particularly among the younger segment of the population. Overall, the trend was toward the development of a typically bilateral system consistent with that of the English-speaking world. For example, many of the younger Choctaw speakers did not refer to father's sister's sons and father's sister's daughters as "fathers" and "mothers" respectively, as had once been customary.

Choctaw communities are still generally closed and endogamous. Outsiders, Choctaw and non-Choctaw alike, are discouraged from settling into and becoming part of the local group. As is to be expected, Choctaws tend to marry members of their own communities. For example, as late as 1968, 63.8 percent of all the couples in one of the Choctaw communities consisted of men and women born in that community. This trend, however, is more characteristic of the larger communities than of the smaller ones for the simple reason that the latter often lack suitable mates for young adults, male or female, aspiring to matrimony.

Also, many members of the more traditional Mississippi Choctaw communities often refuse to cooperate with persons from other localities on tribal projects or other occasions that bring the several villages together, often expressing open hostilities toward kinsmen residing in other areas. Derogatory stereotypes are often developed within one community to be used in reference to persons from another. While the advent of tribal government (1945) and the construction of the new high school (1964) have served to adumbrate community lines and defuse related prejudice, the boundaries are still clearly recognized, and local biases persist.

Marriages are now performed in either civil or Christian ceremony, and the newlywed couples generally establish their own households, independent of those of their parents. Occasionally, traditional wedding ceremonies are staged in some of the more conservative Choctaw communities but more for nostalgic than customary reasons (see Thompson, 1975).

Team Sports and Social Organization

The formal Choctaw stickball match of centuries past was often characterized by the opposition of kin groups, for example, representatives of one of the moieties versus those of the other. The kin orientation of stickball teams was similarly evident in more recent history when contests pitted one local group against another.

Modern team sports (e.g., baseball, softball, and basketball) among the Mississippi Choctaws also manifest kin dimensions, define social boundaries, and operate within the rules prescribed by the overarching social system.

Because of the extensive interrelatedness of the members of the several Choctaw communities, the representative teams are usually composed of closely related individuals. For example, there were thirteen teams participating in the 1973–74 men's basketball program, and of the 129 players, 118 were Choctaw. Of the latter, 68 were related to at least one person of their own team, in a total of 89 intrateam pairings: fathers, sons, uncles, cousins, and in-laws (Blanchard, 1974a:6).

In the summer of 1975 the women's softball team from the Standing Pine community had a total of fifteen persons on its roster. Twelve of these were aware of significant kin ties to one or more other members of the team. The remaining three, sisters to each other, could not document any ties necessary to link them genealogically to the rest of the team, but speculated that these existed at second or third ascending generation levels (see Figure 11) (Blanchard, 1976:66).

Because of the pervasive kin definition of these groups, like the communities they represent, the teams are tightly knit and essentially closed to outsiders, especially among the isolated and more conservative localities. In Pearl River, however, recreation team memberships reflect the greater heterogeneity of community composition, and the problem of intrarelatedness is approached with a more relaxed attitude. Still, when queried as to whether or not they felt that recreation teams should be made up of persons from the same community, 54 percent of a large random sample from six of the seven major villages responded in the affirmative. However, when the question was posed in a different framework—"Should teams be made up of related individuals?"—79 percent of the same sample answered "no." In offering explanations for this seemingly paradoxical response, most of those questioned suggested that kinfolk do not get along, and that such an arrangement would engender an undue amount of friction. Apparently, most of those questioned were not immediately aware of the kin networks that existed within the current Choctaw recreation league units.

The teams representing the traditional communities among the Mississippi Choctaws appear to be significantly more enthusiastic about tribal recreation activities than are those from progressive Pearl River. This greater excitement is reflected in several areas. The more traditional teams are less likely to forfeit games by failing to meet schedules, even when threatened by bad weather or forced to travel great distances. Individual players maintain consistently higher levels of excitement regarding league events, and the outcomes of particular games are of greater community-wide concern. Also, while the kin factor in team composition may be incidental at this point, groups from the outlying areas have fared better in final league standings during the past few seasons than the athletic units from Pearl River.

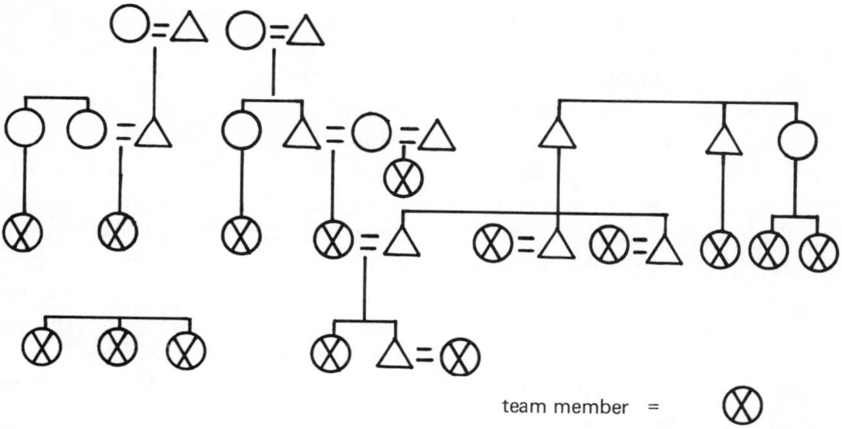

team member = ⊗

Figure 11. Standing Pine Women's Softball Team, 1975: Kinship Definition

When questioned directly about the role of kinship rules and regularities within the playing process itself, Choctaw sport enthusiasts
chuckle at the notion that they might be influenced by genealogical
realities in decisions made during the game. This contention was
reinforced by an analysis of actual play patterns. When on-court
exchanges between members of the same basketball team were analyzed during the 1974 Choctaw recreation league season, it was discovered that there was not a disproportionate control of the ball by
members of the same immediate family or kin group (see p. 79).
This situation contrasts with that of the Rimrock Navajos, where a
similar analysis revealed a very kin-oriented pattern of on-court exchange and decision-making (Blanchard, 1974:11). Unlike the Navajos, the Choctaws appear not to consider the details of kinship
reality within the basketball playing process. It may be that the
greater consistency of the Choctaw teams as community/kin-group
units makes the more specialized distinctions characteristic of the
Navajo ball-playing pattern unnecessary.

On the other hand, Choctaw spectators at local athletic events
tend to recognize and relate to individual players. They call out to
them and refer to them during the course of play, using the players'
personal names. Likewise, they frequently express personal concerns, praise, encouragement or ridicule unique to the individual
athlete in a fashion not as characteristic of the non-Choctaw fan-
player relationship. In other words, in a sense, the role of the spectator gives the typical Choctaw ball game the air of being a big family
event.

Also, the kin variable as a facet of team sport behavior among the Mississippi Choctaws often makes itself evident in the occasional controversies surrounding league play. For example, in the summer of 1975, a women's softball game was interrupted by one manager's complaint regarding a minor rule infraction. One team had allowed one of its players to come to bat out of turn, and the incident eventually led to an exchange of blows between the two team leaders. In the ensuing debate over the issue, community opinion generally placed the entire blame for the incident on the manager who had registered the initial complaint. Even the latter's own team was slow to come to her defense, in some cases footnoting their mild disapproval with the comment, "Well, anyhow, she's an outsider."

In the same sense that the kinship factor is vital to the structure of Choctaw play, the family bond creates a feeling of obligation that in many cases overrides a person's more immediate desires. As a member of a particular ball team an individual has a responsibility or commitment to his teammates (i.e., his family) that he would not have were he playing with a group of unrelated persons. For this reason, he must be careful to observe schedules and perform to the best of his ability whether or not such behavior conforms to his initial impulses in any given situation. As Gloria York says of her own experience as a teenager aspiring to play on a recreation league softball team:

> When I first thought about playing softball, I wanted to be on my sisters' team. . . . My grandfather's first cousin was the manager of this particular team. I wanted to play on his team. I felt like if I could play really good I could be on that team with my sisters. . . .
> Now, I feel like I belong in this particular group more than with somebody you don't know. . . . Most of the teams that I have played with are family kinds of things. . . . I feel obligated to go because Stella or Dessie [her sisters] might not make it, and so I feel like I should be there in case they're not there.

Kinship realities thus serve to generate a sense of commitment to team sport activities as well as to structure actual play. So strong is this commitment that many Choctaws openly admit that the obligation they have to their respective teams is more binding than that which they feel toward their jobs. One can be late to work or simply fail to report without violating any familial responsibility. Such is not the case with a ball game.

The quality of rivalry or competitiveness in Mississippi Choctaw sport behavior is also related to community identification. With some of the same eagerness and aggressiveness characteristic of the traditional stickball contests, today's Choctaws manifest a strong will-to-win in intercommunity ball games. As one contemporary Choctaw athlete suggests:

> The community thing has existed for a long time on the reservation. One community always feels that they're better than another. Pearl River always felt that they were the best, in anything that came up. We had that stigma that we had to win. Of course, we enjoyed it, but winning was the key for us, I think, in the sense that sometimes they beat us, and we tried to get even somehow, in a game. . . . A lot of times, parents would tell us, in a mildly critical way, that we couldn't beat another team, like Connehatta; just stating a fact, but it made us feel bad. So we tried our best. . . .

The importance of the local group as the basic unit of contemporary Choctaw social organization beyond the nuclear family is put in clearer perspective by the sport phenomenon. If the Choctaw world is analyzed in terms of what Sahlins (1972:198) calls "kinship-residential sectors," one can see a correlation between kin distance and sport competitiveness that underscores the significance of the community (see Figure 12).

The outcome of athletic competition within the family unit itself is of little consequence, and only slightly more so within the local group. However, as they occur within the intercommunal sector, the results of total team confrontations became extremely important. Finally, the non-Choctaw area is characterized by a more subdued will-to-win. On the other hand, while team competitiveness is deemphasized at this level, the individual will-to-excel becomes paramount, personal athletic skills are more explicitly developed, and there are fewer attempts to manipulate or rationalize outcomes ritually. In the end, what such a model suggests is that the local group, as the fundamental unit of Choctaw social life, defines its boundaries vis-à-vis other Choctaw communities in the sport encounter.

In addition to the local group identification and solidarity factors, the outcome of any particular sporting event reflects not only the relative abilities of the two teams but also the status of the two communities represented. In essence, it is an expression of their relative prestige within the entire Mississippi Choctaw social system. As one older athlete whose community affiliation is obvious informed me, "It is important to show which community is best. Pearl River is the best, and we have to prove it every time we play ball."

While some Choctaws are more hesitant than others to be explicit

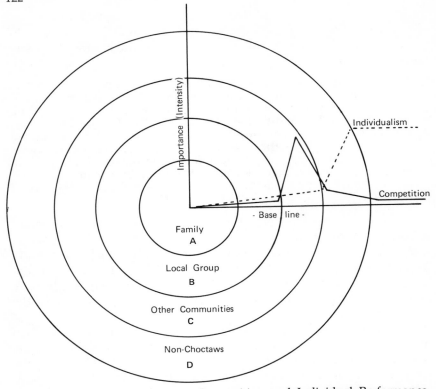

Figure 12. Importance of Team Competition and Individual Performance Factors in Mississippi Choctaw Sport Behavior, (defined by intensity of expression in each of the four basic kinship-residential sectors); (concept adopted from Sahlins, 1972:199)

on this matter, many of them admit that there is a tendency for everyone to rank the several communities in terms of overall prestige. When I asked different informants to list the seven contemporary villages according to relative social standing, I received a variety of responses. If the informant would admit to the existence of such a prestige scale, he or she would usually list his or her own community of provenience at the top. However, most of the responses were fairly consistent in the way that they ranked the remaining six communities (see Table 13). In all cases, the lists suggested a movement from large to small, the greatest amount of social prestige accruing to members of the more heavily populated localities.

In pursuing this idea with the same informants as it applied to sport and recreation among the Choctaws, I discovered another in-

Table 13. Ranking of Mississippi Choctaw Communities Relative to
Overall Social Prestige as Perceived by Four Informants, 1977

Informant A (Pearl River)	Informant B (Pearl River)	Informant C (Bogue Chitto)	Informant D (Connehatta)
1 Pearl River	Pearl River	Bogue Chitto	Connehatta
2 Connehatta	Bogue Chitto	Pearl River	Pearl River
3 Bogue Chitto	Connehatta	Connehatta	Bogue Chitto
4 Tucker	Standing Pine	Tucker	Tucker
5 Red Water	Red Water	Standing Pine	Red Water
6 Standing Pine	Tucker	Red Water	Standing Pine
7 Bogue Homa	Bogue Homa	Bogue Homa	Bogue Homa

teresting pattern. In any athletic contest between the representative
teams of two local groups, the play of the unit from the community
ranking lower on the prestige scale is characterized by a greater sense
of competitiveness and desire to win. The small, traditional, and
closed Mississippi Choctaw communities predictably tend to take
their ball-playing more seriously than the others, primarily Pearl
River. The team sport phenomenon is one of the few ways left by
which community identification can be expressed. The same sense
of urgency that prompts the Bogue Chitto mother to warn her daughter against dating a boy from Connehatta gives the Connehatta softball player a compelling drive to defeat his Bogue Chitto opponents.

Community identification, which some informants claim is visible
in dress styles and mannerisms, also overrides the significance of
more immediate kinship realities in some circumstances. This is
clearly illustrated in the team sport setting. In many cases, where
individual family members have migrated away from their community of orientation, intrafamilial ties have eventually been
superseded by community allegiance. In a ball game, then, it is not
unusual to see members of the same extended family—genealogical
rather than residential—who are playing for different community
teams manifest basic antagonisms toward each other. "Even though
he's our cousin, he's not one of us anymore."

The integration of the team memberships across community lines
has in many cases lowered enthusiasm, aggressiveness, and the will-
to-win, primarily because this cross-cutting counters the effect of the
traditional community factor in Choctaw team sport competition.
This apparently is the reason for the more lackadaisical attitude of
Pearl Riverites, many of whom are playing on ball teams made up

of persons of different community backgrounds and only limited kinship identification. Also, this may be a factor in the general lack of excitement shown by many young Choctaws for high school athletics. Many Choctaw Central students show a much greater interest in the tribal recreation program than in that of the school. In fact, in some cases in which young athletes were not allowed to play on both the school and recreation league teams, they have asked to be removed from the high school roster. As Carl Tubby has observed, "They're [the high school football players] not too crazy about it. They love to play, but the desire to win is not there like in some of the players I've met. But, if they were playing community against community, that would be a different ball game. It wouldn't be just a football game; it would be community and community fighting each other to see who's superior."

One of the reasons often given for this lack of enthusiasm for the athletic program at Choctaw Central is that it is too formal, impersonal, and structured. As Tubby has suggested, "Choctaws have always been serious about things like that [games]. As long as things are not too organized, they are very competitive. They're not as serious about it when it gets too organized."

Then he notes, with reference to his own experience, "The backyard ragball game was more fun [than high school baseball]. The idea was to hit that ball as far as you can. I like to hit home runs. That was my goal. But, in baseball, the coach would make me sacrifice or bunt sometimes. I didn't want to bunt. My idea was to knock the hell out of that ball, out of the park."

Some older members of the community claim that even the contemporary tribal recreation program has become too highly formalized and has thus lost much of its traditional color and excitement. For example, in 1972–73, the Bureau of Outdoor Recreation spent almost $300,000 to build and improve ball parks in the several Choctaw communities. Prior to this, most of the local groups had played on makeshift fields owned by individual community members and used for years. The BOR met stiff opposition in most of the villages as they took it upon themselves to design, locate, and build the new playing fields with no input from the local group memberships. In one particular situation, an adamant landowner stood guard with a shotgun over property that he felt was threatened by the BOR project.

In the aftermath, many of the adults in the Choctaw recreation program became increasingly disaffected. One of those who remembers a time when he got more excited over playing ball than he does now comments:

> It's just not the same. People like the way things were: tradition. They like the old fields. They had played there for many years; they felt they owned something. It belonged to them. It was something to pass on to your children, your boy; to be remembered.
> The BOR came in and leveled the fields, put up lights. They really didn't ask anybody what they wanted. . . . It took something away from the game. They, the older people, liked it the way it was; the rough fields, holes, weeds, rocks. But that was important: tradition.

The strength of community identification among the Mississippi Choctaws, especially as manifested in the sport environment, suggests several observations about the nature of their traditional social organization. The extent to which the Choctaw people viewed themselves as a unified group or tribe is definitely minimized by the observation that local groups (*iksa*) view themselves as virtually independent and closed, even to those within recognizable kin distance. However, it must also be admitted that the evolution of clearly defined and impenetrable community boundaries may be purely a phenomenon of the past 100 to 150 years and reveal little about the nature of earlier social process.

From another perspective, team sport events among the Mississippi Choctaws today provide an opportunity for people to get together, both as a community and as a tribe. Despite a variety of tribal-wide functions and the many activities of the high school, interaction between memberships of the more isolated communities is limited. This is one reason why recreation league events are so well attended. On a nice summer evening, for example, as many as 150 spectators may come to the ball park at Pearl River to watch the two or three scheduled softball games. People sit in the stands, stay in or around their cars, or simply wander around the perimeters of the general playing area. Small groups of children play their own games at several locations around the field. To an outsider, in many cases the game seems to be but an incidental focus of a wide range of social activities.

Similarly, basketball contests are marked by large crowds, intercommunal participation, and very casual atmospheres. Players often drink wine or smoke between quarters and during time-outs, officials flirt with young women in the stands, and the spectators are entertained by the game as well as the activities off court. Children play, young people congregate in tight bunches in the upper levels of the bleachers, women huddle in small groups and converse among themselves, while the men sit behind the player benches and around the scorer's table talking to the teams as well as to each other. Every game is a broad complex of entertaining events, and while community boundaries are being defined by the confrontation of opposing teams on the playing floor, individuals from different localities are provided an opportunity for meaningful discussion and exchange across these lines as well as within their own primary groups.

However, these contests are limited in their effectiveness as means of fostering intercommunity interaction and cohesion. Certainly, they do provide a context within which members of different localities can exchange formalities and occasionally develop productive relationships. Still, the intracommunal aspects of the events are viewed as more important than the broader intergroup dimension. Within the past few decades at gatherings such as the picnic or Gala Day, parents have guarded against social intercourse among the children of the different communities represented and have limited their own interaction with members of other communities. In fact, it is said that at the classic picnics of the '40s and '50s, visiting groups would normally participate only in the affairs surrounding their own scheduled baseball contests, departing soon after they had been eliminated from the tournament. Often, certain communities would purposely not be invited because of pre-existing antagonisms between their population and that of the host group.

In the end, any intertribal goodwill generated by the total team sport encounter is at best limited, but the interaction does make the event more attractive and entertaining for the spectator and participant alike.

Successful individual participation in team sports can provide a feeling of personal accomplishment and is an important source of social prestige among the Mississippi Choctaws. Being athletic is a positive characteristic for both male and female alike, and is often a fundamental element in the Choctaw self-concept. For this reason, to be called a "jock" or "star" is to be highly complimented.

During the summer of 1974, while I was working for the Choctaw tribal recreation program, one of my assistants, a young man in his mid-twenties, failed to report for work one morning. When he appeared in the office that same afternoon, he was practically ecstatic. He had just returned from the hospital, having gone to see about a rash on his feet. The condition had been diagnosed as "athlete's foot." Relating the incident with prideful exuberance, he made it obvious that the event was a highlight in his career; he had been formally recognized as an athlete. One of his more sophisticated co-workers quipped, "I can hardly wait till he gets jock itch."

The importance of the "athlete" model in Choctaw society was illustrated in a study conducted in the early 1970s on the "occupational orientations of Choctaw Indian High School students in Mississippi" (Spencer, 1973). Most of the males at Choctaw Central were generally "attracted to 'athletics,' " primarily because of the role models this area represented, persons "they would like to fashion their lives after" (Spencer, 1973:56). On the other hand, few of them aspired to specific occupations in the sport field, such as physical education instructor or recreation leader. It has been suggested that the reason for this discrepancy is related to the fact that Choctaw youths have direct access to very few, if any, full-time recreation-related professions (John Peterson, personal communication, October 20, 1977). Also, it reinforces the notion that the Choctaw athlete takes his ball-playing very seriously, but only as he perceives the activity within the total tribal setting.

CHOCTAW SPORT AND SOCIAL BOUNDARIES

As suggested earlier (p. 88), sports, in particular Mississippi Choctaw stickball, can be seen as a form of conflict, both from emic and etic perspectives. In the first place, some Choctaws contend that because the formal stickball match was organized explicitly in some cases to avoid more serious intervillage conflict, it was more than simply sport behavior. On the other hand, physically combative sports such as *toli* can be viewed as having conflict dimensions that make them not unlike more openly aggressive encounters, for example war.

Anthropologist Richard Sipes (1973:80) has demonstrated the tendency for societies having physically combative sports to engage in abnormal amounts of warfare. Testing the hypothesis that such sports lower aggression levels in human society, he finds instead that sports do *not* "act as alternative channels for the discharge of accumulable aggressive tensions. Rather than being functional alternatives, war and combative sports activities in a society appear to be components of a broader cultural pattern."

Further, competition can be viewed as a form of conflict in which "two or more persons struggle to attain a given object" with the emphasis resting "entirely on the object itself rather than the persons themselves as antagonists" (Nisbet, 1970:77). This suggests again that sport, as a special form of competition, can be treated as social conflict.

The treatment of sport and war in the some general conflict category is given additional credibility by analyzing tribal forms of armed conflict which have obvious sport or play dimensions (Blanchard, 1976a:69). In many cases, these events appear to be more like games than serious conflict encounters.

Consider the so-called "warfare" of the Plains Indians in the early nineteenth century. One of these groups, the Cheyenne, was noted for its military prowess and was frequently involved in altercations with neighboring tribes, yet "the fighting patterns of the Cheyennes are embellished with virtuosities that go beyond the needs of victory. Display in bravery tends to become an end in itself. Prestige drives override the more limited military requirements for the defeat of the enemy. The show-off tends to supersede the mere soldier. War has been transformed into a great game in which scoring against the enemy takes precedence over killing him"(Hoebel, 1960:70).

Scoring was accomplished by the "counting of coup," a tactic involving the touching of an enemy with one's hands or weapons without suffering direct physical reprisal in return. As a result, Cheyenne warriors attempted to steal horses out from under their riders, touch the thrusting arm of a jousting opponent, charge enemy groups individually, and accomplish other feats having limited logistical value but great social prestige potential.

In other areas of the world, such as the North American Northwest Coast and in the New Guinea highlands, it is likewise difficult to understand patterns of tribal warfare if they are not allowed that competitive or sport dimension. The similarities of team sports and certain types of warfare, specifically those that Wright (1942:56–61) classifies as social, suggest again that combative team sports can be treated as forms of social conflict.

If team sports are treated as conflict forms, then their function in a particular social setting can only be understood as one defines the broader realm of conflict behavior in the specific cultural system. The way that conflict is structured varies significantly from one cultural setting to another, and this can be demonstrated by an analysis of the way that different groups perceive the conflict component in particular athletic activities. As suggested in an earlier chapter, the Mississippi Choctaws, when compared to non-Choctaws, can be seen as conceptualizing sport competition in a uniquely Choctaw way.

If conflict is structured differently from one society to the next, it is reasonable to assume that it is structured toward the resolution of particular sociocultural needs or groups of needs. In other words, institutions and their related behaviors that persist within a specific cultural setting over a long period of time are assumed to be important to maintaining the total cultural system. In this case, it is assumed that conflict behavior among the Mississippi Choctaws, in particular that associated with sport activities, has a significant social function. The question to be raised at this point is one regarding the specific nature of that function.

At a theoretical level, it is generally agreed among anthropologists and sociologists that social conflict is not only ubiquitous in human society but also an essential ingredient in the social process. As Coser (1956:31) suggests, "Conflict as well as cooperation has social functions. Far from being necessarily dysfunctional, a certain degree of conflict is an essential element in group formation and the persistence of group life." The specific ways in which conflict functions to facilitate social process has been elaborated in several contexts, but the theory most appropriate to this discussion is that of social psychologist Muzafer Sherif, who has suggested that competition increases harmony and decreases hostilities *within* the competing groups. Specifically, "when groups in a state of conflict are brought into contact under conditions embodying superordinate goals, which are compelling but cannot be achieved by the efforts of one group alone, they will tend to cooperate toward the common goals" (1958:355).

This hypothesis has been tested in several situations, including a team sport context (McClendon and Eitzen, 1975). Competitive conflict breeds camaraderie and ultimately cooperation within competing factions as internal hostilities and frustrations are directed toward the opposition. This can mean, at broad social levels, the cementing of relationships between kin units in tribal society and between ethnic, racial, or political groups in the urban state.

The many forms of culturally structured conflict can thus be viewed as mechanisms for the ultimate generation of intragroup cooperation, the reinforcement of social cohesiveness, and the maintenance of group boundaries. Among the Mississippi Choctaws this process was manifested in the traditional, formal *toli* match which provided a competitive confrontation between the different Choctaw communities. As a result of competing together, members of the same community developed a greater sense of cooperation and harmony among themselves. At the same time, the increased camaraderie reinforced individual local group boundaries and underscored the closed nature of the typical Choctaw community.

At the same time, however, in those matches involving competition between Choctaws and non-Choctaw groups, such as the Creeks, communities would pool their talent and energies. In these contests it is to be assumed that, temporarily at least, community lines were overlooked and one's sense of Choctawness was reinforced as he cooperated with his distant kinsmen from other local groups in the intercultural competition.

One example of such an intertribal contest was reported by H. S. Halbert (in Cushman, 1899:131–35). According to this account, an incident occurred in Noxubee County, Mississippi, around 1790, involving a dispute between Choctaws and Creeks over the rights to a large beaver pond. After some discussion between leaders of both sides, it was decided that the matter would be settled by a ball game. The best players from each nation were selected, and on the scheduled day approximately 10,000 persons representing the two tribes were in attendance at the ball ground on the Noxubee River. After a four-hour contest, the Creeks were declared the winners, but the Choctaws were greatly humiliated and in retaliation attacked their opponents. "The contagion spread, and a general fight with sticks, knives, guns, tomahawks and bows and arrows began among the ball players. Then warriors from each tribe commenced joining in the fight until all were engaged in bloody strife" (Halbert, in Cushman, 1899:133). The fight continued through the night and into the next day, by which time over 500 warriors had been killed. The following day a council was held and peace was declared, the Choctaws eventually getting undisputed possession of the beaver pond. Such intertribal conflict was frequent in the historic Southeast and apparently served to reinforce intertribal ties and commitments as well as to maintain tribal boundaries.

While the classic stickball match was an eighteenth-century phenomenon, there is still a sense in which that harmony-generating and boundary-defining dimension of the team sport experience functions today in much the same way. Though the games themselves are different, intercommunity contests still breed attitudes of cooperation and camaraderie *within* individual communities as they compete with each other. On the other hand, certain sport activities affecting the whole group and involving representation from several Choctaw communities in a common cause tend to serve a function comparable to that of the intertribal *toli* match of centuries past. For example, the Choctaw Central High School football team is composed generally of players from most of the Choctaw communities, and in its competition with non-Choctaw teams from the surrounding east central Mississippi area it tends to adumbrate community lines and pull together many different interests within contemporary Choctaw society. In these cases, the ball-playing provides a point of reference and a means of individual identification with tribal-wide concerns and goals. Such activities often help to override older local group prejudices, to generate new cooperation in the pursuit of tribal interests, and to reinforce a sense of Choctawness.

While these two functions, maintaining the intra- and intercommunity social boundaries, appear on the surface to be contradictory, in reality they are in most cases compatible. Admittedly, in some situations, local community concerns preclude an individual's participation in a tribal-wide activity or program. For example, some Choctaw parents still resist the notion of their children interacting too freely with those from other communities, such as participating in interscholastic sports. Also, some attempt to avoid intercommunity events altogether (see p. 117). Still, Mississippi Choctaws appear to compartmentalize individual community and tribal-wide issues. Certain activities are defined emically as appropriate to intercommunity cooperation while others are deemed essentially intracommunal. For example, formal education is a common concern and a necessarily cooperative effort of all Choctaws. On the other hand, basic social interactions (e.g., marriage) and economically supportive relationships between kinsmen remain largely individual community matters. In this sense, it is thus possible to conceive of team sports as functioning to achieve intercommunity cooperation at both individual community and tribal-wide levels, simultaneously, though in most cases the former still takes priority over the latter if one is forced to choose.

In summation, the following observations regarding Mississippi Choctaw social organization and sport behavior are in order.

1. The team sport process is largely defined and restricted by kinship rules and regulations.

2. Being an athlete is an important source of prestige among the Choctaws.

3. Physically combative sports are most competitive and thus taken more seriously when one community is pitted against another, demonstrating very clearly the fundamental importance of the local group in Choctaw social life.

4. However, both inter- and intracommunity sporting events have important social conflict dimensions that ultimately function to define social boundaries.

In general, the seriousness with which the Mississippi Choctaws approach their play, specifically their team sport activities, is witnessed to by the integral way in which the events are woven into the very fabric of the social process. Recreation, seen from this perspective, is obviously a vital element in everyday Choctaw life because of what it says about relationships. The "oughtness" underlying the sport experience goes beyond the simple entertainment dimension and assumes "work-ethic" proportions; one has an *obligation* to play. Leisure can be no more serious than that.

Choctaw Sports and Political Organization

Political organization is viewed in this context as "an aspect of social organization" (Fried, 1967:20), and team sports are treated as effective mechanisms within the Mississippi Choctaw political process. It is suggested that the athlete model is an important source of political authority in this context, and that ball games serve as significant conflict-resolving devices both historically and within the contemporary Choctaw world.

HISTORY OF CHOCTAW POLITICAL ORGANIZATION

Among the Choctaws of the seventeenth and eighteenth centuries, when it appears that several different clans were represented within individual Choctaw communities, the basis of power and authority was the exogamous kin unit itself. The heads of the clans in each local group held the major offices and acted to mediate and adjudicate all intracommunal disputes. Usually, the prominent figure from among the group of clan leaders in each town served as the head chief (*tišomįko*). Also, within each local group there was an important war chief (*taškamįkoči*).

Although it may have been under a single administrative authority previously, in the latter stages of its traditional existence the Choctaw world was divided into three district units. The structure of district leadership in many ways was simply a more all-encompassing version of the local pattern. A council of chiefs and a head chief acted to coordinate activities between the several communities within each of the three units.

The following description from the eighteenth-century anonymous French memoir translated by Swanton (1981:54–55) assumes that the affairs of the Choctaw Nation were presided over by a single, supreme chief. However, the characterization can also be applied to the role of district chief. "This nation is governed by a head chief whose power is absolute only so far as he knows how to make use of his authority, but as disobedience is not punished among them, and they do not usually do what is requested of them, except when they want to, it may be said that it is an ill-disciplined government."

Whether or not it is fair to describe the Choctaw chiefdom as "ill-disciplined," it is safe to suggest that the political ties between the many towns were somewhat flexible. Certainly, intracommunal commitments superseded those linked to broader tribal identification.

While the local villages were largely egalitarian, in the sense that everyone had equal access to goods and services, Choctaw society was ranked. At the head of the system were the district, village, and war chiefs. Below them were the *hatak holitopa* or "beloved men." The next rank down included all the warriors (*taška*), and on the bottom rung were the *hatak himmita*, the youth or "those who have not struck blows or who have killed only a woman or a child" (Swanton, 1918:55). In general, "social rank and leadership positions were dependent upon proof of skill and daring in warfare" (John Peterson, personal communication, October 20, 1977).

With the removal of the 1830s, the existing Choctaw political system was virtually destroyed. While some prominent figures, like Greenwood LeFlore, were more influential than others, no formal ties were established between the different Choctaw communities until 1911 (Peterson, 1970:139). That year the New Choctaw Baptist Association was formed, and though it was primarily a religious institution it did serve to facilitate communication between the several local groups in east central Mississippi.

In 1935, the Choctaw Business Committee was formed under the Indian Reorganization Act of 1934. With the approval of the Indian Agency, the committee fulfilled, in limited fashion, the functions of a legislative body, "although in actuality it had little or nothing to govern" (Peterson, 1970:140). While few major decisions were made by the CBC, they did coordinate intercommunity activities and give Mississippi Choctaws some sense of tribal identification.

In 1944, the lands held in trust by the federal government for the Choctaw people were declared reservation area and the following year (1945) the constitution and by-laws of the Mississippi Band of Choctaw Indians were adopted. Since that time, the group has been governed by a sixteen-member tribal council composed of proportional representation from each of the seven localities. Tribal council elections are held every two years, all persons over twenty-one being eligible to vote. Until 1975, the council chose its own tribal chairman.

However, in that year, the constitution was amended and the Choctaw people elected directly their first tribal chief, to serve through 1978.

On October 11, 1977, the Fifth U.S. Circuit Court of Appeals, in overturning a U.S. District Court conviction, ruled that "Choctaw Indian lands in Mississippi are not legally 'Indian Country' subject to federal jurisdiction" (*Choctaw Community News*, November 4, 1977:7). The court reasoned that

> under terms of the 1830 Treaty of Dancing Rabbit Creek, the United States relinquished its claim to the Choctaw lands in Mississippi.
>
> Mississippi Choctaw lands were placed in federal trust in 1939, but . . . the move was a relief measure that helped the Indians in time of need, similar to that provided to disaster victims.
>
> Placing the land in trust, freed it from local, county and state taxes [but] "the specific provisions of the Treaty of Dancing Rabbit Creek with reference to the Mississippi Choctaws were not amended, modified or abrogated by the trust agreement or other federal aid" (*Choctaw Community News*, November 4, 1977:7).

The court claimed that its ruling that Choctaw lands are not Indian Country "in no way affects the legality of the aid being given the group" (*Choctaw Community News*, November 4, 1977:7). However, the decision had a significant impact on tribal affairs. On October 21, 1977, the department of law and order was closed, and the Native Mississippians were brought under the jurisdiction of the sheriff in their respective counties. While the Supreme Court review was pending, the Choctaw people were anxious about the future of their reservation status and the overall effect of the ruling on tribal life.

Fortunately, on June 23, 1978, the Supreme Court, in a unanimous decision, overruled the circuit court decision, contending that the Mississippi Band of Choctaw Indians was a "lawfully reorganized tribe duly formed under the Indian Reorganization Act of 1934" (*Choctaw Community News*, June 30, 1978:1). The high court further ruled that the Choctaw lands were legally "Indian Country" and by definition under federal law. "Indians charged with offenses on such lands are subject only to federal or tribal law and not to state jurisdiction" (ibid.).

SPORT AND POLITICAL LIFE

Because of insufficient ethnohistorical data it is difficult to ascertain the extent to which an individual's athletic prowess affected his credibility and authority within the Mississippi Choctaw community during the past few centuries. According to older informants, the chiefs themselves were generally too old to play stickball. However, since participation in warfare was a vital element underlying one's rise to political prominence in the traditional Choctaw world, it is reasonable to assume that the intercommunity stickball matches likewise provided a conflict setting within which one could achieve fame and popularity that spilled over into the political arena.

According to M'Kenney (1838:32), Pushmataha, the famous Choctaw warrior and leader, was an expert at stickball and spent many hours playing and perfecting his skill at the game. In one incident in the early 1800s, it is reported that he was involved in a ball game when the Creeks attacked, taking advantage of the adept field general's preoccupation with *toli* to initiate their offense. In a later episode (1823), Pushmataha was attending a council of chiefs and government personnel, and it was revealed that he had no horse. One of the agents offered to give him one with the understanding that he would not sell or exchange it for whiskey: "It was not long before he visited the Agency, on foot, and it was discovered that he had lost his horse in betting at ball-play. "But did you not promise Mr. Pitchlynn," said the agent, "that you would not sell his horse?" "I did so, in the presence of yourself and many others," replied the chief, "but I did not promise that I would not risk the horse on a game of ball" (M'Kenney, 1838:33).

The correlation between athletic ability and political success is obvious in the contemporary Mississippi Choctaw situation. Most of the community leaders generally have backgrounds as proven athletes. For example, of all the men on the Tribal Council in 1977, only one did not have a reputation as a ball-player. As one of the younger members of the Pearl River group put it: "A person who is a good athlete, especially in high school, has an advantage over other people. For example, he will be more likely to get a job for which he really isn't qualified, just because of the popularity he had built up as an athlete. People tend to listen to the athlete more than the nonathlete."

The Choctaws give varied reasons for the political advantages of athletic ability. Several have suggested to me that "people respect and listen more to a person who is actively involved in many areas of community life." Since the recreation/sport phenomenon is so thoroughly interwoven with the total fabric of Choctaw culture, it is only logical that a sportsman will be "actively involved in many areas of community life."

On the other hand, some suggest that team sport participation prepares one for the realities of political life. Albert Farve contends:

Being a good sport is related to political life because you have to act the same way in dealing with people. You have to know how to get along with people, to cooperate, and sport helps teach you how to do this.

Also, there is a spirit connected with sports that helps you learn how to try harder, to get ahead, to do your best. "There's always a way" is the kind of attitude I've always had.

People have a tendency to listen to people who have experiences in these areas.

"You've been there," they say.

You learn to compete, and you discover that in working with people, knowing how to compete with other groups and get things for your people is important. For example, where government programs or things like that are concerned, you need to know how to get the most for your tribe.

Certainly, local politicians recognize the importance of the athlete model among the Choctaws. For example, if they themselves are not playing on a softball team in the summer of an important election year, they will undoubtedly make conspicuous appearances at the ball games several times during the course of the season.

From another perspective, the team sport phenomenon can be seen as a setting within which customary political roles in Choctaw society can be acted out, reinforced, and perfected. Leadership styles characteristic of the contemporary Choctaw ball-playing environment, specifically, those of team captains and managers, are amazingly consistent with those of the traditional political process. In the past, political effectiveness among the Mississippian Muskogeans was determined by one's ability to persuade through rational discourse, even among the war chiefs. As one early account of Choctaw life suggests, "Their leader cannot pretend to *command* on an expedition; the most he can do is to endeavor to persuade, or at the extent, he can only pretend to a greater experience in order to enforce his counsel; should he pretend to order, desertion would at least be his punishment, if not death" (Romans, 1775:76).

The Choctaw manager or coach, especially one from a more conservative local group, though not threatened by possible execution, must be careful not to alienate his players by excessive displays of authority. The Choctaw people are still not responsive to direct command (see p. 90). I have on several occasions witnessed a softball or basketball mentor appear to lose his temper or forcefully assert himself in administering his responsibilities, but always he has been careful to couch the whole act in a humorous framework for fear of being taken too seriously.

White employees of the tribe or BIA have often mistaken this hesitancy to command as the inability or simply refusal to accept responsibility. As one former Choctaw Central High School coach once told me:

> I think the Choctaws are followers rather than leaders. Most of the Choctaw kids are followers. . . . I used to operate the recreation program and I would call a meeting of all the managers of the basketball teams to show up and organize a league. I would have two show up. But, I would have about forty teams. Only two managers would show up, and I would ask them, "Why don't you show up?"
> And they would say, "Well, you get it set up and we will play."
> So, rather than meet with the managers, I would get out and scout around and find out who the managers were, and once I found out . . . I found out what the name of the team was and then I drew the schedule. . . . Give them a schedule, and they would play.

Officials in the ball-playing process must also be careful lest they take their enforcement roles too seriously. The basketball referee who is overly conscientious or precise in his judgment and calls very quickly becomes an object of ridicule. Choctaw athletes rarely become unduly excited over official rulings, just or unjust, and likewise expect their referees and umpires to be lenient in the administration of game rules.

TEAM SPORTS AND CONFLICT RESOLUTION

Perhaps the most significant political function of Choctaw sport behavior, both past and present, is its role as a conflict-resolving device. Forms of social conflict not only serve to raise levels of harmony and cooperation among fellow combatants and define social boundaries (see pp. 127–30), but also can generate goodwill and anxiety-relieving distance between opponents and lower tension within competing groups. Sociologist Georg Simmel (1955:33–34) has argued very convincingly that such conflict functions positively in structuring social relations between as well as within societies.

From another perspective, many persons testify to the feeling of camaraderie that develops between two disputants in the wake of a "good fight." Further, it can be suggested that the postgame atmospheres of many classic stickball matches were characterized by positively toned intercommunal attitudes and exchanges, fostered initially by the competition itself. Historical descriptions of the game as it was played among the Choctaws often support such an assumption (e.g., Cushman, 1899:190).

Traditionally, formal stickball matches were often scheduled between two Choctaw communities explicitly for avoiding a threatened outbreak of a more violent and consequential conflict. This process parallels the situation Haas (1940:479) has described for the Creeks, among whom the "two-goal ball game" was used to work out and maintain intercommunity roles and status relationships.

The towns of the old Creek Confederacy were divided into two factions that Haas calls "semidivisions," but are generally known in the literature as Red (war) and White (peace) towns. The Creeks themselves referred to a village other than their own as simply "my friend," if it belonged to its semidivision, or "my enemy," if it were part of the other faction. Relationships between towns of the same classification were generally cordial, while interchanges between those of opposite affiliation were normally hostile. "A legitimate outlet for this feeling was provided by the ever popular two-goal game" (Haas, 1940:479).

The formal stickball match between Creek communities was arranged by elaborate contractual agreement with the implicit understanding that "if either town should defeat the other a given number of times, the losing town would be required to change over to the semidivision of the winning town" (Haas, 1940:481). In this way, intercommunal relations were effectively manipulated, and antagonistic tendencies and hostilities were replaced by cordiality.

While the process was not as clearly defined as among the Creeks, the stickball match was also utilized by the Choctaws as an important mechanism for monitoring, managing, and maintaining intratribal community relationships.

Certainly stickball was a reasonable alternative to war in the Choctaw world, despite the game's cuts, bumps, bruises, and occasional fatalities. War was severe, and even though some writers (e.g., Romans, 1775:72–73) and many members of today's Choctaw community suggest that the Native Mississippians were pacifists who fought only in defense of their homes and families, there is evidence to the contrary (Bossu, 1768:89–94). Many of the Choctaw battles were bloody, brutal affairs, and the chiefs who opted to use the stickball field as a stage on which to act out potentially explosive disagreements were acting in their respective communities' best interests.

Admittedly, the contest was not always an ameliorating event. Sometimes "a ball game was an occasion which allowed old feuds to come to the surface and . . . sometimes gave rise to [new] feuds"

(Swanton, 1931:141). Still, it appears very likely that, consistent with the contemporary emic view, stickball in Choctaw society during the early centuries of the historic period was seen by both spectators and participants alike as a logical and less disruptive alternative to war.

On the other hand, it has been suggested that in the past many stickball games were not intercommunal or conflict-resolving by design, but instead were structured with the deliberate intent of avoiding unnecessary violence between social units. Simpson Tubby (in Swanton, 1931:153) in his conversations with Swanton claimed that before the coming of the white man, the Choctaws played stickball only with "squads drawn from any source," what he called "the peace game." The description sounds very much like that which Fox (1961:10) provides for the competitive games of the traditional Cochiti Pueblo peoples in the American Southwest: "The old competitive games of the Pueblo . . . were never played between any two formal groups. For races and shinny games the categories of "married" versus "unmarried" were employed, or teams were picked from the young men on a count-out method. There was never a competitive alignment in terms of the existing social groupings, and teams were not permanent affairs."

Also, Haas (1940:479) claims that the Creeks made a very clear distinction between the formal match, that played between two communities, and the practice stickball game of opposing intracommunal factions. "For example, men of the White clan moiety might oppose men of the Foreign Speech clan moiety" (Haas, 1940:479n.).

If such "peace games" were the rule in prehistoric Choctaw society, they were no longer the norm when the first outsiders described the game in the eighteenth century, nor are they recounted by older members of the contemporary community. The conflict-resolving, intercommunity stickball contest is the one most frequently related in ethnohistorical accounts and local folklore.

Certainly the traditional stickball conflict functioned to improve relationships and lessen potential conflict levels *within,* if not *between,* communities by promoting integration and solidarity among local group memberships (see p. 129). This process in many ways parallels that of intertribal warfare among the Mundurucú in the Amazon region of South America.

Anthropologist Robert Murphy (1957:1018), utilizing Simmel's (1955:33–34) model of social conflict in which the phenomenon is treated as having the positive consequence of promoting group cohesions and defining boundaries, has analyzed Mundurucú patterns of war. These violent, often bloody encounters had religious and sportive as well as important economic and social prestige aspects.

According to Murphy (1957:1029–30), the Amazonian tribe had "patrilineal clans" but a matrilocal residence pattern. Male solidarity was fundamental to the working of the political system because the authority of the central chief depended on his ability to enlist the support of members of other patrilineages as well as his own. Obviously, the matrilocal definition of village boundaries in some ways militated against the continuity of the chief's administrative effectiveness, giving Mundurucú leadership "a potentially centrifugal nature."

In such a system, warfare functioned to buttress the strength of the chief's position because of his role as war leader. It also gave otherwise fragmented male descent groups an occasion for collective activity, and served in addition as a means of releasing the intratribal tensions and hostilities that had to be "rigorously suppressed" in such a society if the fabric of the kinship structure were to be maintained.

Murphy (1957:1034) concludes with the suggestion that

> . . . matrilocal societies must repress the open expression of intrasocietal conflict and that this repressed hostility, variable in intensity, will be released through acceptable and nondisruptive means within the society, or through warfare, or through both. But warfare . . . is an especially effective means of promoting social cohesion in that it provides an occasion upon which the members of the society unite and submerge their factional differences in the vigorous pursuit of a common purpose.

Traditional Choctaw society was also characterized by a matrilocal residence pattern, but unlike the Mundurucú, the Muskogean group had a system of matrilineal rather than patrilineal clans. Still, there is a sense in which persistent potential conflict existed between clan and resident allegiance within the early local groups of the Native Mississippians that threatened the authority of community leadership. The classic stickball match was simply one way in which community interests may have been placed above those of clan affiliation.

Modern team sports among the Mississippi Choctaws, like their racket-game forerunner, serve similar functions in conflict resolution, although events are not deliberately scheduled with such a goal in mind. Even though the Choctaws often argue that traditional stickball games were qualitatively different from the sporting events of today, they use similar conflict language in discussing Western athletic activities and behave in ways consistent with the older phenomenon, especially in intercommunal confrontations.

Certainly, many areas of potential conflict affect intercommunal relationships among the Mississippi Choctaws, although most are different from those of previous centuries. Problems of recognition, representation, and differential resource allocation are just a few of the possible provocations of discord between local groups.

How, then, do sporting events among today's Choctaws affect the resolution and avoidance of more violent forms of conflict? In the first place, the Mississippi Choctaws find recreation league events tremendously entertaining, in spite of their seriousness. This in itself tends to lower the frequency of disruptive discord in other areas of social interaction. Also, the opportunities provided by athletic activities, at both high school and recreation league levels, for members of the tribe to get together help to lower tensions in some instances, the competitive focus of the contests themselves notwithstanding. Ball-game participation can likewise "allow for the acting out of aggressive and competitive tendencies" that might otherwise be expressed in other less acceptable forms of behavior, a function Fox (1961:15) credited to Cochiti Pueblo baseball.

Reflecting the conflict-resolving potential of team sport participation, the high school athletes, both male and female, at Choctaw Central have been found to manifest fewer negative attitudes than do their nonathletic counterparts. In the spring of 1974, I administered the General MAACL (Multiple Affect Adjective Check List) to large samples of students at Choctaw Central, Philadelphia, Riverdale (Murfreesboro, Tennessee), and Zuni (New Mexico) high schools. The results suggested that levels of anxiety, hostility, and depression were all significantly lower among the students who could be classed as "athletes"—those participating in any formal sport activity at the high school—than among those who could not (see Table 14). Differences in the scores of athletes and nonathletes were more pronounced than those of any other intragroup comparisons (sex, ethnic group, age), and more significant in the Choctaw case than in all the non-Choctaw situations. These results suggest that there is something about the athlete role in Choctaw society that breeds healthy interpersonal attitudes and in turn militates against a predisposition to violence.

Some psychologists might question my interpretation of the MAACL results. Certainly I am aware of the fact that those who emulate the athletic ideal might tend to be more reserved about admitting and expressing basic feelings, and that this might have an effect on the

Table 14. Multiple Affect Adjective Check List (MAACL): Scores of Athletes Compared to Those of Nonathletes among Choctaw and Non-Choctaw High School Students, 1974[a]

Choctaw Central High School Students

	Anxiety	Depression	Hostility
Athletes (n = 21)	7.38	13.33	7.28
Nonathletes (n = 48)	8.12	16.60	8.96

Non-Choctaw High School Students

Athletes			
Philadelphia (n = 27)	7.33	13.48	9.85
Riverdale (n = 16)	7.15	11.92	7.00
Zuni (n = 16)	5.56	10.63	7.50
Total (n = 59)	6.44	11.68	8.44
Nonathletes			
Philadelphia (n = 82)	7.96	14.94	10.39
Riverdale (n = 123)	5.86	10.64	7.88
Zuni (n = 34)	7.59	16.06	9.56
Total (n = 239)	6.83	12.89	8.98

Percentage Differences of Athlete and Nonathlete MAACL Scores:

	%	%	%
Choctaw athletes lower than nonathletes by:	9.2	19.7	18.8
Non-Choctaw athletes lower than nonathletes by:	5.8	9.4	6.1

[a]The higher the score, the greater the measured level of anxiety, depression, or hostility.

outcome of a test like the MAACL. However, the range of adjectives employed in that particular schedule include many that are consistent with the masculine dimensions of the athlete image (e.g., agressive, mean, angry). Also, since both males and females are included in the "athlete" samples from the several high schools, and the differences between the athletic and nonathletic student responses are so pronounced, I feel that the effect of any such hesitancy, if it does exist, is not significant. At the same time, I would admit that there may be a better explanation for the different anxiety, hostility, and depression scores of the two groups, but certainly the status of the athletic model must be viewed as an important factor.

If one assumes that personality traits are primarily products of social interaction, and concomitantly, personal attitudes are the result of interpersonal contacts, then positive feelings are stimulated by positive reinforcement from other members of one's group. Also, in most social settings there are valued statuses, and those who occupy them are in turn recipients of consistently supportive reinforcement. This manifests itself through the attitudes of the status occupant. So, in systems that assign a high priority to athletic ability, it is reasonable to assume that athletes will be revered and at the same time tend to have and express more positive feelings about themselves and their lives than would someone of less-valued status in the same general social environment. In the Choctaw high school situation, then, this would mean that athletes would be *expected* to score lower than nonathletes in categories reflecting negative personal attitudes.

While the ball games in today's Choctaw world serve to release frustration and channel aggressive hostility, it must be admitted that, like their stickball forerunner, they also often generate conflict that ultimately spills over into extrarecreational areas. The seriousness of these activities often leads to disputes, accusations of witchcraft, and outright violence. Still, it is safe to conclude that these events are exceptions to the rule and do not deny the conflict-resolving function of modern intercommunal sport activities among the Mississippi Choctaws.

Some of the Choctaw tribal leaders take this idea even further and claim that the full-scheduled recreation program is a major deterrent to crime in the area. According to Doyle Tubby, tribal law-enforcement planner, the crime rate on the reservation is one of the lowest in the nation; "this is a very safe place to be." From 1972 through the middle of 1977, only three major crimes were reported, and these were murders. Most offenses are minor and predominantly liquor-related. Tubby notes that the average offender tends to be male, in his thirties, a nonparticipant in community affairs, consistently unemployed, and of limited social status. It is significant that most of the lawbreakers do not play on any of the high school or recreation department ball teams.

With this in mind, a tribal planning committee recommended in 1971 that additional monies be spent to expand and improve recreational facilities on the reservation as a means of dealing with the problem of alcoholism (Mississippi Band of Choctaw Indians, 1971). It was assumed that one who played ball would have less need and time for drinking.

A.S. Spaulding, often called "the father of professional baseball," once planned and developed a small community called Faywood Springs, near Silver City, New Mexico. He included many ball fields but made no arrangements for any type of law enforcement. Spaulding claimed that the town that played enough baseball would have no crime and thus no need for policemen. While Faywood Springs was a short-lived experiment, the Mississippi Choctaws, with their high rate of sport participation and low crime rate, give some credibility to Spaulding's notion.

Play is a serious element in the Mississippi Choctaw political world. Indeed, the sport model has become an important means of structuring authority roles and managing conflict relationships, both between and within the seven local groups under tribal jurisdiction. Nothing could be more vital.

CHAPTER 6

Sport, Myth, and Ritual in Choctaw Society

The seriousness with which Choctaws take some of their leisure activities is manifested in the way that their recreational pursuits are couched in the broader world of myth and ritual. Their team sport behavior provides a fruitful perspective on this aspect of Choctaw life, both within and beyond the athletic arena.

Traditionally, Choctaw ritual life revolved around a concept of a supreme deity who was treated as identical to the sun in some situations, but only associated with it in others, a pattern typical of many southeastern tribes (Hudson, 1976:126). Symbolically, the sun was represented on earth by fire. The supreme being's existence did not preclude that of the many other lesser spirit figures and required no form of propitiation or worship.

One of the most persistent roles in Choctaw mythology is that of the *bohpoli*, or "little person." Halbert (1895:157) described the dwarf-like figure as he was perceived by the nineteenth-century Choctaws:

> The Choctaws in Mississippi say that there is a little man, about two feet high, that dwells in the thick woods and is solitary in his habits. This little sprite or hobgoblin is called by the Choctaws *Bohpoli*, or *Kowi anukasha*, both names being used indifferently or synonymously. . . . *Bohpoli* is represented as being somewhat sportive and mischievious but not malicious in nature. The Choctaws say that he often playfully throws sticks and stones at people. Every mysterious noise heard in the woods, whether by day or night, they ascribe to *Bohpoli*. He takes special pleasure, they say, in striking the pine trees. . . . *Bohpoli* . . . is never seen by the common Choctaws. The Choctaw prophets and doctors, however, claim the power of seeing him and of holding communication with him. The Indian doctors say that *Bohpoli* assists them in the manufacture of their medicines. Most Choctaws say or think that there is but one *Bohpoli*. In the opinion of others there may be more than one.

Among the Choctaws of centuries past there were many types of ritual specialists, but the most prominent were the doctors (*alikči*), prophets (*hopaii*), and rainmakers (*hatak umba ikbi*).

The *alikči*, sometimes referred to as the "physic doctors," dealt

145

with disease and prescribed natural cures: herbs, roots, sucking, sweating. Cushman (1899:199–200) has provided a colorful description of the nineteenth-century Choctaw doctor and the art of "dry-cupping":

> . . . sucking that part of the body of which the patient complained, or where, in his own judgement, the disease was located, making a gutteral noise during the operation that reminded one of a dog worrying an opossum; at different intervals raising his head a few inches and pretending to deposit into his hands, alternatively in the one and the other, an invisible something which he had drawn from his patient, by a magic power known alone to himself.
>
> After sucking a sufficient length of time to fill both hands, judging from the frequent deposits therein made, with great apparent dignity and solemn gravity, this worthy son of Esculapius arose and stepping to the nearest tree, post, or fence, wiped the secret contents of his apparently full hands thereon, then with an air of marked importance walked away to the enjoyments of his own reflections, while the sufferer, in real or fancied relief, acknowledged the efficacy of the physician's healing powers by ceasing to complain, turned over and sought forgetfulness in sleep.

Another type of Choctaw ritualist, the prophet, appealed even more directly to the occult in order to divine, cast spells, and impart supernatural power to his clients.

The Choctaws also believed in the existence of witches (*hatak holhkonna*), sorcerers or wizards who lived in their midst and cast spells on unsuspecting victims or exercised their magic to counteract that of other witches. Though many Choctaws often sought the aid of *hatak holhkonna*, theirs was seen as an evil practice, and those suspected of witchcraft were often put to death.

Myth and Ritual among Contemporary Choctaws

For the most part, traditional cosmologies and origin myths have been forgotten by the Mississippi Choctaws. Metaphysical questions are generally addressed in theological terms. Catholic and Protestant missionaries have been active among the Native American group in the state since the 1870s, and today most Choctaws claim to belong to one of several churches represented in the area: Baptist, Methodist, Church of God, and Mennonites, as well as Roman Catholic.

Nevertheless, certain aspects of the traditional belief system have persisted. For example, the *bohpoli* concept is very much alive and basic to explanation, especially in those unknown or mysterious areas of Choctaw experience. The small, human-like figure is now generally viewed as living in groups, but still stays in the deep woods, performs superhuman feats, throws large rocks against trees, and intervenes in human affairs predominantly through his influence over the Choctaw doctors or medicine men.

One young women who had previously aspired to be a doctor described her experience with the little people to me in the summer of 1977:

> When I was a little girl, I thought I wanted to be a doctor. . . . I couldn't sleep at night. Choctaw doctors don't sleep, you know. I used to get out of my bed and go for a walk in the woods. I used to go far into the woods, but I wasn't afraid.
>
> One night I meet with these green dwarfs. They were short [about three feet tall] and like adults. I played with them. They were really eager to show me their medicine and to play with rocks. They wanted to show me how to use the rocks. . . . You could throw them anywhere, any direction, and hurt somebody if you wanted to. I really didn't want to hurt anybody.
>
> I used to meet them regular. There were four of them. They were all men and had names, but that's my secret. I can't tell anyone their names. They tried to teach me to catch snakes, but I could never do that. They used to yell at each other. . . .
>
> They dressed like normal dwarfs, a nice green outfit; you know that kind of material. A hat [felt]. They played like kids, even though they were adults.
>
> They used to come and meet me, but they wouldn't take me where they lived unless I was willing to become a real doctor. If you become a doctor you can own them; that's what they told me. . . .
>
> I didn't understand them at first. I don't know what language they spoke; it was just a jabber, but finally I began to understand it. If I had stuck with it, I would be able to speak their language. Choctaw doctors speak their language.
>
> They also taught me the weeds. They could talk to the plants and make them stand up and grow and blossom out real pretty. . . .
>
> They wanted to put me through a lot of tests. One was a test to see if I could find my way out of a forest where I had never been. They would just take me there and leave me, and I would have to find my way back. Another test was where I would meet different and strange animals; animals that I had never seen before. They also told me to go to the graveyard and talk to dead people. . . .
>
> I can still contact them if I want to. I go back to the old place and wait five or ten minutes. They come back.

The *bohpoli* are often used to explain otherwise unexplainable events. The following story and interpretation, related to me by a Choctaw male of college age, is typical:

> Once when we were kids, we were running through the woods behind our house. There was a bunch of us. My sister was behind

us and kept getting farther behind, and then all of a sudden we heard her cry out. We thought she had just fallen down or something, and we went back to where she was and she had been hit on the forehead with a big rock. It couldn't have been any of us; we were running way ahead of her. . . . It had to be them [the *bohpoli*]. They throw rocks like that, you know. A big lump came on her head. . . .

My mother had told us about them. They lived in the rocks out behind the house, in the woods. We never saw them, but we could hear them out there playing a lot.

Although most Choctaws contend that only the medicine man or doctor sees and really knows about the *bohpoli*, many laymen have stories about their own encounters with the little people. In the following account, the dwarfs are seen as having female counterparts, the ability to move through solid objects, and superior strength.

One time when we lived over there in the log cabin, my mother told me that the cabin was built on a trail that belonged to the little men. She said one day their dog was out a little ways from the house and started barking. When she went out there, she saw two of the little people, a man and a woman. The woman was really pretty: blond hair, bright red lips, round cheeks. They were just standing there, probably wanting to walk down the trail. . . .

She [the mother] says that even though the cabin was built across the trail, they [the *bohpoli*] still used it anyhow. They just walked through the walls like they weren't there. . . .

One day this man . . . started bragging that the next time those little men came around he was going to beat them up. So, the next time he saw one he went up to him and started wrestling him. That little man beat the crap out of him. He could really wrestle.
. . . They're strong!

The ritual personnel in the contemporary Mississippi Choctaw world parallel those of tradition, but there is much disagreement among the Choctaws as to their perception and classification of these roles. Most of those who talked to me about this aspect of cultural reality recognized two distinct types of ritual specialist, the Choctaw doctor or medicine man (*alikči*) and the witch doctor (*hatak holhkonna* or *hopa alikči*—"One who hides behind the owl). The first has inherited a "god-given" talent and generally works to heal, divine, or otherwise improve the lot of his patients. The witch, on the other hand, exploits, debilitates, and destroys his subjects; often, but not always, on behalf of a client. One is good; the other bad.

In some instances, Choctaws have told me that the medicine man and the witch doctor are the same. The two roles, for these individuals, are both *alikči*. Either type of practitioner can be good or bad, depending on whether or not he uses magic, medicine, or both, and to what extent. The medicine man is the *alikči* as healer; the witch doctor is the *alikči* as sorcerer.

In additon, some of the older members of the Native Mississippian community make a distinction between the medicine man and herb doctor. Both are referred to as *alikči*, but one uses more plants and herbs to effect his cures, while the other relies more heavily on sucking techniques. Also, there is a sense in which the medicine man is viewed as having more supernatural power at his disposal.

In this particular analysis, I am using the more specialized classification system for describing Choctaw ritual personnel. In the first place, the notion that there are several distinct categories of specialists is more consistent with tradition than the tendency to lump all into a single role. Second, the more precise terminology makes it easier to describe the ritual dimensions of sport and recreation phenomena among the Mississippi Choctaws.

Every Choctaw community has one or more doctors. Both men and women can be doctors, but most are males. The position of witch is also open to either sex, but Choctaws who make a clear distinction between this role and that of doctor will rarely hazard a guess as to how many doctors and how many witches there are in any particular Choctaw community.

The normal procedure is for someone who has a condition that cannot be readily diagnosed and cured by physicians at the Public Health Service Hospital in Pearl River to visit the family's Choctaw doctor. At that point, the most common practice is for the *alikči* to divine the nature of the condition, locate its focal point on the patient's body, scratch a small X on the skin with a sharp piece of broken glass, and then employ the "horn." This technique involves placing the large end of a specially prepared cow horn over the broken skin and sucking through a hole cut at the opposite end of the device. Once a sufficient vacuum has been created, the small hole is filled with cloth or paper, and the horn is held in place for fifteen or twenty minutes. Then it is removed, and its contents, a sizeable lump of coagulated blood, analyzed. Depending on the situation, this process works either as a cure in itself or as an instrument of further divination. In the latter instance, the *alikči* will make suggestions as to the nature of the condition (e.g., the patient is the subject of a witch's spell) and recommend additional remedy. This is essentially the same process witnessed by the anonymous Jesuit priest in the early 1700s (Swanton, 1918:62).

The reputation of particular Choctaw doctors is related to the power and range of skills they are reported to have. This also determines the amount of money they can charge for their services. Some medicine men are noted for their ability to cure diseases that the PHS physicians can only treat. For example, one such specialist reportedly healed several diabetics during his career, and his fees were legitimately higher. Also, some doctors claim they can bring people back to life. One of the more famous of recent Choctaw medicine men once offered to revive a man who had expired from self-poisoning, but refused to do so when the family of the deceased could not raise the necessary fifty-dollar fee. In other cases, Choctaw doctors have suggested that if they had been called in time they could have brought the recently dead back to life, especially in situations where death had been diagnosed as the result of witchcraft. Still, I have had no one relate an incident to me in which he or she actually saw a dead person revived by an *alikči*.

One does not become a Choctaw doctor simply because he aspires to the profession. It must happen to him. In the words of one member of the Pearl River community:

> They say you have to have a sign. It can be a snake, an owl, maybe the little men. Something that pulls you away. . . .
> They say that you can tell when a kid's little if he's going to be a medicine man. He usually likes to go into the woods by himself and stay for a long time. He might go out at night a lot. Sometimes he will walk in his sleep and go out into the woods. That's where it happens. He can go and be gone for a long time, but come back. If he wakes up when he's out there, he can't find his way back. Also, he'll get sick if he wakes up.
> Everybody thought————was going to be a medicine man. He used to go into the woods a lot and started to walk in his sleep at night. His folks would see him walk out of the house at night and they would follow him down to the pond and bring him back. But one night, they let him go, or didn't know he'd gone. He got about a mile from home and woke up. He finally got home, but they knew he wasn't going to be a medicine man. . . . He got real sick, too.

Apparently, it is during these sleepwalking episodes that one encounters the *bohpoli,* who in turn introduce him to the occult arts and direct his professional training.

Despite their prestige in the community and their collection of fees, Choctaw doctors generally suggest by their appearance that they are abnormally impoverished. Consistent with Victor Turner's (1974:265–66) model of "liminal poverty," the *alikči* reinforces his status by rejecting basic material values.

You can usually tell if somebody's a medicine man.

They just look a certain way. . . . They dress poorly, really bad. My mother's grandfather was that way. He was shabby all the time. He used to eat junk, too. He used to carry the stuff he picked up to eat in a brown burlap bag he carried around. He came to the house once with that bag, with stuff that he had picked up in garbage cans; some of those onions with plants growing out of them. He had these three rats he had killed, too. He wanted my mother to cook them for him. She threw them out.

While Choctaw doctors are generally viewed as valuable members of the community, they are often accused of misusing their powers. Medicine men reportedly have the ability to render a person sexually irresistible or, conversely, administer aphrodisiacs to unsuspecting women. While this is seen as legitimate when done for a patient, it is unethical when the doctor uses the power for his own gratification, and stories are often told of medicine men who put women to sleep and then take advantage of them sexually. In one case, an *alikči* was treating a couple in their home, and on repeated occasions would put them both to sleep and molest the woman before they awoke. The husband was beginning to suspect something and soon went to another doctor who was able to divine the real nature of the repeated house calls. The next time the philandering physician made his rounds, the offended husband was ready. On this occasion he only pretended to fall asleep. And as the culprit lowered his trousers and prepared to mount the unsuspecting wife, the now wiser patient grabbed a specially prepared pan of scalding water and dashed it against the exposed groin and sexual expectations of the unprofessional medicine man.

The herb doctor is less colorful and not as esoteric as the medicine man in his practice. He prescribes and administers a variety of concoctions designed to treat basic maladies from the common cold to backache. Items like rabbit tobacco, snakeroot, wild cherry, and goldenrod are just some of the botanical materials felt to possess significant medicinal powers. One of the most common potions is the "black root." Jim Gardner says:

A lot of doctors tell you to drink black root. They find them in the woods, in a special place, a special kind of soil, and they boil it. You take about half a cup like you take pills. You use it like castor oil, to clean your stomach. It makes you feel good. You take it for headaches, backaches, sore joints. . . .

You have to mix it with another weed to make you vomit. If you do that it makes you come out of both ends.

During the early years of their work among the Choctaw people, Public Health Service personnel made many attempts to discredit native doctors and dissuade patients from employing them. The PHS argued that there was a danger in relying too heavily on traditional medical techniques, especially when serious illness was involved, and they encouraged the state legislature to prohibit its practice. While no legal ban ever evolved, the PHS did manage to create anxiety and an unfair dichotimization between modern and traditional medicine in the community mind. As a result, Choctaw doctors and their patients simply became more secretive about their activities.

More recently, the Public Health Service has ceased debunking Choctaw medicine. In many ways, its personnel have become more humanistic and sophisticated, appreciating the effectiveness of traditional cures and in some cases recommending that patients see a native curer. Also, many PHS employees are either Choctaw or of other Native American heritage and themselves often use the professional services of the local practitioners. Then there are those members of the community who still refuse to visit a modern physician or hospital under any conditions and continue to rely on the traditional therapist for all their medical needs.

The witch (*hatak holhkonna*), though not as visible as the Choctaw doctor, is still a prominent figure in community life. His actions serve to explain unusual acts or events, and his services are available to one wishing to right a wrong or correct an imbalance in his social world.

Because of the stigma attached to the witch's role, few persons openly admit that they themselves belong to the mysterious order, and seldom will one Choctaw accuse another. However, they will tell you that each community has one or more witches, and often they will name names and relate stories of their feats. There is always the fear, however, that the accused witch will know that he or she is being talked about and will put a spell on the one telling the story or making the accusation. For this reason, it is safer to talk about witches who are now dead.

Among their many powers, the witches supposedly have the ability to fly. Some Choctaws say that you can see them in the evening, especially during July and August, as they soar through the air with a blue glow around them. They also claim that you can see them come crawling out of the woods shortly after they flash across the sky. Jim Gardner contends:

> Around dusk you can see them. They go through the air like a star or a Roman candle. I've seen it.
> One time I asked my grandfather, "What's that?"
> "It's a witch doctor."
> "There's a man flying around? A man can fly?"

"Yes, a witch man can fly. He fixes up himself and flies, and the blood drips off and sparkles [with a whirring sound].

According to other informants, the witch doctor goes into the woods and removes his visceral organs by literally cutting his stomach open before he flies. Some report having seen a witch return from his flight and reinsert his "insides." One Choctaw friend of mine once told me about his great-grandfather, who was reputed to be a witch: "He used to go into the woods, way in the woods where nobody could see him, and cut open his stomach and take his insides out and stuff them in a can and hide that can where nobody could find it. Then he'd fly. One time he came back, and somebody had found it [the can] and poked holes all in it. . . . He died right after that."

It is also thought that witch doctors can put many different spells on people, effecting almost any evil imaginable. A variety of pathological conditions can be perpetrated, love relations torn asunder, marriages broken apart, automobile accidents staged, outcomes of otherwise chance events predetermined, psychological disorders instilled, and persons killed by a wide assortment of methods. If anything of an unusual nature occurs it is because someone has put a spell on the victimized party. The following is a typical incident:

> Once I was walking up to my house and I fell down and couldn't walk. My mother took me to the hospital, and the doctor there told me that I had a sprained ankle. He treated it, but for a month I couldn't walk on it, and it hurt. Finally, I went to the Indian doctor; my mother took me. He looked at it and he told me, "You hurt your ankle when you were walking up to your house last month and fell down."
>
> He knew, even though he hadn't seen it happen. He also told me it was not an accident. Another doctor [witch] had done it to me. Some girl was jealous of me because the boy she liked had a crush on me, so she had him do it to me.
>
> He [the doctor] boiled some roots and put it on my ankle, and it was better in three days. In four days I was walking again.
>
> He asked me if I wanted to so something to that girl, but I told him "no."

Another power presumed to be unique to the Choctaw witch doctor is the ability to assume the forms of different animals, specifically, the owl, rabbit, whippoorwill, and white dog. Any time one sees one of these ominous creatures in his yard, he is suspicious that he is being threatened by supernatural forces. However, if the suspicious victim attempts to harm or kill one of these witches in disguise, it is very unlikely he will succeed. Guns jam, thrown rocks go awry, and fired bullets ricochet off target. Occasionally, though, an attack on a witch is successful.

> Once we lived in the old log cabin . . . we lived across the road from the old———woman who was a witch.
> My father said every night when they'd be sitting on the porch, this rabbit would come across the road and sit on the other side of the ditch and just laugh, like an old woman.
> Finally, my dad got tired of this, so one night he got his shotgun and sat on the porch and waited. This time when the rabbit came and started laughing he took the gun and shot at it, but he missed. The rabbit just turned around and ran off. . . .
> He told me this, and I've heard other people say this too, that if you don't aim right at a witch, just to the side of them or something, you can hurt them. . . .
> So, the next time he shot at the rabbit he aimed just to the side of its head. It hit the rabbit this time, but didn't kill it. It just ran across the road and disappeared.
> About one week later the old woman died.

According to Choctaw amateur philosophers, the source of both the witch's and the doctor's power is supernatural. Most put it into a theological context: "They go into the woods, pray to God, and ask for power." No one seems to know to what Choctaw ritualists appealed in the pre-Christian era, although ethnohistory suggests that the sun was the effective force underlying their cures and magic. One woman told me once that although she thought that Choctaw religious personnel all "prayed to God," she saw a definite conflict. "In the Bible, it says that you should love your neighbor. Witch doctors try to hurt people, and that's not loving your neighbor, so it's not the same thing."

The ability to interweave traditional ritual roles with those of modern Christianity, though seldom explicitly verbalized, is witnessed to in the local folk belief that even clergymen can be witches. For example, one native preacher of a Protestant church in one of the Choctaw communities has a reputation as a sorcerer. Several persons have told me of his talent, one claiming to have seen him gliding along in a seated position, suspended only two feet above the pavement as though he were in an invisible automobile. At the same time, however, they say they see no conflict of interest between his role as witch doctor and his position as minister.

A symbol basic to the witch doctor's power is blood. The witch sucks blood from his neighbors, especially healthy babies, and drips blood as he flies through the sky. When one decides to become a sorcerer, he must begin by working on and exploiting members of his own immediate family. He will even put a curse on his wife and children or extract their blood. Choctaws claim that this type of behavior is the ultimate expression of greed and selfishness and the basis of community disdain for witch doctors.

After they have developed and demonstrated their ability within the kin circle, witches move out into the local group and the broader tribal context and accumulate increasing power through continued success. Throughout the process they are very careful not to let others know that they have become sorcerers. To broadcast the fact is not only to risk community reprisal and ostracism but also to invite attacks from more experienced practitioners threatened by new competition.

On the other hand, much of the witch doctors' power depends upon their reputation. Often they brag about their exploits and take the responsibility for unexplained events. Despite the need to remain incognito, the size of their clientele depends on their visibility. The paradox of a witch's need for both popularity and anonymity is manifested in the claim made by many Choctaws that on the one hand they do not know who the witch or witches are in their particular communities, but on the other, they know where to go to get one if they need the type of assistance a sorcerer has to offer.

Despite the changes occurring in the religious/ritual life of Choctaws, resulting primarily from the impact on Western technology and its associated ideology, certain patterns of traditional Choctaw thought and behavior persist. The change that has taken place in the belief system can be correlated with the continual shrinking of the unknown areas of experience in the Native Mississippian's world. As one reflective Choctaw suggests: "Many things used to go on in those woods over there, but now all the highways and buildings have come along and changed that." In other words, the area of the dark or spiritually distant, as represented by the heavy undergrowth of the unpenetrable forest, is shrinking, and along with it the awe-inspiring bewilderment. The mysterious no longer has a place; at best its space is limited.

Sport and Ritual in Choctaw Society

Team sport behavior is constrained and in some ways defined by the realities of Choctaw ritual life. Ball game outcomes are often explained by witchcraft. Both Choctaw and black witches in east central Mississippi offer to throw ball games for a price. Players appeal to medicine men for special treatments to improve playing skills and visit these same doctors to be treated for ailments contracted in the sport context.

Traditionally, the role of the various ritual specialists among the Choctaws was explicitly defined within the setting of the formal stickball match (see pp. 35–36). Choctaw doctors prepared the players on their community teams by giving them special medicine to make them stronger, swifter, and more skillful with the stick. The *alikči* could, in addition, treat the ball to make it *isht albi* ("ball witch") so that the players on the other team could not throw it against the post. It would veer to one side or the other of the pole, but never touch it for a score under such a spell. Before the game began the players would lay their rackets on the ground, and the *alikči* would "put 'good medicine' on the rackets of his team of players" and watch "for a chance to put 'bad medicine' on the rackets of the opponents" (Densmore, 1943:128).

According to Densmore's (1943:128) informants, every team had a contingent of five or six medicine men that "had two or three whistles, a drum, and a wand with some small object at the tip," in one case, something that looked like a redbird. They made their presence obvious throughout the ball game and the festivities preceding it, blowing their whistles and beating their drums. By her description, however, it is obvious that Densmore's (1943:128) "medicine men" actually covers several categories of specialists, including the witches or sorcerers.

Witch doctors were accepted at ball games though nowhere else "because there they had to fight other wizards" (Swanton, 1931:240). They put spells on members of the opposing teams and devised other techniques for the magical manipulation of eventual contest outcomes. The stickball match was a safe context within which to allow explicit witchcraft performances. As Jim Gardner notes, "The witch would try to hurt people on the other team so they couldn't play. Each team had a witch, and if one witch did something to the other team, the other witch would know it and hurt somebody on the other team."

In this sense, the competing witches acted as controls on each other in limiting the extremes of their destructive behavior.

Rainmakers and other ceremonial practitioners likewise were involved in the application of their professional specializations in the attempt to "cause" a victory for the stickball team representing their local group. During the *toli* match itself the ritual personnel were as active as the players. The witch doctors were particularly conspicuous. Walking up and down the field, gesticulating violently, and acting out the symbolic dimensions of the event, they pitted their power against that of their professional adversaries from the competing village.

The formal competion among traditional Choctaws amounted in many ways to a contest between the ritualists of the two communities involved. This is similar to what anthropologist Raymond Fogelson (personal communication, April 6, 1977) has suggested relative to Cherokee stickball matches. In the formal Choctaw match, the community that won was seen as the group having the greatest amount of power on that particular occasion. If nothing else, the extent to which ceremonial manipulations were a part of the game suggested the degree of community involvement and level of seriousness characteristic of sporting events in early Choctaw history.

While many Mississippi Choctaws argue that medicine and witchcraft do not play as vital a role in the contemporary sport and recreation setting as they did in previous years, they admit that there is an important ritual dimension to today's ball games. While this phenomenon is not unique to the Choctaws, it does offer a rare opportunity to analyze the continuity of ritual meaning within the total context of sport change (see Scotch, 1961).

Choctaw athletic contests pitting teams from different local groups against each other are still viewed in a broader, supernatural setting. As several of the Choctaws have admitted, each community represents a certain quantity of mystical power. Although it eludes definition, everyone "knows that they use it," and approaches that particular group with a certain awe and misgiving. The spiritual anxiety that is generated obviously affects the ball-playing experience. For example, when an outsider is playing a softball game in Connehatta he has a feeling that "something is going on"; that a power pervades the atmosphere, superseding the actual athletic ability of the team.

When the outcome of the ball game is "unusual" or "unexpected," many Choctaw sport enthusiasts suspect witchcraft. Obviously, if your team has better players and a superior won-lost record, you should win, especially in a crucial tournament or championship game. If not, you would assume there has been obvious foul play. For example, in the summer of 1974 there was an important men's softball match between Tucker and Connehatta. Tucker had an exceptionally good team that year, undefeated up to that point, and after four innings they had built up a ten-point lead. Then it started to rain, and the game had to be postponed. After a brief interval, the skies cleared and the game was resumed, but during that time

Connehatta [had] switched balls. After that Tucker couldn't do anything right. The ball kept jumping out of their gloves or over their heads. I saw it myself and I know something was wrong. You know ——. He was playing shortstop, and I swear, the ball jumped right over him several times. Something had to be going on. Connehatta finally won the ball game twenty-to-ten, or something like that. Everybody was talking about it; it was the way they switched that ball. There was a spell on it; that's what caused it.

In the summer of 1977, several instances during the course of the softball season, important game outcomes were explained by witchcraft. Apparently, the outcome of athletic contests, like those of any significant, unpredictable events, do not just happen; they are caused.

Still, in accusing another team of using medicine or magic, one must be very careful. If you antagonize a powerful witch, he or she might make it even worse. You might appeal to the ritualists in your own community to validate the reality of a game-winning act of sorcery and enlist their help in retaliation, but that is risky business. "You can get another witch doctor to do something, but he may not have enough power. Really, it's best to leave it alone. . . . Usually, if you just forget it, it will finally go away, but if you try and get back it can cause more problems."

It is partly for this reason that no Choctaw recreation league team has ever filed a formal protest over the suspected use of witchcraft, even though they often contest outcomes over other, sometimes minor, issues: player ineligibility, poor field conditions, officiating error. It is also doubtful that such a protest could be adequately investigated, so it is better left alone.

Even though today's sport-related bewitching activities are usually performed incognito, it was only a decade or two ago among the Mississippi Choctaws that individuals claiming to be witch doctors made their presence obvious at important athletic events. As one now-retired Choctaw baseball player told me: "I remember at Standing Pine, they had a witch. He thought he could turn a ball game around. He used to walk up and down the baselines going through all kinds of motions, blowing through his hands and waving them around. When his team was at bat he would make all these motions and sometimes he would point out toward the field, way out. Then, the next batter would come up and hit a home run. Maybe he didn't, but it sure looked like he made it happen."

It seems that magic and sorcery still have a degree of legitimacy in the ball game context among the Choctaws, even though they are considered inappropriate anywhere else. However, for a witch to harm an individual player, as opposed to simply manipulating the total game context, is an unforgivable offense but a difficult one to vindicate. Unfortunately, if an athlete is too talented or too visible, he is frequently the likely victim of a malevolent witch doctor's jealous wrath.

One middle-age Choctaw baseball player recalls a critical day during his prime when his career was cut short by a painful arm injury that resulted from his being "witched" by an envious opponent. He had played in Meridian that day and had been largely responsible for his team's victory, having amazed fellow players and spectators alike with his sterling play in center field.

We didn't get home until really late that night. It was after dark. We didn't have any electricity then, only lamps. I had been home for a little while, but couldn't go to sleep. I kept hearing this dog barking; just barking and barking. He wouldn't quit. Finally, I decided to go out and see what was going on.

I walked out into the yard and there was this big white dog standing in the yard, barking. He was almost glowing in the dark; a bright white. I'd never seen that dog before. I walked up to him. I was only about five feet away. I looked down and saw this round, smooth rock lying there, so I picked it up, and threw it at the dog. I missed him, and at the same time, something snapped in my arm. It really hurt. I had thrown it out.

I missed the dog, but he took off. He ran a few feet and disappeared right in front of me.

The next day I looked for the rock, but couldn't find it. . . .

My arm was never the same after that. . . . I think somebody had that dog and rock placed there so that I'd pick it up and throw it at him. They wanted me to ruin my arm. I still believe it had to be that way.

Local athletes, in particular the persistent standouts, are always in danger of being the target of a witch's evil power, often for reasons totally unrelated to the sport scene. Many Choctaws have stories to tell about situations in which an injury to a superior ball-player, though it appeared to be natural on the surface, was actually magically induced. For example, the starting quarterback at Choctaw Central in the early 1970s

was dating this one girl pretty regularly. There was another girl from another community who wanted to date ———, but he never asked her out. Because of that, ——— hurt his arm, his throwing arm. It swelled up right here [around his bicep] and hurt really bad. He didn't know exactly what was wrong, but everybody knew that somebody had done it to him for that girl that wanted to date him. . . .

He had the arm treated and wrapped by the trainer at Mississippi State, but it really didn't work. He played some after that, but his arm kept bleeding around the swollen area.

If one is willing to take the chance and risk possible community disapproval and victim reprisal, he or she can very easily enlist the help of an appropriate specialist to "fix the game" or "hurt" a key player on the opposing team. Within each local group there are still witch doctors who for a fee, usually commensurate with their reputed power, can bring about the desired results, in many cases appealing to the *bohpoli* for help.

Many of the Choctaws engage the services of one of the several black witch doctors in east central Mississippi. For reasons that I have been unable to isolate, the Choctaws feel that the magic of the Blacks is superior to their own in the athletic environment. This respect and awe may underlie the intimidation that Choctaw Central High School ball-players often reflect in head-to-head competition with black athletes, even though contests with white opponents are approached with no undue anxiety or sense of powerlessness.

One of the best-known black witches lives in the Stallo area, north of Philadelphia, and openly solicits the patronage of Choctaw athletes. For a fee of from fifteen to twenty-five dollars, depending on the seriousness of the event, he will see to it that his client's team wins. Putting a curse on the other team, witching the bat, or putting a hex on the game ball, he is so confident of his ability that he will refund his fee if he fails to bring about the desired results. The story is told about a situation that occurred in the 1960s in which the managers of two Choctaw teams scheduled to compete against each other in a critical baseball tournament met unexpectedly in Stallo prior to the game only to discover that they both had employed the noted witch doctor and had been given the security of the money-back guarantee. This experience and others like it are related in a humorous vein, but also in a way that suggests that this dilemma is typical of what the athlete encounters if he dares to dabble in the world of the occult and attempt to outmaneuver fate.

Some of the traditionalists among the Choctaws are very hesitant about approaching black witch doctors. They argue that the Choctaws have their own magic, and it works best when applied in familiar surroundings. They admit that black witchcraft can be effectively utilized in a Choctaw setting, but it is dangerous: "That kind of magic can turn on you. Bad things can happen to you for using it when you don't understand it or can't control it, because it's foreign; it's different."

While the use of magic in the sport context is generally frowned upon by contemporary Choctaws, there is a degree of legitimacy in the attempt to increase one's ability and playing power by recourse to medicine. Even more is it appropriate to attempt to protect oneself against the effects of an opponent's magic.

A good Choctaw doctor can improve the quality of the athlete's game, in many ways, even to the point of making him invincible. In baseball, arms are treated to help pitchers and batters perform better. Legs are doctored to improve the runner's speed. Knowledge is injected into the athlete's mind to help him master the strategic dimensions of the game. Indeed, the physiological prerequisites and basic skills underlying team sports can be medically manipulated to the benefit of both the individual and his squad. One successful Choctaw athlete told me about his first encounter with medicine in the Choctaw world:

> When I was growing up, my mother was in bad health, and the medicine man used to visit her a lot. One Saturday, before noon, I was getting ready to go to the ball field when the doctor was there. He asked me where I was going. I told him I was going to the ball field.
>
> "What kind of ball-player are you?"
>
> I told him that he would just have to watch. I told him that I liked to play, but that it might sound like I was bragging if I said anything else.
>
> He asked me, "Do you want to be a better player?"
>
> I said, "Naturally."
>
> He said he would be back next week. He had something to make me a better ball-player.
>
> Sure enough, he came the next week. We had a ballgame that day. He started walking along with me. When we got a little way from the house, he told me he had it ready.
>
> "It will cost you, but it will work. If you have the ability and the desire it will make you better. If you want to be a home-run hitter, if you want to be a fielder and not drop the ball, or a pitcher. . . ."
>
> I said I'd like to be all those things and then I asked him, "How much is it going to cost me?"
>
> "About ten dollars."
>
> Well, I didn't have any money, but I did have a suit, one of those blue serge suits, that I never wore. I told him I didn't need it, and he could have that.
>
> He said, "All right, but you're going to have to tell your mother something."
>
> I told him I could tell her something. . . . I was giving it to him as a present for all the things he had been doing for my mama.
>
> So, I got the suit and told my mama. Then I gave it to him, and

he gave me a small piece of sewed-up cloth and told me to put it in my back pocket and carry it there all the time. He said it was also good for something else. "You can have any girl you want and you'll be able to make friends real easy."

. . . I was real happy. I walked down toward the field feeling like I was going to be a super ball-player. But I got to thinking about it and started to wonder whether I should accept it. If I was really confident about my own ability, why should I worry about something like that? . . .

I walked across a small creek and kept thinking about it. Finally, I took it out and threw it into the creek. I don't know what would have happened if I'd kept it. I've often wondered what it would have done for me.

While the use of this type of medicine and the intrusion of the *alikči* into the athletic arena do not meet with the same degree of disapproval as do similar actions of the witch doctor, it is still viewed as a minor violation of the rules of good sportsmanship. The good athlete doesn't use medicine because he does not need it. One female Choctaw athlete claims that "they use medicine in women's softball games today. Some teams do. We don't. . . . I don't think it's good to do that. We have a good team, and we get accused of using medicine sometimes. Not too long ago this team accused us of using it, but then the lady on the team that accused us came by the house of one of our players and told her that she had her hands fixed to pitch. And she had. She won the game that day."

This same Choctaw woman who told me that she was opposed to the use of medicine in softball games admitted that the *bohpoli* had once given her some special training. "They used to teach me how to play ball their way, throwing and catching things. But their way is different. They would make me jump over logs or wood to catch the ball. Also, they played with a little rock. I had to catch a little rock instead of a ball."

Using medicine to ward off or counter enemy spells is an acceptable practice for those Choctaw athletes who feel that they must compete at supernatural levels in order to equalize or beat the odds of the actual sport encounter. The *alikči* and the witch both have many techniques to equip their clients in the defense against the power of the opposition. One form of magic common to the Choctaw ball game is the amulet or charm that individual players carry in their pockets. The following incident took place in the early 1950s and illustrates the typical battle of the fetishes characterizing the Native Mississippian baseball contests of recent decades:

We used to play a lot of black teams, and the Choctaws thought they [the Blacks] had some special magic. They used a "lodestone" that each player carried that gave them extra power. . . . The only way we could stand up to them was to use our own magic. Every night before we played one of their teams, like Kosciusko, our manager would tell us to be sure and get a dried, hot pepper, put some salt or pepper on it, and sew it up in a piece of cloth— a red cloth is best—and put it in our back pocket. We would also rub it on our gloves during the warm-up before the game. . . . It kept the other team's power from working.

I used to do this and I believe it worked. . . . I remember one time we were playing a team from Kosciusko, and we had gone with our cloth in our pockets. After the first four innings, we were winning, and the other team couldn't do anything. But then this black batter comes to bat. . . . After the first strike he called time-out and walked out toward the mound, right up to our pitcher. He told him to turn around. When he turned around he grabbed the cloth out of his back pocket and threw it on the ground.

I don't know how he knew it was there, but after that they [the black team] started to get some hits. . . .

We still won the ball game, but it was proof to me that it worked.

At another level there are techniques that the layman himself can use, without professional help, that will improve his playing ability. For example, if one comes across the dried, flattened carcass of a toad lying in the road, he is advised to pick it up and rub it into the pocket of his ball glove. The rationale is simple: "A toad can catch a fly."

Likewise, many mysterious events that occur, beyond the conscious control of individual players, communicate ominous meaning to participants, just previous to an important sporting activity. The unusual presence of a rabbit or a whippoorwill in one's yard on the night before a "big game" is interpreted as a message that magic is being used in the impending ball game. "If an owl returns to the same spot near your place two or three times in a row, it means something bad is going to happen to you or your family. I've seen it happen. . . . Sometimes it's a way of letting you know you're going to lose a ball game."

Using medicine, carrying charms, using any available mystical aids, employing witches to throw ball games or harm an opponent, appealing to the *bohpoli*, applying magical technique, and reading telltale signs in daily events are all part of the Choctaw sport ritual process.

The Symbols of Sport Seriousness

One dimension of sport ritualization among the Mississippi Choctaws is manifested in the wide range of symbols that surround the phenomenon. Of the many symbolic categories that underscore the seriousness of the athletic affair, the most obvious and perhaps the most important are the "uniform" and the "trophy."

Choctaws take their game-playing apparel very seriously. Persons who are normally nonchalant about the clothes that they wear to work are often extremely fastidious about what they wear on the ball field or basketball court. Also, expense is rarely a factor in making sure that one is properly outfitted for the game. An older Choctaw athlete, who has spent a large portion of many paychecks in the past for equipment, claims:

> A good uniform says that a player is trying to look his best and to be better than the other team. It says that you're putting out a little extra effort. It's also important to your own confidence.
> If a team has sloppy uniforms, it tells me that they are not that interested in playing. If you're totally involved in the game, you'll put effort into your uniform. . . .
> A uniform is also important to the unity of the team and your community. . . . It just adds something to the spirit of the game.

This same sport enthusiast claims that he once walked twenty miles one morning just to buy a seventy-five-cent baseball cap to complete his uniform for a game that afternoon.

Trophies are also vital to maintaining the Choctaw sport mystique. Every athlete, male or female, has a collection of these memoirs that decorate his living room and validate his prowess on the ball field. In some Choctaw homes, I have counted as many as thirty trophies on display, scattered over mantels, bookshelves, television stands, and refrigerator tops. These monuments of wood and gold-colored alloys range in size from eight to thirty inches in height and may or may not be engraved. Those appropriately labeled refer to playing roles, the sport, and the particular contest, tournament, or season. Every sporting event, no matter how small or insignificant, must promise trophies to its successful participants. In many cases, potential entrants in proposed tournaments will make sure that trophies are to be given to the winning team, and in some instances to the runners-up as well, before they will commit themselves to participate.

Also reflecting its importance is the tendency for the trophy to be used to commemorate or recognize an important nonathletic event. For example, in the early summer of 1977, a tragic traffic accident claimed the life of a young Mississippi Choctaw athlete, and his softball teammates bought an expensive trophy, had it engraved, and presented it to his family. While it had little if anything to do with his prowess on the ball diamond, it did serve as a significant way of expressing the team's appreciation for their deceased colleague.

As with uniforms, cost is of limited importance when it comes to buying trophies, the symbols of success. During the summer of 1974, one of the Choctaw employees working with me in the tribal recreation office took it upon himself to order the prizes for a league softball tournament to be held several weeks later. When the shipment arrived, to the dismay of the tribal business office, it included a bill for over $450, along with massive trophies for first- and second-place teams in both the men's and women's tournaments, their managers, and each individual player. Despite a mild reprimand, the ambitious employee still felt he had acted in the tournament's best interest. "Folks have to have those trophies or they won't play."

The Sport Perspective on Ritual

The analysis of Choctaw ritual behavior within the context of the athletic environment not only provides significant insight into the nature of the medicine and magic employed in the sport setting, but also serves as a perspective on Choctaw ritual in general.

It is apparent that Mississippi Choctaws still put a premium on certain forms of traditional ritual. However, the actual, demonstrable effectiveness of these elements is not the issue. In other words, whether or not a witch doctor's perceived attempt to influence a particular ball game does in fact predetermine its outcome is of little consequence. Rather, this ritual process is important as a means of underscoring the seriousness of the team sport experience. Such activities are more than physically rewarding ways to spend a pleasant afternoon. They are important community events that amplify social boundaries, enforce kinship rules and regularities, and keep the relative prestige of individuals and local groups in proper perspective. In many ways, the ritual trappings that surround the sport phenomenon are merely symbolic expressions of that gravity.

On the other hand, the ritual framework provides a convenient rationale with which to explain ball game results. "Connehatta beat Bogue Chitto in last week's stickball tournament, not because they had a better team, coach, or players, but because Connehatta used sorcery." Such a justification, very consistent with the Choctaw world view, makes defeat more tenable and likewise makes more acceptable the inequities of intercommunity social prestige and political power implicitly expressed within the athletic encounter.

From another perspective, it is possible to look at Choctaw athletic behavior as a type of ritual itself, as others have done for sport in general (Kilmer, 1976:32). Mary Douglas (1970:42) treats ritual forms "as transmitters of culture, which are generated in social relations and which, by their selections and emphases, exercise a constraining effect on social behavior." Ball games function to validate and reinforce the fundamental premises of Choctaw life, and explicitly or implicitly, regulate social behavior in many ways both on and off the playing field. The mechanics and repetitiveness of team play in and of themselves mandate an adherence to a traditional pattern of rules governing everything from relationships among kinsmen to the individual's interaction with the supernatural world.

The ritual significance of ball-playing was even more explicit in previous centuries. In fact, stick-game matches were in some contexts viewed as actual religious ceremonies. Culin (1907a:484), speaking of Native American games in general and stickball in particular, contends that

> back of each game is found a ceremony in which the game was a significant part. The ceremony has commonly disappeared; the game survives as an amusement, but often with traditions and observances which serve to connect it with its original purpose. The ceremonies appear to have been to cure sickness, to cause fertilization and reproduction of plants and animals, and, in the arid region, to produce rain. . . . These observations hold true both of the athletic game as well as of the game of chance. The ball was a sacred object not to be touched with the hand, and has been identified as symbolizing the earth, the sun, or the moon.

Perhaps of greatest importance to the anthropological discipline is the observation that team sport behavior provides a valuable setting within which to explore the realm of myth and ritual. Reflecting many of the characteristics of fundamental, traditional values, sport behavior, viewed as an aspect of the total social process, provides a useful perspective by which anthropologists can analyze the many dimensions of the cultural experience.

CHAPTER 7

Change and the Significance of Sport

Mississippi Choctaw culture has changed significantly over the past two centuries as the Choctaw people have gradually been drawn into the larger Anglo-American system. As parts of the total Choctaw cultural pattern, sport and leisure-time activities have likewise undergone change and in some ways provide unique perspectives for the analysis of Choctaw culture change in general. On the other hand, participation in these same events has in some ways served as an important adjustment device and as a stabilizing force in that change process. The overall meaning and significance of the Choctaws' serious commitment to sport vis-à-vis the phenomenon of change is the subject of this chapter.

The Mississippi Choctaws and Change

The changes occurring in Choctaw society over the past 200 years have been dramatic. Economically, the group has moved from a horticultural and hunting-gathering subsistence base through marginal agricultural roles as squatters and sharecroppers to the contemporary participation in a full-scale wage-market system. Socially, they have witnessed the replacement of the exogamous clan/moiety pattern by endogamous local groups or communities. Also, traditional kinship distinctions have increasingly succumbed to the pressures exerted by English prototypes. Politically, the chiefdom was essentially lost in the confusion of removal in the 1830s, and only in the last few decades has the ensuing leadership vacuum being alleviated with the advent of a new tribal constitution and government. Ideologically, the basic tenets of Christian theology have had a significant impact on Choctaw world view and ritual practice.

However, as Peterson (1972:1286–87) notes, the dominant theme throughout Choctaw history has been the tribesmen's attempt to maintain their cultural integrity and identity amidst the uncertainties of changing circumstance:

Prior to Reconstruction, the Choctaws occupied the locally incongruous position of being defined as non-White, but being nonslave. As such, there was no established position for them in a local society based on White landowners and landless Negro slaves. Participation in any of the institutions of the dominant society required that Choctaws either accept the position of slaves or that they acquire land and be accepted as White. The latter alternative was impossible, and the former was unacceptable to the Choctaws who remained in almost total social isolation until the end of the slave system.

Peterson further suggests that the sharecropping system that developed in the late 1800s made it possible for the Mississippi Choctaws to move into an agricultural role that did not require the sacrifice of their identity. It is also significant that the advent of Choctaw land ownership and tribal government in the twentieth century created new mechanisms facilitating the maintenance of tradition. By virtue of their determination, the Mississippi Choctaws are still Choctaws despite the fundamental changes characterizing both their world and those of others around them.

While, as Peterson (1971:124) has concluded, many of the changes taking place in Choctaw society during the nineteenth and early twentieth centuries seem "to have been part of a more general restructuring of human relations throughout the Southeast," there were many developments unique to the Native American contingent in Mississippi. While specific causes are difficult to isolate, it is safe to suggest that the most visible, external factors in this change were the federal government and the church.

Changing Patterns of Sport

The sport behavior patterns of Mississippi Choctaws have changed dramatically in the past two centuries. Though stickball is still being played, in many ways it is not the same game that made possible the formal confrontation of traditional communities in the 1700s and early 1800s. Recently, Jim Gardner, after looking at several photographs of stickball players in the first decade of this century, commented on how much even the rackets (*kapoča*) had changed in their shape and construction since he was a young man. Now, baseball, basketball, softball, and football, all introduced within the past seventy-five years, dominate the Choctaw sport scene.

The major factors underlying changing patterns of Choctaw sport behavior include (1) the increasing contacts between the Native Mississippians and their white neighbors; (2) the mobility fostered by the advent of the automobile, which in turn brought the Choctaws into Philadelphia and other towns in the area more frequently; (3) the increased exposure of the Choctaw population to the public media and their coverage of national and regional sporting events; (4) the opening of the agency schools and the related development of athletic programs; (5) the impact of tribal members returning to the reservation after being away at school or serving in the armed forces; and (6) the work of Christian missionaries among the Choctaws.

The church had a dramatic impact on Choctaw leisure-time activities, especially around the turn of the last century, when the Catholics and the Baptists began to make significant headway in their attempt to "convert" the Mississippi group. As part of their efforts to "spread the light" the missionaries tried to discourage participation in stickball games and traditional dances. As a result, the church was viewed locally as an institution "rivaling traditional Choctaw activities and forms of association" (Peterson, 1970:69–70). In fact, "the key conflict from the 1880's on . . . was between Choctaw dances and ballgames and church attendance" (Peterson, 1970:70). Church leaders of the period argued that their programs provided ample opportunity for social interaction and thus negated the need for the *toli* matches. Also, it was felt that the influence of the local Whites, their whiskey, and their frequent attempts to sexually solicit and abuse native women, had so corrupted the stickball contest that it had become morally degrading in and of itself. Reflecting the outcome of the ensuing conflict between the conservative and the missionary factions among the tribe, there is "some indication that the rise in Choctaw Baptist churches was associated with a decline in traditional stickball games and dances" (Peterson, 1970:73).

On the other hand, the church had become a principal force underlying the proliferation of modern sport activities among the Choctaws by the 1950s. The Baptists and the Methodists reasoned that there was something wholesome about participation in formal basketball or baseball games. Several church leagues were organized, and interdenominational competition became part of community recreational life. While church leaders have at times expressed concern over issues they consider to have moral implications, such as female basketball players wearing shorts or ball games conflicting with the mission program, they have generally supported the growing popularity of Western sports in the Choctaw world, at least in recent years. In some ways this new emphasis in the religious programs can be seen as a reaction to the fact that within the past two decades the school has begun "to rival the churches as the center of community life" (Peterson, 1970:164).

Despite external pressure, not all the sporting activities introduced into Choctaw society within the past few decades have caught on with the enthusiasm characteristic of the major team sports. For example, swimming is still an event popular only with the children and some teens.

In 1972, a large pool was built in Pearl River under the supervision of the tribal-based Chata Development Company. Every summer this large facility, featuring a "kiddy pool," a twenty-five-meter racing area, and a diving section with both low and high boards, is cleaned and opened to the public for a low daily entry fee. On a typical warm, sunny day in June, the pool may attract as many as 200 paying customers, predominantly public school- and college-aged youths, with some women and their small children. Most of those over the age of twelve, however, are usually Anglo, although Choctaw parents occasionally accompany their youngsters poolside, remaining fully clothed and simply supervising from a lawn chair or picnic bench.

When I inquired as to why so few Choctaw adults took advantage of the swimming facilities, I got several responses. In the first place, few of them have had an opportunity to learn to swim because of the unavailability of either pools or sufficiently large and safe rivers, lakes, and ponds. Also, both Choctaw men and women tend to be a bit modest and hesitant about donning a bathing suit in public. The females are more likely than their male counterparts to admit to this modesty, many of them claiming that they could override that constraint if their husbands were not opposed to their being seen so scantily clad by other men. Another reason that the Choctaws give for avoiding a refreshing plunge, even on those hot and muggy Mississippi summer afternoons, is that the tribal pool is so often overrun by local Whites. The constant clowning, splashing, and general boisterousness of the high school and college crowds in particular can be intimidating when one is contemplating that first uncertain but committal leap into the water. Several of the Pearl River residents have further suggested that the Choctaw people do not relish an afternoon at the pool as much as their Anglo-American neighbors because they are obviously less interested in getting a suntan.

For whatever reason, swimming has yet to capture the Choctaw imagination as an important leisure-time activity, and as a result, the Pearl River pool continues every summer to operate in the red. Even with ticket and concession stand sales, income is insufficient to cover the total cost of water, chemicals, cleaning, lights, management fees, and lifeguard wages.

Once new games and sports are accepted and begin to be played among the Mississippi Choctaws, they in turn become part of a continuously changing process. For example, while basketball is essentially the same sport that was introduced into Choctaw society in the early part of this century, the total meaning and purpose of its play is perceived differently now than then.

While the initial introduction of new sport activities was primarily the result of outside influence, the changing patterns of recreational behavior merely reflect the changes taking place in other dimensions of Choctaw life. For example, a partial breakdown in intercommunity competition has resulted not from any changes in team sports themselves, but rather from a steady out-migration pattern of the smaller Choctaw communities and a blurring of local group allegiances in the larger communities, especially Pearl River (Peterson, 1972:1291). Economic realities are forcing many Choctaw wage earners to relocate and eventually to abandon previous community commitments. Team sport behavior simply manifests the results of this mobility well after the fact. As a result, patterns of sport competition have been altered, although not critically. Still, some Choctaws suggest the changes have been radical. For example, one recently retired local athlete has observed:

> Basketball has lost a lot in recent years. It used to be more a community-versus-community kind of thing. Now, the teams start real early recruiting and bringing outsiders into the league. After a while, the teams are really not community teams anymore.
> It all started when they opened the Choctaw league to outsiders. At first it was Whites, then the Blacks, and you had managers going out into the area and recruiting players for their teams. They got them from all over; college, junior college. These guys were hard to compete with, so a lot of Choctaws were forced to quit. I really think the league has lost something. The attendance may have gone up in some cases, but the community pride and respect isn't there anymore.

Sport in the Total Change Process

Given the nature of the changes that have affected Choctaw sport behavior in recent decades, what can one conclude about the nature of sport as a stabilizing influence in the broader pattern of general Mississippi Choctaw culture change?

One of the assumptions often made by coaches and physical educators is that modern, Western athletic activities function as very effective, almost invincible, change agents. As one commentator has noted: "It is my contention that, whatever else their outcomes, interscholastic athletics serve first and foremost as a social device for steering young people—participants and spectators alike—into the mainstream of American life through the overt and covert teaching of 'appropriate' attitudes, values, norms and behavior patterns" (Schafter, 1974:6–7).

It is thus assumed that when modern team sports are introduced into a non-Western area they bring with them a complete package of Western values, specifically those of the white, Protestant middle class.

But this is not the case. When confronted with the novel options presented by the introduction of Anglo-American sports, Native American peoples have generally adopted them, but on their own terms. In other words, they have tended to take only those aspects of the games that are essential and/or fit conveniently into a traditional framework. In the end, the forms that have actually been played amount to an amalgamation of the new and the old, syncretistic phenomena that use new equipment and physical skills but do not violate customary cultural patterns.

For example, after basketball was introduced into the Rimrock (New Mexico) Navajo setting several decades ago, it very quickly became a uniquely Navajo sport. Now, in comparison to their Anglo-Mormon counterparts in the same community, the Navajos play the game using different styles of play, strategy, and management techniques. Similarly, their perception of the sport's nature and purpose is distinctive to the point that it is reasonable to speak of a "Navajo basketball," something very different from the Anglo-Mormon variety. As a result, it is obvious that

> basketball, in light of its inherent flexibility and the way that the Navajos deal with novelty in general and this sport in particular, is of little culture-change significance. The Rimrock Navajos have simply borrowed a new form of play and molded its essentials to fit ongoing needs and values. In this sense, basketball is providing recreational and entertainment opportunities for members of the Navajo community without forcefully subjecting them to the Wall Street ethic of White America [Blanchard, 1974:12].

The introduction of Western sports into other contact situations has been analyzed, and the results have been very similar (Tindall, 1975). The role of modern recreational activities among the Mississippi Choctaws leads one to the same conclusion and suggests that Choctaw sports are significant factors in the total change process.

The Significance of Choctaw Sport

The sport activities engaged in by today's Mississippi Choctaws, both the revitalized stickball and modern games like basketball and softball, can be viewed as having a significant stabilizing influence within the process of cultural change. As suggested earlier, Choctaw sports, even those introduced by Anglo-Americans in recent decades, are uniquely Choctaw. As such, these activities manifest norms and values fundamental to tradition and serve primarily as cultural maintenance devices rather than as avenues of acculturation. In particular, the team sports among the Choctaws define social boundaries and maintain the proprieties of kingroup relationships. Whether one is playing basketball, softball, or stickball, the social mechanisms and the meanings are the same.

The nature of political relationships is also afforded a traditional model by the exercise of authority and power within the ball-playing context. The manager manages, the coach coaches, the official officiates, and the teammate admonishes, all in a way consistent with the workings of the Choctaw political mind that abhors coercion but responds to logical advice and instruction by demonstration.

Similarly, traditional ritual concepts and practices are maintained in the athletic arena. The *bohpoli*, the witch doctor, the *alikči*, and the customary notions of supernatural power are important to modern sports, even though these elements had no meaning for those who first introduced them into the Choctaw setting. In this same sense, participation in these sports, from stickball to baseball, serves to underscore the Choctaws' distinctive identity as a separate cultural entity within the multiracial and multicultural complexity of the rural South.

Sport, and the seriousness with which the Mississippi Choctaws approach their recreational activities, can also be viewed as an adaptive mechanism, a valuable means by which one copes with the forces of change. Sport participation provides frequent opportunities for relating to persons outside the Choctaw community in ways that transcend traditional dominant-subordinate interracial social relationships. In recent years, when Choctaws have competed against non-Indian athletes, they have done so on an equal basis, generally, without intimidation. This has been especially true since 1964 and the passage of the Civil Rights Act and the recent emergence of Choctaw Central High School as a power in east central Mississippi athletic circles. These experiences allow for an exposure to a non-Indian world, yet on Choctaw terms, thus permitting the individual

Choctaw to be more selective in dealing with external forces of change.

Also, sport participation is a particularly important coping device for Mississippi Choctaw women. As has been suggested for Navajo women (Blanchard, 1975a; Hamamsy, 1957), changing patterns of economic and social organization among the Choctaws have had a particularly significant impact on females. As wage labor and tribal government forms of employment continue to limit the reliance on agriculture and other traditional forms of subsistence, Choctaw men have simply changed jobs and generally maintained their roles as productive members of individual households. Women, however, have seen their traditional economic roles within the household deteriorate in this process without the substitution of new opportunities. In recent years, many Choctaw women have resolved this dilemma by taking jobs outside the home. However, another legitimate way for a woman to underscore her personal worth and achieve recognition and a sense of importance within the community, as well as to establish new types of social relations, is by participating in formal recreation activities such as basketball and softball.

The seriousness with which Choctaws approach their sporting has a fundamental significance for Choctaw life in the twentieth century. The Choctaws are more committed to a year-round participation in sport activities than is true of other groups in the rural South. This is reflected in both the level of participation in any given sport and the attitudes expressed by the Choctaw people themselves.

While in some ways this seriousness can be viewed as a product of the Mississippi Choctaw simply having fewer outside activities in which to engage during their leisure time, it is certainly a fundamental part of Choctaw culture. With distinctive traces in prehistory and ethnohistory, this attitude has become a fundamental dimension of contemporary Choctaw sport behavior. Indeed, this sport seriousness has become an integrated element of Choctaw culture.

To argue that this working-at-play attitude is a positive feature of Choctaw life is not to simply rationalize or attempt to justify the economic problems of the Mississippi Choctaws. Certainly, one cannot ignore these problems nor in any humane way suggest that they be overlooked. On the other hand, to fail to treat the mechanisms that have been developed by the Choctaws to deal with these problems, to note the efficacy of these methods, and to underscore the valuable lesson to be learned from the Choctaw experience is equally as irresponsible.

A serious commitment to community sport and recreation activities provides the individual Choctaw with a sense of meaning often lacking in a work-oriented world marked by frequent unemployment. This commitment brings with it certain predictability not available for most adults in the Choctaw world of work. Jobs come and go, tribal programs change, and federal funding fluctuates, but ball teams generally remain the same from year to year. The development of a sense of obligation to one's leisure-time activities brings with it a sense of importance and meaning not available in a temporary work situation.

Participation in team sports also provides a constructive way to handle leisure time, especially for those faced with abnormally large amounts of such time for reasons beyond their control. Taking this participation very seriously allows one to better take advantage of all the physical, mental, and emotional benefits of recreation, for Choctaw and non-Choctaw alike.

In general, the Choctaws' serious approach to sport may offer a valuable message to those of us whose behavior is dictated by a basic work ethic and for whom meaning is a by-product of work. Working at play may be a very appropriate response to the realities of the late twentieth and early twenty-first centuries as the world is faced with shrinking resources, a technology that is taking over many jobs previously performed by humans, and longer life expectancies that tend to increase the retirement years. The Choctaw model of serious play can thus be viewed as a very valuable model by which human beings might address the economic realities of the future.

Conclusion: Summary

The serious side of leisure among the Mississippi Choctaws finds its most consistent expression in their team sport competition. Traditionally, it was stickball; now it is baseball, basketball, and softball that dominate the local recreation scene and serve as mechanisms with which the Choctaws act out their devotion to certain forms of play.

Most Choctaws, male and female, young and old, are sport enthusiasts. They participate, either as spectators or players, in a year-long round of activities. Athletes rarely question the cost of sport activities, and for many, tribal life revolves around recreation league contests. Of these, many actually "live to play ball," and games become more important than work and other commitments. One might miss a day on the job, but never a ball game. Jobs come and go, but teams are forever.

The seriousness of athletic competition is rooted in the most vital facets of Choctaw culture. Team sports are important in the economic system, in the past affecting the distribution of goods and services, and now tribal investment and cash flow. Social and political organization regularities structure ball-playing events, while the outcomes of these same contests are rationalized and manipulated with Choctaw ritual belief and practice. Athletic symbols permeate the total complex of the Choctaws' social life. Indeed, sport and recreation are inextricably interwoven with all aspects of the Mississippi Choctaw cultural experience.

While it is difficult to demonstrate that the Choctaw's work-ethic approach to team sports is the result of any single cause or group of causes, it is safe to suggest that it is related to the phenomenon's integrative function. As an important dimension of economic, social, political, and ideological realities, the ball game serves to define and ritually maintain that unique Choctaw cultural identity.

At a more specialized level, community allegiance tends to be the more vital factor underlying the typically Choctaw sport seriousness. For this reason, as local group lines are continually adumbrated by population movement, it is probable that the sense of intercommunity competition will wane. However, just as new sport and recreation opportunities are being adopted periodically by the Choctaw tribe, new allegiances may evolve that support in similar ways the on-going preoccupation with athletics. For example, in 1977 a bowling alley was constructed in Philadelphia, and shortly after its grand opening a Choctaw bowling league was initiated. Within a few months, a team bowling excitement had given a new dimension to the Choctaw sporting experience, even though the squads were structured along occupational and departmental rather than community lines.

I predict that as sport and recreational alternatives increase, the competitive units will likewise become more diversified, either representing social units smaller than the entire local group or overlapping community affiliation. However, neither this nor the increasing availability of new forms of entertainment (e.g., television sports) should dampen enthusiasm for group sport activities.

On the other hand, any predictions at this point should take into consideration the possible effects of the energy crisis. As gasoline becomes scarcer and thus more expensive, intercommunity sporting events may become more of a luxury, forcing recreation officials to plan more intracommunal activities and thereby minimize athletic competition and social interaction between Choctaw local groups. Such a turn of events would have a significant impact on Choctaw life in east-central Mississippi.

Nevertheless, the Choctaws remain committed to playing ball. The Monday nights on the softball fields, the weekend high school football game, the marathon basketball tournaments, and the occasional stickball match may have been forgotten by next year, but the dedication to play will remain. Likewise, the satisfaction that comes with the serious approach to leisure will continue to fill that void created and left empty by the periodic unavailability of meaningful employment.

Albert Willis will be an old man some day. He will keep alive the myth of the ball game and his skill as a player by telling his story to grandchildren, age-mates, and an occasional anthropologist. He will talk sometimes of how he met his wife, the job he had for several months in New Orleans, and where he went to school as a boy. But even more, he will reminisce about those times he stood on the mound, threw the ball with a fluid, almost machine-like motion, watched it dance above a determined batter's swing, and heard it smack solidly against the catcher's mitt to validate the success he had felt already in the release. Then he will smile and dream again that dream of Yankee Stadium, the roar of crowd approval, and the celebration of greatness. He will speak of many games, of players who are now a part of local lore, of winning, and perhaps of losing. After he tells again the story of the ancient rivalry between Connehatta and Tucker, he will pause, and then digress for a moment to bewail the passing of that community spirit so vital once to competition.

Albert Willis, the old man, will no longer play ball, but he will still live in a sport-conscious world. Week nights will find him in the local gymnasium or at the ball park watching a game and telling younger men about the way it used to be. He will be seemingly unaware of the anxieties that are expected to come with retirement and old age. Retirement will have come for him much earlier than most; sometimes around his forty-fifth birthday when he will have been forced to leave the strenuous games to those younger and more agile.

The fact that old age means having no job will not bother him. He will be accustomed to long periods of unemployment and job uncertainty well before he reaches that arbitrary and almost incidental passage of sixty-five years.

Albert Willis, the aging sport enthusiast, will reflect on his life and feel good about himself, his contributions to the community, and his legacy to his descendants.

> *Someday, when I am gone, they will talk; they will say, "Do you remember Albert Willis?"*
> *And someone else will say, "Yes, I remember him. He was a good baseball player and he was good to his family."*

Could it be any better than that?

The Football Game Projective Test

In the fall of 1974, while studying the cultural dimensions of sport conflict, I developed a projective picture testing technique that I administered in both Native- and Anglo-American settings in the rural South. Taking a cue from the recent use of projective plates in anthropology field work (Tindall, 1974), I had an artist sketch five pictures roughly depicting football game scenes (see Figures 5–8). Following my instructions, the drawings were done in such a way that unnecessary information (e.g., facial detail, uniform symbols) was omitted.

The sketches were first used among the Mississippi Choctaws during the first week in October. Setting up my equipment in a small office in the library of Choctaw Central High School, I used the pictures as a basis for an extensive interviewing of a sample of juniors and seniors who were in the library during their normal "study hour" or who had come to work on special projects. During a two-day period, I conducted a total of thirty-eight of these interviews, the first four of which were ultimately rejected because I had to conduct several practice sessions before I had decided on the standard questions to be posed relative to each picture (see Appendix B) and become comfortable with the procedure.

Each interview lasted from five to fifteen minutes and was tape-recorded in its entirety.

Later that same month, I enlisted the cooperation of the history department at Riverdale High School in Murfreesboro, Tennessee. I then spent several hours in that setting over a two-day period interviewing juniors and seniors, using a small office and techniques similar to those I employed among the Choctaws. In this phase of the study, twenty-nine Anglo-American students were questioned, the general problem of sport conflict and violence was discussed, and the complete conversations were recorded.

Before the data were studied, it was determined that both groups interviewed could be treated as random samples of junior and senior high school populations. Then, specific responses and the volume of related comments were analyzed.

Where justifiable information was involved, results from the two interviewing sessions were compared, with the two sets of responses being treated as independent samples. Expected frequencies were then determined, and chi-square tests were performed to weigh the significance of the findings. These results, along with the percentage calculations and the volume of supportive discussion, I believe are sufficient to justify the conclusions I have drawn from this particular analysis.

Football Projective Plate Schedule: Interview Format

Subject name: _____   Date: _____

Location: _____   Sex: _____

Plate 1

    A. Event: what?
    B. Team identification (same, different, etc.)
    C. Why are they fighting?
    D. Is this normal?
    E. Is this good or bad?
    F. Why good or bad?
    G. Additional comment

Plate 2

    A. Event: who?
    B. Event: what?
    C. Attitude of participants?
    D. Attitude toward whom (officials, team, etc.)
    E. Why attitude?
    F. Is this normal?
    G. Is this good or bad?
    H. Function?
    I. Why good or bad?
    J. Additional comment

Plate 3

    A. Event: what?
    B. Event: who?
    C. Is anyone mad?

   D. Is this necessary?
   E. Is anyone trying to hurt anyone?
   F. Is it necessary to try and hurt someone in order to play good football?
   G. Do you try to hurt anyone when you play games?
   H. If so, why is it bad to try and hurt?
   I. Additional comment

Plate 4

   A. Event: what?
   B. Event: who?
   C. Mood of primary actor?
   D. Voice level?
   E. Good or bad as technique?
   F. Why good or bad?
   G. What would you do if you were the coach?
   H. What are the players thinking?
   I. How will the players respond; play better?
   J. Do you think you would like him (the coach)?
   K. Additional comment

Plate 5

   A. Event: what?
   B. Event: who? (same or different teams)
   C. Are they mad?
   D. Why or why not?
   E. What are they saying?
   F. Is this normal?
   G. Is this good or bad?
   H. Do you have to get mad to play good football?
   I. Do you get mad when you play football or other games?
   J. Additional comment

REFERENCES CITED

Aberle, David F.
1963 "Some Sources of Flexibility in Navajo Social Organization." *Southwestern Journal of Anthropology* 19:1–18.

Adair, James
1775 *Adair's History of the American Indians.* Ed. Samuel Cole Williams. New York: Promontory Press (1930 edition).

Avedon, Elliot M., and Brian Sutton-Smith
1971 *The Study of Games.* New York: John Wiley.

Beckett, Charles M.
1949 "Choctaw Indians in Mississippi since 1830." Unpublished MA thesis, Oklahoma A and M, Stillwater, Okla.

Blanchard, Kendall A.
1973 "Run, Jump, and Shoot: Basketball and the Rimrock Navajos." Unpublished paper presented at the annual meeting of the American Anthropological Association, New Orleans, November.
1974 "Basketball and the Culture-change Process: The Rimrock Navajo Case." *Council on Anthropology and Education Quarterly* 5(4): 8–13.
1974a "Team Sports and Conflict Resolution among the Mississippi Choctaws." Unpublished paper presented at the annual meeting of the American Anthropological Association, Mexico City, November. ERIC.
1975 "Choctaw Conflict Language and Team Sports: A Problem in Language Borrowing." In *Views on Language,* ed. Reza Ordoubadian and Walburga Von Raffler Engel. Murfreesboro, Tenn. Inter-university Publishing. Pp. 166–81.
1975a "Changing Sex Roles and Protestantism among the Navajo Women in Ramah." *Journal for the Scientific Study of Religion* 14:43–50.
1976 "Team Sports and Social Organization among the Mississippi Choctaws." *Tennessee Anthropologist* 1(1):63–70.
1976a "The Cultural Dimensions of Competition: An Ecological Analysis." *National College Physical Education Association for Men, Proceedings* 79:68–74.
1977 "The Cultural Component in Physical Fitness." In *Studies in the Anthropology of Play,* ed. Phillips Stevens, Jr. West Point, N.Y.: Leisure Press. Pp. 42–49.

1979 "Stick Ball and the American Southeast." In *Forms of Play of Native North Americans*, ed. Edward Norbeck and Claire R. Farrer. 1977 Proceedings of the American Ethnological Society. St. Paul, Minn. West. Pp. 189–208.

Bossu, M.
1768 *Travels in the Interior of North America*. Trans. and ed. Seymour Feiler. Norman: University of Oklahoma (1962 edition).

Catlin, George
1844 *Letters and Notes on the Manners, Customs, and Conditions of the North American Indians*. Vol. 2. New York: Dover (1973 edition).

Charlesworth, James C., ed.
1964 "Leisure in America: Blessing or Curse?" *American Academy of Political and Social Science*, Monograph 4.

Charlevoix, Father Pierre Francois
1721 "Historical Journal." In *Historical Collections of Louisiana*, ed. B. F. French. Vol. 3. New York: D. Appleton (1851 edition). Pp. 119–96.

Choctaw Recreation League
n.d. "Independent Basketball Program Operational Policy." Mimeo. Philadelphia, Miss. Mississippi Band of Choctaw Indians.

Coe, Pamela A.
1960 "Lost in the Hills of Home: Outline of Mississippi Choctaw Social Organization." Unpublished MA thesis, Columbia University, New York.

Coser, Lewis
1956 *The Function of Social Conflict*. New York: Free Press.

Csikszentmihalyi, Mihaly
1975 *Beyond Boredom and Anxiety*. San Francisco: Jossey-Bass.

Culin, Stewart
1907 "Games of the North American Indians." *Bureau of American Ethnology, Annual Report* 24.
1907a "Games." In *Handbook of American Indians*, ed. Frederick W. Hodge. Bureau of American Ethnology, Bulletin 30. Pp. 483–86.

Cushman, Horatio B.
1899 *History of the Choctaw, Chickasaw and Natchez Indians*. Stillwater, Okla.: Redlands Press (1962 edition).

de Brébeuf, Jean
1636 "Relation of 1636." In *The Jesuit Relations and Allied Documents*, ed. Reuben Gold Thwaites. Vol. 10. Cleveland: Burrows Bros. (1897 edition).

de Grazia, Sebastian
1962 *Of Time, Work and Leisure*. New York: Twentieth Century Fund.

Densmore, Frances
1943 "Choctaw Music." *Bureau of American Ethnology, Bulletin 136*. Pp. 101–88.

de Paina, Father Juan
1676 "Origin and Beginning of the Ball Game Which the Apalachee and Yustaga Indians have been Playing from Pagan Times up to the Year 1676." In *Archivo general de Indias, Seville*, Escribania de camara, legajo 156.XXX. Julian Granberry, transcript and translation, for incomplete study by John M. Goggin. Photostats in Stetson Collection, University of Florida Library, Gainesville.

Douglas, Mary
1970 *Natural Symbols*. New York: Random House.

Dumazedier, Joffre
1968 "Leisure." *Encyclopedia of the Social Sciences*. Vol. 9. New York: Macmillan. Pp. 248–53.

du Peron, P. Francois
1693 "Lettre au P. Joseph-Imbert du Peron." In *The Jesuit Relations and Allied Documents*, ed. Reuben Gold Thwaites. Vol. 15. Cleveland: Burrows Bros. (1898 edition). Pp. 147–90.

Dutton, Denis
1977 "Art, Behavior, and the Anthropologists." *Current Anthropology* 18(3):387–94.

Edwards, Harry
1973 *Sociology of Sport*. Homewood, Ill.: Dorsey Press.

Eggan, Fred
1937 "Historical Changes in the Choctaw Kinship System." *American Anthropologist* 39:34–52.

Firth, Raymond
1931 "A Dart Match in Tikopia." *Oceania* 1:64–97.

Fogelson, Raymond D.
1962 "The Cherokee Ball Game: A Study in Southeastern Ethnology." Unpublished Ph.D. Dissertation, University of Pennsylvania, Philadelphia.

Fox, Robin
1961 "Pueblo Baseball: A New Use for Old Witchcraft." *Journal of American Folklore* 74:9–16.

Fox, Steven J.
  1977 "A Paleoanthropological approach to Recreation and Sporting Behaviors." In *Studies in the Anthropology of Play*, ed. Phillips Stevens, Jr. West Point, N.Y.: Leisure Press. Pp.65–70.

Fried, Morton
  1967 *The Evolution of Political Society*. New York: Random House.

Geertz, Clifford
  1973 *The Interpretation of Cultures*. New York: Basic Books.

Gini, Corrado
  1939 "Rural Ritual Games in Libya (Berber Baseball and Shinney)." *Rural Sociology* 4:283–99.

Haas, Mary R.
  1940 "Creek Inter-town Relations." *American Anthropologist* 42:479–89.

Halbert, Henry S.
  1888 "The Choctaw Achahpih (Chungkee) Game." *American Antiquarian and Oriental Journal* 10:283–84.
  1897 "Indian Schools." In *Bienniel Report of the State Superintendent of Public Education to the State Legislature, for the Scholastic Years 1895–96 and 1896–97*. Jackson, Miss.
  n.d. Unpublished Manuscript. In Swanton, Source Material for the Social and Ceremonial Life of the Choctaw Indians. *BAE Bulletin* 103 (1931). Pp. 148–49.

Hamamsy, L. S.
  1957 "The Role of Women in a Changing Navajo Society." *American Anthropologist* 59:101–11.

Harris, Marvin
  1968 *The Rise of Anthropological Theory*. New York: Crowell.

Heider, Karl
  1970 *The Dugum Dani*. Chicago: Aldine.

Hoebel, E. Adamson
  1960 *The Cheyennes*. New York: Holt, Rinehart and Winston.

Hoffman, Walter J.
  1896 "The Menomini Indians." *Bureau of American Ethnology, Annual Report 14*.

Hudson, Charles
  1976 *The Southeastern Indians*. Knoxville: University of Tennessee Press.

Huizinga, Johan
  1949 *Homo Ludens*. Trans. R. F. C. Hull. London: Routledge and Kegan Paul.

Joe, Ava Dee, Lorne Nussbaum, Edmond Lewis, et al.
1976 "Čahta icowah holisso (Choctaw Alphabet Book)." Mimeographed book-
let. Philadelphia, Miss: Bilingual Education for Choctaws of Mississippi.

Jones, Charles C., Jr.
1873 Antiquities of the Southern Indians, Particularly of the Georgia Tribes. New
York: Appleton Press.

Kando, Thomas M.
1975 Leisure and Popular Culture in Transition. St. Louis: C. V. Mosby.

Kaplan, David, and Robert A. Manners
1972 Culture Theory. New York: Prentice-Hall.

Kilmer, Scott
1976 "Sport as Ritual: A Theoretical Approach." In The Anthropological Study
of Play, ed. David Lancy and B. Allan Tindall. West Point, N.Y.:
Leisure Press.

Kraus, Richard
1971 Recreation and Leisure in Modern Society. New York: Appleton-Century-
Crofts.

Lancy, David F., and B. Allan Tindall, eds.
1976 The Anthropological Study of Play. West Point, N.Y.: Leisure Press.

Laudonniere, Rene
1562 "History of the First Attempts of the French to Colonize the Newly
Discovered Country of Florida." In Historical Collections of Louisiana
and Florida, Trans. Richard Hakluyt, ed. B. F. French. New York: J.
Sabin and Sons (1869 edition). Pp. 165–362.

Leach, Jerry W.
1976 "Structure and Message in Trobriand Cricket." Unpublished paper
written to accompany the movie Trobriand Cricket. Berkeley: University
of California Extension Media Center.

Loy, John W.
1969 "The Nature of Sport." In Sport, Culture and Society, ed. John W. Loy
and Gerald S. Kenyon. London: Macmillan. Pp. 56–71.

McClendon, McKee J., and Stanley D. Eitzen
1975 "Interracial Contact on Collegiate Basketball Teams: A Test of Sherif's
Theory of Superordinate Goals." Social Science Quarterly 15:926–38.

Mergen, Bernard
1978 "Work and Play in an Occupational Subculture: American Shipyard
Workers, 1971–1977." In Play: Anthropological Perspectives, ed. Michael
Salter. West Point, N.Y.: Leisure Press. Pp. 187–200.

Merton, Robert
1968 *Social Theory and Social Structure.* New York: Free Press.

Mississippi Band of Choctaw Indians
1971 "Position Statement on Local Alcoholism and Alcohol Related Problems and Proposed Corrective Measures." Unpublished document.

1977 "Recreation Master Plan." Unpublished document.

M'Kenney, Thomas L.
1838 *History of the Indian Tribes of North America with Biographical Sketches and Anecdotes of the Principal Chiefs.* Vol. 1. Philadelphia: Frederick W. Greenough.

Mooney, James
1890 "Cherokee Ball Play." *American Anthropologist* 3:105–32.

Murphy, Robert F.
1957 "Intergroup Hostility and Social Cohesion." *American Anthropologist* 59:1018–35.

Nisbet, Robert A.
1970 *The Social Bond.* New York: Alfred A. Knopf.

Norbeck, Edward
1974 "The Anthropological Study of Human Play." In *The Anthropological Study of Human Play,* ed. Norbeck. Rice University Studies 60(3). Pp. 1–8.

Peterson, John J., Jr.
1970 "The Mississippi Band of Choctaw Indians: Their Recent History and Current Social Relations." Unpublished Ph.D. Dissertation. University of Georgia, Athens.
1970a "Socio-Economic Characteristics of the Mississippi Choctaw Indians." *Mississippi State University Social Science Research Center, Report 34.* Starkville.
1971 "The Indians of the Old South." In *Red, White, and Black: Symposium on Indians in the Old South. Southern Anthropological Society, Proceedings 5.* Pp. 88–98.
1972 "Assimilation, Separation, and Out-Migration in an American Indian Group." *American Anthropologist* 74:1286–95.

Pitt-Rivers, Julian
1967 "Contextual Analysis and the Locus of the Model, *Archives Europeenes de Sociologie." European Journal of Sociology* 8:30–32.

Richardson, Miles
1975 "Anthropologist—the Myth Teller." *American Ethnologist* 2(3): 517–33.

Roberts, John M., Malcolm J. Arth, and Robert R. Bush
1959 "Games in Culture." *American Anthropologist* 61:597–605.

Romans, Bernard
1775 *A Concise Natural History of East and West Florida*. Vol. 1. New Orleans: Pelican (1921 edition).

Sack, Allen
1977 "Sport: Work or Play?" In *Studies in the Anthropology of Play*, ed. Phillips Stevens, Jr. West Point, N.Y.: Leisure Press. Pp. 186–95.

Sahlins, Marshall
1972 *Stone Age Economics*. Chicago: Aldine.

Salter, Michael A., ed.
1978 "Play: Anthropological Perspectives." *Association for the Anthropological Study of Play, Proceedings 3*. West Point, N.Y.: Leisure Press.

Schafter, Walter E.
1974 "Sport, Socialization and the School: Toward Maturity or Enculturation?" *Oregon School Study Council, Bulletin 17(5)*.

Schwartzman, Helen
1976 "The Anthropological Study of Children's Play." *Annual Review of Anthropology* 5:289–328.

Scotch, N. A.
1961 "Magic, Sorcery, and Football among Urban Zulu: A Case of Reinterpretation under Acculturation." *Journal of Conflict Resolution* 5(1):70–74.

Sheldon, William H.
1940 *The Varieties of Human Physique*. New York: Hafner.

Sherif, Muzafer
1958 "Superordinate Goals in the Reduction of Intergroup Conflict." *American Journal of Sociology* 63:349–56.

Simmel, Georg
1955 *Conflict*. Trans. K. H. Wolff. Glencoe, Ill.: Free Press.

Sipes, Richard
1973 "War, Sport, and Aggression: An Empirical Test of Two Rival Theories." *American Anthropologist* 75:64–86.

Skeat, Walter
1911 *Concise Etymological Dictionary of the English Language*. New York: American Book Company.

Southern California Research Council
1967 *The Challenge of Leisure: A Southern California Case Study*. Claremont: Pomona College.

Speck, Frank G.
1909 "Ethnology of the Yuchi Indians." *Anthropological Publications of the*

University Museum. Philadelphia: University of Pennsylvania Press. Vol. 1, No. 1.

Spencer, Barbara G.
1973 "Occupational Orientation of Choctaw Indian High School Students in Mississippi." Unpublished MA Thesis, Mississippi State University, Starkville.

Spencer, Barbara G., John H. Peterson, Jr., and Choong S. Kim
1975 *Choctaw Manpower and Demographic Survey, 1974.* Philadelphia, Miss.: Mississippi Band of Choctaw Indians.

Spradley, James P., ed.
1972 *Culture and Cognition: Rules, Maps, and Plans.* San Francisco: Chandler.

Stern, Theodore
1948 "The Rubber Ball Game of the Americas." *American Ethnological Society Monograph 17.* Seattle: University of Washington Press.

Stevens, Phillips, Jr., ed.
1977 *Studies in the Anthropology of Play: Papers in Memory of B. Allan Tindall.* Association for the Anthropological Study of Play, Proceedings 2. West Point, N.Y.: Leisure Press.

Swanton, John R.
1918 "An Early Account of the Choctaw Indians." *Memoirs of the American Anthropological Association* 5(2):53–72.
1931 "Source Material for the Social and Ceremonial Life of the Choctaw Indians." *Bureau of American Ethnology, Bulletin 103.*

Thompson, Peggy
1975 "Choctaw Wedding." *Nanih Waiya* 2(1–2):19–26.

Thompson, Bobby, and John H. Peterson, Jr.
1975 "Mississippi Choctaw Identity: Genesis and Change." In *The New Ethnicity: Perspectives from Ethnology,* ed. John W. Bennett. 1973 Proceedings of the American Ethnological Society. St. Paul, Minn.: West. Pp. 179–96.

Tindall, B. Allan
1974 "The Anthropological Usage of Non-standardized Projective Pictures in Cross-Cultural Research." Unpublished paper presented to the Second International Conference of the International Association for Cross-Cultural Psychology, Kingston, Canada. April.
1975 "Ethnography and the Hidden Curriculum in Sport." *Behavioral and Social Science Teacher* 2(2):5–28.
1976 "Questions about Physical Education, Skill, and Life-time Leisure Sports Participation." Position paper presented to UNESCO on behalf of the Association for the Anthropological Study of Play for the First International Conference of Ministers and Senior Officers Responsible for Physical Education and Sport for Youth, April.

Tubby, Simpson
1975 "Early Struggles." Religious tract, n.d., reprinted in *Nanih Waiya* 2(1–2):33–43.

Turner, Victor
1973 "Liminality, Play, Flow and Ritual. An Essay in Comparative Symbology." Unpublished paper presented at the annual meeting of the American Anthropological Association, New Orleans, November. Also in *The Anthropological Study of Human Play*, ed. Edward Norbeck. Rice University Studies 60(3). Pp. 53–93.
1974 *Dramas, Fields, and Metaphors*. Ithaca: Cornell University Press.

White, Leslie
1965 "Anthropology 1964: Retrospect and Prospect." *American Anthropologist* 67:629–37.

Wright, Quincy
1942 *A Study of War*. Vol. 1. Chicago: University of Chicago Press.

INDEX

Adair, John, 25
Ačaphi (chunkey stone), 25
Alikči (doctor), 145, 148, 149, 156, 173; training,150; sexual powers, 151; use of medicine in sport, 161–62
Anglo: defined, xiv
Anthropology of sport, xiii; history, 13; foci, 14–15; theory in, 15–16
Apalachee, 24
Apisači (scorekeeper), 35
Athlete: importance of role among Choctaws, 126–27
Athletics: defined, 20

Baggataway, 26
Baptists: as factor in sport change, 169
Baseball. *See* Choctaw—baseball
Basketball. *See* Choctaw—basketball
Beckett, Charles M., 53, 104, 106
Blowgun, 103
Bogue Chitto, 3–4, 6, 44, 69, 123, 165
Bogue Homa, 4, 6, 123
Bohpoli, 145, 146, 147, 148, 149, 160, 162, 163, 173
Bossu, M., 39
Bowling. *See* Choctaw—minor sport activities
Bryant, Paul ("Bear"), 43
Bureau of Indian Affairs (BIA): Choctaw agency established, 44, 105; schools, 44, 52, 54; basketball league, 53; land purchase program, 106
Bureau of Outdoor Recreation (BOR), 124, 125

Catlin, George, 35
Charlevoix, Pierre Francois, 27

Chata Development Company, 170
Cherokee Conference, 59
Cherokees, 27, 43, 108; stickball, 157
Cheyenne, 128
Chickasaw, 24
Choctaw
—baseball: introduction, 43–44; intercommunity competition, 45; socialization, 45, 46, 48; importance of, 1–3, 46; influence of veterans, 49; skills, 51; pre-game restrictions, 52
—basketball: introduction, 52; socialization, 53; marathon tournament, 54; described, 75–77; distinctive characteristics, 77–81; woman's, 79; role of kinship, 79, 117–18; managerial styles, 79–80
—community: as basic social unit, 114; boundaries, 117; differential enthusiasm for sport competition, 118; as factor in competitive spirit, 120–21; relative prestige, 121–23; identification, 123
—culture change, 167–68
—economics: employment, 8–10, 106, 107; unemployment, 8–10; occupations, 9; subsistence, 103
—gambling, 25, 41, 57, 71
—general information: orthography, xiv; location, 3, 4, 5; communities, 3, 4, 5, 28; language, 4; population, 6; work ethic, 6–8; marriage, 8
—leisure, 175–76
—medicine. *See Alikči*
—minor sport activities: rings, 56–57; golf, 57; swimming, 170; bowling, 176

Choctaw (*continued*)
—political organization: traditional, 132–33; constitution, 133; reservation status, 133, 134; tribal council, 133–34, 135; war, 138; crime, 143
—physical fitness: values, 97–101; ideal female body types, 98–101
—recreation: terms, 21; tribal expenditures, 110–11
—ritual: origin myth, 24; specialists, 145–46; change, 146, 155
—social organization: clan (*iksa*), 113, 114, 115, 116, 125, 132, 140; family, 114; kinship terminology change, 115-16; marriage, 114, 117; moieties, 113, 114, 117; kinship residential sectors, 121; ranks, 133
—softball: introduction, 55; as women's sport, 55; popularity, 60; described, 82–83; distinctive characteristics, 83–86; kinship factor, 83–84, 118; managerial styles, 84; controversy, 120
—sport: ritual, 52, 115–63, 165–66; community participation, 10, 60, 61; seriousness, 61–63, 173, 175; as vital element in culture, 63, 65; distinctive characteristics, 86–101; competition, 88; conflict language, 90, 97; traditional economics of, 107–10; seasons, 108; equipment expenses, 11; as means of upward mobility, 112; kinship factor, 117–24; social functions, 125–26; as conflict and aggression, 127–30; political organization factor, 132–44; as conflict resolving device, 132, 137–41; relation to political success, 134–35, 136; role of coach, 136–44; symbols, 163–65; change, 168–69, 171–72; general significance, 175; future, 176–77
—stickball: history, 24–43; rules, 26–27, 34–35, 40, 68; as conflict resolving device, 28–29; pregame ritual, 30; dress, 30, 67;

son, 32; playing field, 34; gambling, 32, 40, 41–42, 71; drummer, 35–36, 67; singers (*italowa*), 36; clowns, 36; spectators (*okla yopísa*), 36; types of players, 37; killing, 39; fighting, 39, 130; demise of traditional game, 42; at the picnic, 49; style of play, 68–71; contemporary compared to traditional game, 71–73; as conflict, 127, 138–39; peace game, 139; ritual, 156–57
—women's sports and games: women's game, 26; socialization, 55; equality with men's activities, 56, 88; in the change process, 174
Choctaw Business Committee (CBC), 133
Choctaw Central High School, 61, 67, 87, 88, 97, 111, 124, 127, 130, 137, 159, 160, 173, 179; opening, 57
Choctaw Community News, 85
Choctaw demographic survey, 8
Choctaw fair, 42, 50, 67, 71
Choctaw Independent League, 51, 74
Choctaw Recreation Board, 60
Choctaw Recreation League (Department), 75, 79, 81, 82, 124
Choctaws: Oklahoma, 4, 42, 104, 105
Chunkey (*čąki*), 7; described, 25
Civil Rights Act (1964), 106, 173
Cochiti Pueblo, 139, 141
Connehatta, 1, 4, 6, 44, 67, 74, 83, 123, 157, 158, 165, 177
Coser, Lewis, 129
Coushatta, 43
Creeks, 27, 130; formal stickball match, 138; Red and White towns, 138
Crow kinship system, 115
Csikszentmihalyi, Mihalyi, 12, 13
Culin, Stewart, 34, 37, 64, 166
Culture: defined from ethnoscience perspective, 16
Cushman, Horatic B., 40, 103, 146

Dancing Rabbit Creek: treaty, 4, 104, 134
de Grazia, Sebastian, 18
Densmore, Frances, 30, 156
de Paina, Father Juan, 24
de Soto, Hernando, 24, 102
Dixie Youth Basketball Association, 59
Douglas, Mary, 165
Dry-cupping: description, 146
Dutton, Denis, 17

Edwards, Harry, 20
Eggan, Fred, 114
Emic, 16, 17, 98
Ethnoscience: as theory, 16–17; as method, 17–18
Etic, 17

Fabossa (goal posts), 34
Farve, Albert, 45, 47, 51, 135
Faywood Springs, New Mexico, 144
Fifth U. S. Circuit Court of Appeals, 134
Firth, Raymond, 15, 65
Flatheads, 23
Fogelson, Raymond, 39, 157
Football: Choctaw Central High School, 58, 59; socialization, 58
Fox, Robin, 14, 139, 141
Fox, Steven, 23

Gala Day, 50, 54, 126
Gambling. See Choctaw—gambling
Game: definition, 20; corn and moccasin, 26
Gardner, Jim, 8, 39, 49, 103, 114, 151, 152, 156, 168
Geertz, Clifford, 109
Gini, Corrado, 14
Golf. See Choctaw—minor sport activities

Haas, Mary, 138
Halbert, Henry S., 26, 32, 41, 42, 130, 145
Handball game: described, 26
Hatak holhkonna (witch), 146, 148; flying, 152–53; placing spells,

153; killing, 153–54; source of power, 154–55; in sport, 157–60
Hatak umba ikbi (rainmaker), 40, 145, 156
Herb doctor, 157
Horn technique: described, 149
Hucks, Lonus, 78
Huizinga, Johan: definition of play, 12

Indian Reorganization Act (1934), 133, 134
Isaac, Jackson, 37
Isht albi ("ball witch"), 156
Itakobi (laziness), 7
Ìtibbi (fighting), 90

Jimmie, Leonard, 78

Kaplan, David, and Robert Manners, 15
Kapoča (racket), 26, 168; described, 32–33

Laudonniere, Rene, 24
LeFlore, Greenwood, 104, 133
Leisure: seriousness of, xiii, 1–3; defined, 11, 18; history of concept, 18–19
Lodestone, 162
Loy, John, 20, 21

Medicine. See Alikči
Mergen, Bernard, 13
Methodists: attitude toward sport, 169
Mìko (chief), 4, 7, 29
Mississippi Athletic Association (MIA), 57, 58, 59
Mississippi Choctaw Bilingual Program, xiv
Mississippi Recreation Program, 59
Mooney, James, 14
Multiple Affect Adjective Check List (MAACL), 141, 142
Mundurucú, 139–40
Murfreesboro, Tennessee, 88, 98, 141, 179
Murphy, Robert, 139, 140

Nanih Waiya, 113
National Indian Activities Association (NIAA), 61
Native Mississippians: defined, xiv
Navajos, Rimrock: basketball, 20–21, 65–66, 119, 172
Neshoba County, Mississippi, 4, 104
New Choctaw Baptist Association, 133
Newton County Choctaws, 42
Noxubee County, Mississippi, 130

Pearl River, 3, 6, 7, 41, 44, 53, 54, 57, 58, 63, 69, 75, 80, 104, 118, 121, 123, 135, 149, 170, 171
Pearl River School: sports program, 57
Peterson, John J., Jr., 104, 107, 115, 167, 168
Philadelphia, Mississippi, 53, 83, 98, 160, 176
Picnic, 49–50, 122
Pitt-Rivers, Julian, 17
Play: defined, 12–13; and sport, 22
Projective picture testing technique, 179–80
Public Health Service (PHS), 149, 150, 151, 152
Pushmataha, 135

Rabbit Stick, 103
Ragball, 47, 48, 124
Rainmaker. See Hatak umba ikbi
Recreation: defined, 21–22
Red Water, 4, 6, 44, 87, 123
Removal, 104, 105, 114, 133
Rings. See Choctaw—minor sport activities
Roberts, John, 65
Romans, Bernard, 6, 25, 26

Sack, Allan, 20, 21
Sahlins, Marshall, 121
Seminole, 43
Sheldon, William, 98
Sherif, Muzafer, 129
Simmel, George, 137, 139
Softball. See Choctaw—softball
Spaulding, A. S., 144

Sport: as integral element of primitive culture, 15; definitions, 19–21; as work and play, 20; defined, 22; as conflict, 22; in the archeological record, 23; as war, 128. See also Anthropology of sport, Choctaw—sport
Stallo, Mississippi, 160
Standing Pine, 4, 6, 74, 123, 158
Stern, Theodore, 27
Stickball. See Choctaw—stickball
Swanton, John, 27, 114, 132, 139
Swimming. See Choctaw—minor sport activities

Talowa (chanter), 49
The Association for the Anthropological Study of Play (TAASP), 14
Theory: defined, 16
Thompson, Bobby, and John Peterson, 64
Tikopian dart game, 15
Timucuan handball: described, 24
Tindall, B. Allan, 14, 21
Tọksali (work), 7
Toli (stickball), xiv, 26. See also Choctaw—stickball
Towa (ball), 26; described, 34
Tribe: defined, xiv
Trophy: importance as Choctaw symbol, 164–65
Tubby, Carl, 48, 57, 58, 124
Tubby, Doyle, 143
Tubby, Simpson, 41, 139
Tucker, 2, 4, 6, 40, 44, 82, 83, 123, 157, 158, 177
Turner, Victor, 10, 150

Uniform: importance as Choctaw symbol, 164
United Southeastern Tribes (USET), 55
Utes, 21

Warfare: as sport, 128
Wášoha (play), 10
White, Leslie, 65
Willis, Albert, 1, 2, 3, 177, 178
Witch. See Hatak holhkonna
Witches, black, 155, 160

Women's sports. *See* Choctaw—
    women's sports and games
Work and play: the distinction,
    18–19
Working at play, 10–13
Wright, Quincy, 128

York, Baxter, 30, 33, 35
York, Gloria, 56, 120
Yuchi, 108

Zuni, 141

A Note on the Author

Kendall Blanchard's professional interests span the fields of anthropology and leisure studies. His current work on the importance of sport in Choctaw Indian society grew out of several extended stays among the Choctaws as a recreation consultant, giving him an inside view of the Choctaws at play. He currently serves as professor and chairman, Department of Sociology, Anthropology, and Social Work, Middle Tennessee State University, Murfreesboro. After receiving M.A. and Ph.D. degrees in anthropology from Southern Methodist University, he did a year's postdoctoral work at Johns Hopkins University with a postdoctoral fellowship from the National Endowment for the Humanities. In addition, he is a fellow of the American Anthropological Association and the Association for the Anthropological Study of Play. His previous publications include *The Economics of Sainthood: Religion Change Among the Rimrock Navajos* by Fairleigh-Dickinson University Press.